Software Exorcism: A Handbook for Debugging and Optimizing Legacy Code

BILL BLUNDEN

Apress™

ISBN-13 (pbk): 978-1-4302-5107-1

ISBN-13 (electronic): 978-1-4302-5108-8

President and Publisher: Paul Manning
Lead Editor: Dominic Shakeshaft
Technical Reviewer: Doug Holland
Editorial Board: Steve Anglin, Mark Beckner, Ewan Buckingham, Gary Cornell, Louise Corrigan, Morgan Ertel, Jonathan Gennick, Jonathan Hassell, Robert Hutchinson, Michelle Lowman, James Markham, Matthew Moodie, Jeff Olson, Jeffrey Pepper, Douglas Pundick, Ben Renow-Clarke, Dominic Shakeshaft, Gwenan Spearing, Matt Wade, Tom Welsh
Coordinating Editor: Kari Brooks
Copy Editor: Ami Knox
Compositor: Kinetic Publishing Services, LLC
Indexer: Carol Burbo
Cover Designer: Anna Ishchenko

Distributed to the book trade worldwide by Springer Science+Business Media New York, 233 Spring Street, 6th Floor, New York, NY 10013. Phone 1-800-SPRINGER, fax (201) 348-4505, e-mail orders-ny@springer-sbm.com, or visit www.springeronline.com. Apress Media, LLC is a California LLC and the sole member (owner) is Springer Science + Business Media Finance Inc (SSBM Finance Inc). SSBM Finance Inc is a Delaware corporation.

For information on translations, please e-mail rights@apress.com, or visit www.apress.com.

Apress and friends of ED books may be purchased in bulk for academic, corporate, or promotional use. eBook versions and licenses are also available for most titles. For more information, reference our Special Bulk Sales–eBook Licensing web page at www.apress.com/bulk-sales.

Any source code or other supplementary materials referenced by the author in this text is available to readers at www.apress.com. For detailed information about how to locate your book's source code, go to www.apress.com/source-code/.

This book is dedicated to bad kung fu movies.

Contents at a Glance

Contents

Chapter 4   Debugger Internals *157*

Chapter 5   Optimization: Memory Footprint *215*

About the Author

REVEREND BLUNDEN has spent much of his life wandering through the subterranean catacombs of system software. At an early age, he discovered the DOS debug program, and he has been trying to peek behind the curtain ever since. Along the way, he received a degree in physics from Cornell University and a masters in operations research from Case Western Reserve University. Having narrowly escaped a lifetime of servitude to the Society of Actuaries, Reverend Bill fled westward. After ten years of searching in the desert, Reverend Bill was visited by an epiphany: a great smiling head named J. R. "Bob" Dobbs. Through Dobbs, Reverend Bill has learned the true nature of what makes software evil. He has come back to civilization to spread the word.

Acknowledgments

WRITING A BOOK IS ALMOST like being pregnant. For months you feel tired and sleep deprived. You have strange mood swings and food cravings. When you are finally done, you're exhausted and overjoyed that the tribulation is over. Yet people still continue to write, even after the first ordeal. I believe that the need to write must be an inveterate quality in some authors.

I would like to thank all the people at Apress who encouraged me and put up with all of my shenanigans. Specifically, I would like to thank Gary Cornell for giving me the opportunity to write for Apress. I would also like to thank Jim Sumser and Hollie Fischer for entertaining my lengthy diatribes and offering feedback on my dubious cogitations. Finally, I would like to thank Ami Knox, Kari Brooks, Beth Christmas, and Jessica Dolcourt for their assistance during the production process.

Praise Bob,
Rev. Bill Blunden
Church of the SubGenius

Introduction

IT HAS BEEN DOCUMENTED[1] that the maintenance phase of the typical software project's life cycle accounts for over 60 percent of the total cost incurred. For all the pomp and circumstance heaped upon the design phase, once the first release has been deployed, most of the resources will be spent on fixing bugs, adding new features, and fixing bugs resulting from those new features. The post-release development cycle of the average software application resembles that shown in Figure 1.

---

1.   Don Coleman et al., "Using Metrics to Evaluate Software System Maintainability," *IEEE Computer,* August 1994, pp. 44–49

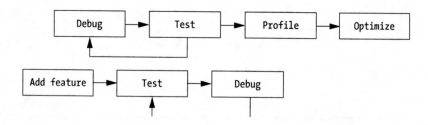

Figure 1. Post-release life cycle of the average software application

The post-release cycle can be initiated by the addition of a new feature or the submission of a bug report. In either case, unit and system tests are used to determine if the patched code is doing what it is supposed to. Once the paths of execution have been sufficiently stabilized, the application can be profiled to locate performance bottlenecks. A variety of optimization techniques can then be implemented to increase execution speed and decrease memory footprint. As customers demand new features and report new bugs, the cycle will repeat itself and the application will evolve.

Most books on software engineering focus intently on the phases of development leading up to the release of an application (e.g., requirements, analysis, use cases, implementation, and so on). Everyone knows that it's much easier, and more gratifying, to write a program from scratch. Software maintenance, on the other hand, is the ugly stepchild of computer science. Most professors would prefer not to mention it in public. This is because discussing the rigors of maintenance work might raise questions . . . dangerous questions. Why spend four years completing a degree in computer science when the fruits of your labor land you in an insanely frustrating maintenance role? If professors told their students the truth about software engineering as a profession, there would be a mass exodus out of computer science courses. A smaller department would translate into budget cuts and loss of prestige, so you'd better believe that the professors are more than willing to sidestep a few unpleasant truths to bolster the size of their classes.

This book is different. Rather than shield your eyes from the sordid realities of the software industry, I am going to dust off my old 8mm films and let you take a good look at the uncensored truth for yourself. You may want to keep a paper bag handy in case you get sick. This book examines the tools that engineers can use to facilitate the debugging and optimization of legacy software. In other words, this is a book on maintaining software that has been hacked to death by other people. Grab a bowl of popcorn and have a seat, but don't complain that I didn't warn you.

A Marine Corps Recon officer once told me that martial artists should not talk about techniques that are "combat effective" unless they have used those techniques under the threat of being killed. In this spirit, I feel that a book on software maintenance should not offer advice unless it has been used in the field, by the author, under stressful circumstances. This book intentionally avoids ivory tower abstraction in favor of field-ready tactics. I stick to simple tools that have worked for me in the past. The average maintenance engineer does not have time to waste on cloud diagrams or fashionable development methodologies. Maintenance engineers have a job to do and an immediate need to get it done. This book presents tactics that may be used, in the trenches, with little or no preparation.

Historical Motivation

Back in the Iron Age (i.e., the late 1960s and 1970s), most software engineers did not have much computational real estate to play with. Room-sized computers like the CDC 6600 had only 65,000 60-bit words of memory (less than a megabyte). In this type of environment, every single bit counted, and engineers went to extraordinary lengths to save space. At the same time, processor speed was also a serious issue. Most people dropped off their programs with the system operator in the afternoon and came back the next day to pick up the results. Hence, engineers in the days of yore had to meticulously balance memory usage with the need to minimize the number of CPU cycles consumed.

This situation has changed. In 1998, I was working on a Windows NT workstation that had dual 450 MHz Pentium processors and 2GB of RAM. The CDC 6600 sold for $7,000,000 dollars. My NT workstation cost a little under $5000. Engineers today are not faced with the same pressures to squeeze every ounce of performance out of their programs (I can almost hear the CDC engineers grumbling, "Back in my day . . ."). To put it bluntly, we can be lazy if we want to and let the hardware pick up the slack. If a program doesn't run quickly enough, we can always throw more hardware at it, and with the emergence of cheap commodity parts, this is a realistic, short-term solution.

In the future, we are bound to hit a wall. The laws of physics require an electron to have a circuit path that is larger than three hydrogen atoms across. Once the path becomes smaller than this, the electron stops behaving like a particle and starts to behave like an escaped convict (i.e., quantum tunneling occurs). This means that the hardware industry will only be able to make computer processors shrink to a certain size. There will come a day when the processor manufacturers will no longer be able to have their cake and eat it too. At a certain point, increasing computing power will require processors to become larger in order to accommodate more transistors.

When this wall is hit, the responsibility for improvements will shift back onto the shoulders of software engineers. Better algorithms and better ways of implementing algorithms will need to be invented. The focus on optimization that occurred in the 1960s will reemerge as the next generation of pioneers pushes the envelope for application performance.

NOTE *When exactly will we hit the wall? I'm sure a lot of chip vendors don't like to think about it. In 1989 the Intel 80486 was released with a design rule of about a micrometer, which is a millionth of a meter. The anthrax bacterium is roughly 1 to 6 micrometers in length. A human hair is about 100 micrometers in diameter. According to Gordon Moore's observation, known as* Moore's Law, *the number of transistors in a given area doubles every 18 months. In other words, the design rule of a transistor should be cut in half every 3 years. If we take 1989 as a starting point, where the design rule of a transistor was 1 micrometer, then you should be able to plug through the math and see that the show will be over by 2022. Even if CPU vendors drag things out, I doubt if things will continue to shrink after 2100.* Also sprach Zarathustra.

During the Iron Age, debugging often entailed reading hex dumps and reconstructing stack frames. The very act of looking for a bug was painfully time consuming. As a result, engineers developed precise strategies for preventing bugs and fixing them quickly when they occurred. Today, most engineers simply place a breakpoint somewhere in their code and start stepping through their program with a GUI debugger. GUI debuggers and shotgun surgery have replaced the detective skills that were so vital to the older generation of engineers.

I'm not saying that GUI debuggers are bad; in fact, I'm a huge fan. I'm just saying that there are times when a GUI debugger by itself won't illuminate the source of a problem. In these situations, what's called for is a set of diagnostic skills that must be honed through disciplined study and practice. These skills, in addition to the GUI debugger, can be used to address tough problems.

Using tools effectively is not a bad thing, unless you become completely dependent upon them. This reminds me of a story that Isaac Asimov wrote called "The Feeling of Power." In this story, future generations become so dependent upon computers that they forget how to perform basic arithmetic. At the end the story, one of the main characters performs multiplication in his head:

Nine times seven, thought Shuman with deep satisfaction, is sixty-three, and I don't need a computer to tell me so. The computer is in my own head. And it was amazing the feeling of power that gave him.

As time progresses, software applications will become larger and larger. The first version of PC DOS was roughly 4000 lines of assembly code.[2] That

---

2.   Andrew Tanenbaum, *Modern Operating Systems*, Second Edition (Prentice Hall, 2001. ISBN: 0-13-031358-0)

was back in 1981. Fast forward to the mid 1990s. Windows NT 4.0 was over 16 million lines of code.[3] In the coming century, we will probably see software applications that top a billion lines of code. Although the current generation of debugging tools is impressive, the casual approach assumed by contemporary developers will not suffice as the complexity curve ramps up towards the stratosphere.

Even if the optimization and debugging skills of the average software engineer have atrophied, in the advent of superior hardware and tools, engineers worth their salt will still take the time to master these forgotten arts. The investment of time and energy will pay themselves off by rewarding the investor with skills that will make them a better engineer. There is nothing worse than being woken up at 3:00 in the morning by an angry client. With this book, you can protect yourself from this kind of interruption and get back to sleeping nights.

Audience

According to the U.S. Bureau of Labor Statistics, there were over a million software engineers employed nationwide in 2001. Easily half of these engineers performed maintenance work of some form or another. Hence, this book targets a sizeable cross-section of software professionals.

Maintenance programming is not a glamorous position. It's more like working in a steel mill: tedious and fraught with danger. The high-paid consultants, whom management recruited specifically to perform the first cut, run from maintenance work like the plague. Why? Well, consulting architects avoid maintenance because it sucks. It's tedious, frustrating, and completely uninspired. That's why they gave it to you, the new guy.

The average maintenance engineer will usually be given a few thousand lines of code, a brief explanation, and then directed to make improvements. They rarely have had the benefit of being a part of the original development team and are often confronted with even stricter deadlines. This book is dedicated to such maintenance programmers, who slog away in dimly lit cubes, drink day-old coffee, and wonder silently to themselves, "How on earth did I ever get into this mess?"

Maintenance engineers of the world: I feel your pain.

Organization

Software, as it is developed today, tends to follow a series of basic dance steps that include construction, testing, debugging, and fine-tuning. A number of models describe the general process. For instance, the venerable waterfall approach (see Figure 2) is one of the oldest models for describing how these development dance steps are ordered.

---

3.   Don Clark, "Windows NT Is Back," *The Wall Street Journal*, July 29, 1996

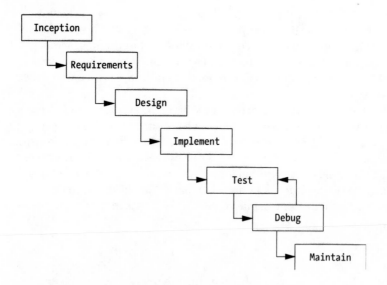

Figure 2. The waterfall development model

Many engineers scoff at the waterfall model, and with good reason. In today's environment, where businesses age in Silicon Valley years, there are really only two steps in the process, implementation and maintenance, and the people who perform the implementation have all made a run for the border.

This book consists of seven chapters. I spend the very first chapter trying to spell out a few tricks that can possibly save you from reading the next three chapters—which is to say that I offer a few pointers on how to write code that is bug resistant. If you are not in the enviable position of writing the first cut of a software program, then you can ignore the first chapter. Chapters 2 through 4 are dedicated to the high art of debugging. I not only look at strategies for debugging code, but I also examine how debuggers function internally.

Besides debugging, most maintenance engineers spend their workday fine-tuning programs to improve their performance. Chapters 5 and 6 are devoted to explaining ways to make more efficient use of a computer's resources. I end the book with an abbreviated final chapter that offers a few words of hard-won advice.

Following is a more detailed rundown of what each chapter covers.

Chapter 1: Preventative Medicine

The original authors of a program are almost always responsible for most of the bugs. Engineers, in the privileged position of building a piece of software from scratch, have the unique opportunity to institute conventions that minimize the number of bugs that they embed in their creation. This chapter is devoted to examining a set of techniques that can be used to construct software that is easy to modify, and hence easy to debug.

Chapter 2: Debugging Tactics

This chapter presents a step-by-step approach for locating and eliminating software bugs. I begin by discussing how to verify that the issue you are dealing with is actually a bug. Next, I examine the scientific method and explain how it can be applied to deal with bugs. To persist in your work and provide a trail guide for the engineers who follow after you, this chapter looks at the methods that can be used to track maintenance work.

Chapter 3: Understand the Problem

In Chapter 2, I mention that understanding the problem, and program, that you are working with is a prerequisite. But how do you "understand the problem" when you are confronted with 50,000 lines of cryptic Kernighan and Ritchie C? Aha! That is the $64,000 question. In this chapter, I provide a number of battle-tested methods that you can use to address this question. At the end of the day, there is no replacement for hard work. However, there are steps you can take to make your job easier. I can only say, in my own defense, that it is easier to write about this topic than it is to actually do it.

Chapter 4: Debugger Internals

Understanding how a debugger works, underneath the hood, is not required to use a debugger successfully. However, there may be a few curious readers who have a nagging desire to know how debuggers operate. This chapter is devoted to explaining the essentials of how debuggers do what they do. I begin with basic features, like breakpoints and single stepping, and then gradually move into more advanced functionality. I conclude this chapter with a discussion of techniques that can be used to protect your program from being reverse engineered.

Chapter 5: Optimization: Memory Footprint

Computers have two resources: memory and CPU cycles. Successful optimization depends upon being able to both minimize the memory footprint of an application and make efficient use of processor cycles. It is a very delicate balancing act. This chapter looks at the first half of this puzzle by offering techniques for reducing the amount of memory that an application uses. All of the standard memory components of a program are examined, including the code segment, data segment, stack, and heap.

Chapter 6: Optimization: CPU Cycles

This chapter is the second half of the discussion that began in Chapter 5. Specifically, Chapter 6 presents a number of ways in which programs waste processor cycles, and then offers solutions in each instance. I begin by analyzing elementary program control constructs, like loops and branching statements, and then move on to more advanced topics, like exception handling and memory management.

Chapter 7: Final Words of Advice

Some things your professors in school will not warn you about, primarily because they can't: they have spent most of their professional lives in academia. There have been those, however, who left the cocoon-like safety of the university to brave the elements in the software industry. In this chapter, I tell you a few things that I, and others like me, have learned.

Typographical Conventions

In this book, the courier font is used to indicate that text is one of the following:

- Console output

- A filename or file extension type

- Source code

- Numeric values

Hexadecimal values are indicated, in this book, by prefixing them with a 0x. For example, the integer value 5689 will, in hexadecimal, look like 0x1639. Words will appear in the *italic* font, in this book, for two reasons:

- When defining a new term

- For emphasis

Prerequisites

The examples in this book are primarily implemented in a combination of ANSI C, C++, and ×86 assembly language. I rely on C/C++ and assembler not only to appeal to the largest number of programmers, but also to provide insight. To see why a certain strategy is effective, there will be times when you will need to see what the compiler is doing behind the scenes. The best way to do this is to take a look at the assembly code that the compiler generates. Having said that, my use of assembly code is fairly pedestrian, and I think that most engineers who have spent any time behind the wheel will be comfortable reading through my code.

Initially, I thought about using Java to implement examples. However, I have found that the flexibility of C and C++ provides greater opportunity for misuse and mistakes. What did Spider-Man say? With great power comes great responsibility? C and C++ are powerful languages. Hence, with C/C++ it's easier to make a mess. Memory leaks and dangling pointers have beset C programmers for decades, not to mention preprocessor pyrotechnics and arbitrary levels of indirection. In short, C and C++ provide fertile territory for discussing debugging and optimization.

I have often listened to debates concerning the relative merits of C++ and Java. As far as I am concerned, these two languages are different tools used for different jobs. It is like asking, "Which is better, a pencil or a pen?" Both languages are object oriented, but the primary difference between them lies in their orientation. Specifically, Java is an *application language* and C++ is a *system language.*

Java programs are compiled to run on a virtual machine. "Write once, run anywhere" is the fundamental benefit of implementing a project with Java. This feature has made the language extremely popular with software companies, like IBM, that strive for cross-platform portability. The downside to this is that you cannot directly interact with native hardware. By striving for portability, Java has insulated itself from the host machine.

Likewise, building system software requires that you have the ability to do things like insert inline assembly code, explicitly manipulate memory, and generate a native executable. It just so happens that C++ provides these features. It is no surprise, then, that almost every operating system currently in production is written in a combination of C and C++. When it comes to handling interrupts and communicating with hardware, there is always some assembly code involved—it's unavoidable. C and C++ allow high-level constructs and assembly code to intermingle so that assembly-level routines can be hidden away in the bowels of the system.

CHAPTER 1
Preventative Medicine

Quite frankly, I'd rather weed out the people who don't start being careful early rather than late. That sounds callous, and by God, it _is_ callous. But it's not the kind of "if you can't stand the heat, get out of the kitchen" kind of remark that some people take it for. No, it's something much more deeper: I'd rather not work with people who aren't careful. It's Darwinism in software development.

—Linus Torvalds on kernel debuggers, Linux Kernel Mailing List

The role of the maintenance engineer is to exorcise the evil spirits that dwell in legacy software. Day and night, maintenance engineers are beset upon, and spited, as they forge a lonely path through the corporate landscape. Every day, they face the challenge of

- Repairing bugs

- Improving performance

1

The first four chapters of this book are devoted to looking at the first task. The final two chapters of this book deal with the second task.

An 1896 electrical handbook entitled Hawkin's *New Catechism of Electricity* states that "The term 'bug' is used, to a limited extent, to designate any fault or trouble in the connections or working of electric apparatus."[1] This term evolved, with a little help from Rear Admiral Grace Murray Hopper (the inventor of COBOL), to denote a malfunction in a computer program.

Dealing with bugs is one of the most odious tasks that a programmer can perform. Given this fact, the best time to deal with a software bug is during the implementation phase. In other words, fix the problems before they become a part of the release build. This saves maintenance engineers from having to deal with them later on, after the bugs have had the chance to burrow deeply and hide. Many professionals, including Linus Torvalds, agree with this train of thought.

Sun Tzu once said, *"You should do something large while it is still small."* In other words, have the foresight to implement corrections and isolate problems early. This way you won't have to worry about getting a phone call at 3:00 in the morning from an angry system administrator.

In this chapter, I will examine preventative measures that can be used to make source code less susceptible to bugs. If you are an engineer in the process of building a brand new piece of software, or adding a new feature, you should read this chapter carefully. On the other hand, if you have been handed an application that you did *not* write (and this is a very common occurrence), then I would recommend that you skip this chapter initially, and go to the next chapter. Once you have dealt with the offending bug, you can come back and use the techniques in this chapter to help you clean up your patch.

1.1 Core Problems

You may be smirking to yourself right about now: "Catch bugs before they occur? Ha, if it were only that simple!" The real world is rife with external pressures that confound this type of measure-twice-cut-once approach to software development. In this section, I will examine real-world problems that can lead to the construction of buggy code, and offer possible remedies when I can.

---

1.   Eric S. Raymond, ed., *The New Hacker's Dictionary, Third Edition* (MIT Press, 1996. ISBN: 0-262-68092-0)

1.1.1 Time to Market Pressure

The problem with using disciplined engineering practices to catch program bugs is that they require extra effort, and extra effort costs time. Time is a valuable commodity in the post dot-com era. Software companies are under intense pressure, from their backers, to beat their competitors to the punch. They aren't given the time to invest in a solid development scheme. Heck, even if they did have the time to utilize a sane development methodology, many companies wouldn't know how because these same companies usually try to save money by hiring inexperienced developers. All that matters is getting a product out the door as soon as possible, preferably under budget. Yes, you're right, it is stupid. Welcome to the business world.

Haste Makes Waste

While the time-driven approach may garner results from a marketing perspective, where perception is everything, over the long run it is a losing strategy. *Haste makes waste,* to the extent that it has been designated as a design antipattern.[2] When software engineers rush to get things done, they work late, they take shortcuts, and this results in bugs. It's as simple as that.

Who cares if a company is the first to release a product, especially if the product being sold is so bug-ridden and clunky that it alienates users? Being first doesn't matter if your execution sucks. It doesn't matter how much buzz the marketing people can generate.

Let's look at a case study. When IBM released OS/2 version 2.00 in 1992, they touted the fact that it was the first true 32-bit operating system for the PC. OS/2 supported legacy DOS applications via a 16-bit subsystem (i.e., a DOS Virtual Machine) and Windows applications on IBM's licensed version of Windows 3.0 (i.e., Win-OS/2). The problem was that the compatibility code was so poor that it forced DOS and Windows applications to slow to a crawl. Not to mention the perplexing peripheral interface, which was an absolute disaster. Adding a new printer on OS/2 was so involved that people literally wrote entire magazine articles on how to do it.

Strictly speaking, OS/2 came to market way before Windows NT 3.1, which was released in 1993. IBM may have beat Dave Cutler to market, but being early didn't help much. OS/2 performed so poorly that customers who could afford 16 megabytes of RAM in 1993 opted for NT. At the time of this

---

2.   William J. Brown et al., *AntiPatterns: Refactoring Software, Architectures, and Projects in Crisis* (John Wiley & Sons, 1998. ISBN: 0-471-19713-0)

book's publishing, IBM is still selling OS/2 Warp 4. Can you believe it? I know an IBM consultant who looked me straight in the face (without smiling) and said, "Inside IBM, OS/2 is still seen as a viable desktop operating system."

Logic Is Not a Factor

After four years of truth tables, and algorithms, and mathematics, most computer science majors expect the world to be run by people who make rational decisions. BZZZZT, sorry, wrong answer. While the argument for using a disciplined development process makes sense, not everything in the business world makes sense. Business decisions often get made that have very little to do with logic. For example, did you know that IBM still sells a version of DOS called PC DOS 2000?

Politics, charisma, and corporate culture can be just as influential as logic. To make matters worse, the executive officers who wield these intangible powers of persuasion tend to have considerably less technical expertise than the engineers. If the slick marketing executive can somehow convince the CEO that they have to get project XYZ to the public before anyone else, then you can expect to be asked to sacrifice everything in the name of expediency. Such is life.

Ultimately, the decision making process in a corporation is run by the golden rule: the person who has the gold makes the rules. Put another way, the person who controls the resources ultimately makes the final decision. Money talks, and logic takes a backseat. You can sulk all you want, but this is how the world runs. Recognizing this will help you understand why things like ridiculous project schedules occur.

Being First Can Backfire

Sometimes being first is actually hazardous, particularly if you get the attention of a larger competitor. It is the pioneers in an industry that have to jump all of the initial hurdles to validate a new product and establish an audience. Large multinational corporations often wait back in the wings, letting the venture startup do the footwork to blaze a new trail. Once the new market has proven to be profitable, the multinationals move in with their salesmen and economies of scale. If the pioneers are lucky, a competing multinational might buy them out.

Let's look back at history again. In December 1994, Netscape released the first version of its Navigator Web browser. This caught the attention of Bill Gates, who not only realized that Netscape was on to something, but that it also threatened his business. Subsequently, Gates unleashed his army of developers and in August 1995 Internet Explorer (IE) version 1.0 was released as a part of the Windows 95 PLUS pack. Not only that, but the price for IE was right. As everyone knows, it is not wise to stand in the way of an oncoming

18-wheel Mack truck. Likewise, it is not very bright to get in the way of Bill Gates. In 1998, after several years of assault, America Online (AOL) acquired Netscape in a transaction worth $4.2 billion.[3] Like I said: if the pioneers are lucky . . .

The moral of this story is not that you shouldn't be first because a larger competitor will crush you. Rather, I believe that if you are going to sell a software application, then you should make sure that it has every advantage possible so that it can stand apart from similar products. This includes taking the time and investing the resources necessary to ensure application stability.

Increased Competition

How did things get so competitive? Why the rush to market? Whatever happened to Ward Cleaver and his nine-to-five job? Well, I don't have a definite answer, but I can speculate. I am of the opinion that the emergence of pervasive networking has allowed consumers to become pickier. This may sound simpleminded, but I think that the aggregate impact of well-informed consumers is more significant that you might suspect. What used to be a seller's market is now a buyer's market.

For example, back in 1970, most consumers trying to buy a television were stuck with the vendors in their immediate vicinity. Finding different purveyors and comparing prices meant digging around for information that was difficult to locate. Today, if you don't like the price that the dealer down the street is selling at, you can crank up a Web browser and check out price information on eBay. Data that was once very time-consuming to obtain is now very easy to acquire.

1.1.2 Fluid Specifications

Sometimes people don't really know what they want, even after they have told you. In pathological cases, the sponsor of a software project may keep adding new requirements while the engineers are in the process of implementing that project. This is known as *feature creep*. It is an insidious project killer.

Feature Creep Causes Premature Code Decay

Most software programs can stand only so much modification before they need to be completely redesigned. Another way of saying this is that change

---

3. Rebecca Sykes, "AOL buys Netscape, joins Sun in Java Deal," IDG News Service, November 24, 1998

can damage the integrity of a program's design. Modified code becomes brittle. By initiating this gradual decay early, during the implementation phase, feature creep makes life more difficult for the maintenance engineer. It's like moving into a new house, only to find that squatters have already lived there and made a few renovations of their own.

There Is Always Something New

The early adoption of new technology is one of the most common causes of feature creep. In the software industry, in general, some new development framework is always waiting around the next corner. It is the nature of the beast. Technophiles, or people who are stalling for time, will often "discover" a new gizmo and then demand that new requirements be added for it (with the justification that it allows for future flexibility). In terminal cases, a project will *never* be deployed because each time it nears code cutoff, a new technology is discovered.

1.1.3 Trade Features for Time

How exactly should an engineer cope with unreasonable deadlines and feature creep? The best way to deal with deadlines is to quantify them in terms of application features. The longer you have to work on a project, the more features you will be able to implement. Likewise, the less time you have to work on a project, the fewer features you will be able to implement. If a project sponsor wants to stick you with a tight schedule, then you should accept the schedule only after doing an analysis to determine which features you can successfully implement in that period of time.

The alternative is to spend the next six months pulling 15-hour days, trying to meet a deadline that may be completely unrealistic. This type of deadline basically forces you to exchange your life for a paycheck, which is a bad deal by any standard. No one lies on their deathbed wishing they had spent more time at the office. If you are a software engineer spending 15 hours a day at work, you need to get a life. Sitting in front of a computer for weeks on end may seem heroic, at first glance, but it is a losing strategy over the long run. Have you ever looked at software that was written by someone subsisting on 3 hours of sleep?

If project sponsors approach you with a request to add a new feature while you are knee-deep in the implementation phase, you should make them aware that this new feature will require the timetable to be adjusted to accommodate the new feature. In other words, tell sponsors that they will not get the new feature for free; it will cost them time. Time translates into money, and money is a language that most business people understand. This is the key to dealing with executives: find a way to speak to them in their native language (i.e., $$).

1.1.4 Get It in Writing

There is a sinister little game that Marine Corps drill instructors sometimes play on candidates in basic training. One day, while a candidate is nervously standing at attention, a drill instructor walks up and says something like this:

"Private Blunden, the other drill instructors tell me that you are a pretty smart guy. Well, private, I have decided that I would like to see this for myself. Private Blunden, I'd like you to demonstrate your renowned brilliance and raise your hand for me."

This is a setup. When the candidate raises one of their hands, the drill instructor will yell at the top of their lungs:

"I meant the other hand, Blunden, you stupid SOB! You raised the wrong *@#$% hand!"

This sadistic trick teaches an important message. Always ask for clarification if you feel like the directions that you have been given are ambiguous. Otherwise, someone can accuse you of doing the wrong thing.

If someone really wants to stick it to you, they will intentionally give you ambiguous orders so that they have an excuse to attack you when you don't do things their way. In other words, both answers are wrong, and they're just looking for an excuse to abuse you. You could breathe air and they'd start criticizing you for breathing out of your nose instead of your mouth.

Nail Down Requirements

You should never make an assumption about a software requirement that you think is ambiguous. Always encourage customers to tell you exactly what it is they want, even if you have to drag it out of them. Better that you annoy them up front than have to spend weeks reimplementing a core product feature.

This is your responsibility as an engineer. Do not sit passively hoping that someone will magically appear at your cube and tell you everything that you need to know. Don't fall into this trap—and it is a trap. You need to be aggressive. If you aren't clear on an issue, relentlessly hunt down the truth until you find it. No one else is going to do if for you, so if you just sit in your cube, scratching your head, you are wasting valuable time.

To be honest, a lot of people have a problem with this, including me. I prefer to be given a well-defined task and then sit down and work on it. I find it aggravating when I have to run around, bouncing from one person to the next, to try and get a straight answer from someone. To me, this seems like a huge waste of time and money. Like I said, the business world does not always make sense.

Get a Signature

Once you have extracted a set of solid requirements, the next step would be to record them as a document and have the project sponsor sign them. This document now constitutes a contract that binds the involved parties. The benefit of such a contract is that it establishes a common set of expectations and decreases the likelihood of a misunderstanding.

But why get a signature? It's not like anyone is getting married? Or is it . . .

Foil Plausible Deniability

During your career you may meet people, particularly higher-ups in the food chain, who do not like to put anything in writing. There is a reason for this preference, a reason that may not be immediately recognizable to more decent and honest members of the audience. The truth is that anything in writing creates a paper trail. Well-maintained paper trails can be used to track down the people responsible for making certain decisions. Responsibility can translate into blame, and blame translates into unemployment. Understand?

> *To err is human. To cover it up is weasel.*
>
> —Scott Adams, *Dilbert and the Way of the Weasel*

The business world has its share of weasels. If the project that you are working on heads south, less scrupulous people may be tempted to switch sides and ridicule a project that they once championed. This reminds me of people who always cheer for the winning team in a play-off series. In a less drastic scenario, a manager may simply deny any responsibility for failure and lay the blame on someone else's shoulders. "It's not my fault, Mr. Gerstner, everyone knows that those guys over in manufacturing couldn't keep to the specifications." Don't think that this doesn't happen. A good paper trail will safeguard you from weasels like this.

People with a propensity to "abandon ship" prefer verbal specifications to written specifications, particularly when there are no witnesses to verify the verbal specification. If push comes to shove, they can always make it their word against your word. This is why you want to bind them with a signature, preferably during a meeting, where plenty of other people are around, in a room with CCTV cameras.

If you cannot get a signature, then at least make sure to schedule a meeting and invite everyone who has a stake in the project. During the meeting you can nail down requirements without having to demand that the project sponsor sign anything in blood. However, make sure to designate someone to transcribe the meeting and then send that transcription, via e-mail, to all of the participants. If people are not adverse, you can opt to tape-record the meeting so that no one is stuck as a transcriber.

In the worst-case scenario, you may be dealing with a *ghost*. In other words, the people dictating requirements may be able to elude making public statements. Or, if they do, they will never say anything incriminating. Ghosts tend to have political savvy and years of experience playing the game. This makes them dangerous. Ghosts prefer to corner you in the hallway and dictate their requirements during an impromptu conversation. This backroom approach to deal making is favored by people who don't like being quoted. Can you spell "plausible deniability"?

Use E-Mail

If you cannot schedule a formal meeting, then follow up the conversations with e-mail. Make sure to send copies of the e-mail to others involved with the project. You want the ghost to know that the conversation is now public knowledge. This will prevent sudden bouts of amnesia. *The basic idea behind all of this is that you need to create some sort of artifact.* If the waters become stormy, you will need evidence to protect yourself. Your credibility depends upon it. Maintain a paper trail and then make copies.

Buy a Home Safe

Once you have generated a paper trail, take it home at the end of the day and store it in a safe place. I prefer a 700-pound TLTR-30x6 vault, which can withstand tools and a blowtorch for 30 minutes on all six sides.[4]

This may sound a little paranoid, but it's not. Trust me. Shredding documents to destroy the paper trail is a time-honored tradition in the business world (uh, ahem . . . Enron, uh, ahem . . . Arthur Andersen). Your desk, chair, computer, and office supplies at work aren't really yours; they are tools for you to do your job and are the property of your employer. There is nothing that prevents a manager from walking up to your desk and taking every last bit of evidence to the garbage bin.

---

4.   Gardall Safe Corporation, P.O. Box 240, Syracuse, NY 13206-0240. Phone: 1-800-722-7233

1.1.5 Complexity

As software technology has evolved, better tools and development environments have allowed us to construct larger applications. Larger applications have more "moving parts," and this makes them more difficult to understand. To get an idea of what I am talking about, compare the source code of a binary search tree (BST) to that of a B*-tree. Compared to a B*-tree, a BST is a walk in the park.

If a program is complicated, then more effort is needed to maintain it. Not only that, but if you can't understand a program, then it is also more likely that you will introduce bugs when you modify it. Complexity is the natural enemy of maintenance programmers.

Complexity Supports Bug Conservation

Most maintenance engineers prefer to get in, make a quick update, and then get out, without having to read the entire application. A complex application can make it difficult, if not impossible, for maintenance engineers to follow this standard modus operandi. Instead, they have to invest time climbing a learning curve, which can take days or even months.

A little bit of knowledge is a dangerous thing. If maintenance engineers try to fix an intricate program that they do not completely understand, the patch can end up creating more problems than it solves. This explains how service packs often introduce the same number of bugs as they solve, such that the total number of bugs remains constant. This phenomenon is known as *conservation of bugs*.

Complexity Undermines System Security

The relationship between complexity and bug cardinality in software development is analogous to the United States federal tax code. The more rules there are, and the more special cases that exist, the easier it is for some sneaky accountant to find a tax code loophole to exploit. Likewise, the more logic there is in a software program, the easier it is for some wily hacker to discover a bug to exploit. Hence, not only is complicated code a royal pain to maintain, but it also undermines security.

By the end of this century, I suspect that we will see software applications composed of billions of lines of code. A billion lines of code is a large piece of software real estate. Do you think that a few security exploits may be hiding in there somewhere?

Microsoft Windows

Let's take a look at Microsoft's operating systems (see Table 1-1).

Table 1-1. The Growth of Windows

OS	Lines of Code	Source
PC DOS v1.0	4,000	Andrew Tanenbaum, *Modern Operating Systems, Second Edition* (Prentice Hall, 2001. ISBN: 0-13-031358-0)
Windows NT 3.1	6 million	"The Long and Winding Windows NT Road," table, *Business Week*, February 22, 1999
Windows 98	18 million	*United States v. Microsoft*, February 2, 1999, a.m. session
Windows 2000	35 million	Michael Martinez, "At Long Last Windows 2000 Operating System to Ship in February," Associated Press, December 15, 1999
Windows XP	45 million	Alex Salkever, "Windows XP: A Firewall for All," *Business Week*, June 12, 2001

In 1981, the IBM PC was released with a version of DOS owned by Microsoft. It consisted of a few thousand lines of assembly language. These were the salad days; hardware interfaces were built on simple BIOS interrupts and memory was defined by a 20-bit address space. Two decades later, Windows XP consists of 45 million lines of code, and has a hardware model that is so elaborate that most engineers have to digest an 800-page book before they can really tackle the problem.[5]

Given that Microsoft's operating systems have grown larger and more complicated, it should come as no surprise that when Microsoft released Windows XP, there were 18 megabytes worth of patch binaries posted at Microsoft's Web site.[6] This is not an isolated incident. Any system administrator who worked with Windows NT during the 1990s will tell you that NT v4.0 was not worth a damn until Service Pack 3.0 was installed (Service Pack 3.0 was roughly 17.5 megabytes in size).

---

5. Walter Oney, *Programming the Microsoft Windows Driver Model, Second Edition* (Microsoft Press, 2002. ISBN: 0-7356-1803-8)

6. Charles Mann, "Why Software Is So Bad," *Technology Review*, June 17, 2002

Perhaps Nathan Myhrvold was right when he said, "Software sucks because users demand it to."[7] Users request new features, which get implemented and cause the application to be bigger. This extra size, as an unintended side effect, makes it more difficult for maintenance engineers to understand, update, and debug.

How do you deal with complexity? That is not a question that I can answer in a couple of sentences. In fact, I will spend most of Chapter 3 on this question. For the time being, all you need to realize is that complexity is the most formidable adversary of a maintenance engineer.

1.2 Defensive Programming

Defensive programming is like driving a car. When I was 16, my father told me to always drive defensively. Initially, I thought he was talking about driving around with a shotgun in the trunk. When I asked him what that meant, he told me, "Cars can be killing machines; you not only have to watch your own driving, but you also have to watch out for the other guy."

Defensive programming is *proactive*; it is utilized during the initial implementation of an application (as opposed to *refactoring*, which is *reactive*). In this section, I will present a collection of defensive programming tactics that you can use to make your code resistant to bugs.

1.2.1 Cohesion and Coupling

Cohesion and *coupling* are qualities that can greatly influence your ability to modify a program's source code. As a general rule, you should always aim to create functions that have *strong* cohesion and *weak* coupling.

Cohesion *A measure of how closely the instructions in a procedure are related to each other*

A function that demonstrates strong cohesion will focus on performing a single task. Cohesive functions do not have unexpected side effects. A function that has *weak* cohesion will attempt to perform a number of operations, not all of which are necessarily related. Cohesive functions discourage cut-and-paste programming by isolating related instructions in one place. This, in turn, fosters reuse and prevents redundant source code fragments from popping up.

---

7.   Ibid.

Consider the following code fragment:

```
int processOrder(char* code, int itemID, int nItems)

{
        int dbHandle;
        char record[REC_SZ];//edit the fields
        if((code[0]!='B')&&(code[0]!='C')){ return(ERR_INVALID_CODE); }
        if((itemID<0)||(itemID>MAX_ID)){ return(ERR_INVALID_ID); }
        if((itemID<0)||(itemID>MAX_ORDER_SZ))
        {
                    return(ERR_INVALID_ORDER_SZ);
        }
        //open the database
        dbHandle = openDB("corporateDB","orderEntry.db");
        if(dbHandle==NULL){ return(ERR_OPENING_DB); }
        //store the customer's order and go home
        sprintf(record,"%s%04X%05X",code,itemID,nItems);
        dbAddRecord(record);
        if(closeDB(dbHandle)){ return(ERR_CLOSING_DB); }
        return(RET_OK);
}
```

The previous code accepts order information for some item, in inventory, and persists the order in a database table named orderEntry.db. This function does a number of tasks, some of which may be invoked again in other places.

It would improve the long-term integrity of the code if snippets of related program logic were placed in their own, small, cohesive functions:

```
int processOrder( char* code, int itemID, int nItems )
{
        FieldEditor edit = FieldEditor();
        try
        {
                    edit.fieldCode(code);
                    edit.itemID(itemID);
                    edit.orderSize(nItems);
                    (*this).addOrderEntry(code,itemID,nItems);
        }
        catch(int error)
        {
                    return(error);
        }
        return(RET_OK);
}
```

Notice how I replaced the set of branching tests with a single `try-catch` block. All told, this looks much better and is easier to understand.

Coupling   *A measure of how closely a procedure's execution depends upon other procedures*

Husbands and wives are strongly coupled, whereas teachers and their students are weakly coupled. A teacher should be able to interface with each student equally well. A husband and wife are more likely to share confidences with each other than with other people.

Coupling denotes semantic connection. Strongly coupled functions are difficult to separate because they are closely related to some common goal. Weakly coupled functions can be mixed and matched like building blocks, and are more capable of standing by themselves.

Objects Have Cohesion and Coupling

The concepts of cohesion and coupling are not limited to the structured programming paradigms of the 1970s. Like functions, objects can be described in terms of cohesion and coupling. The same general ideas apply; it's more a matter of granularity than anything else. An object has strong cohesion if its member variables and functions are focused on providing a specific set of closely related services. Likewise, objects are coupled loosely when the internal operation of an object does not depend heavily on other objects.

Use Mediators to Decouple

One technique to encourage loose coupling between functions is to use a design pattern known as a *mediator*. Specifically, when a function invokes another function, it does so indirectly using the mediator as a third party. If the signature of an invoked function changes, nothing needs to be changed in the invoking function because changes can be isolated to the mediator.

Consider the following class member function:

```
/*
Client::sell
Description: Sells client stock at the stock exchange.

Input Parameters:
```

```
        symbol          stock symbol (i.e. "MSFT")
        nShares         number of shares to sell

Return Value:           The price per share the stocks were sold at.
                        A negative value indicates a failed attempt.
*/
float Client::sell( char *symbol, int nShares )
{
        Broker broker = getBroker();
        return(broker.sell((*this).name,(*this).ID, symbol, nShares));
}
```

The client function (i.e., Client::sell()) invokes a Broker object to sell stock at the stock exchange. The client function returns the price per share at which the stock was sold. The Broker object is an intermediary between the client and the stock exchange.

Let's take a look at the internals of the sell() function in the Broker class.

```
/*
Broker::sell
Description: Sells stock at the stock exchange.

Input Parameters:
        name            name of the customer (i.e. "Smith, John")
        id              customer's ID (i.e. "5678-9939")
        symbol          stock symbol (i.e. "MSFT")
        nShares         number of shares to sell

Return Value:           The price per share the stocks were sold at.
                        A negative value indicates a failed attempt.
*/
float Broker::sell(char *name, char *id, char *symbol, int nShares)
{
        struct MemberInfo info;
        info.license    = (*this).licenseID;
        info.broker     = (*this).brokerID;
        info.company    = (*this).name;
        info.expiration   = (*this).expiration;

        if(authenticate(name, id) && ownsStock(name, symbol, nShares))
        {
                updateClientInfo(name, id, symbol, nShares);
                return(exchange.sell(&info, symbol, nShares));
        }
        return(-1.0);
}
```

The Broker object's sell() function authenticates the client and then sells the stock by invoking a method on its private Exchange object. Any changes to the sell() member function in the Exchange class can be isolated within the Broker class. The client's version of sell() can remain unchanged.

The Bottom Line

Maintaining and debugging code entails making changes. In fact, code is often judged in terms of how well it accommodates modifications. Cohesion makes implementing changes simpler by making routines easier to understand. Loose coupling makes implementing changes simpler by making the connections between different routines malleable. An engineer who is programming defensively will utilize functions that have strong cohesion and weak coupling.

1.2.2 Checking for Bad Input

As I stated earlier, defensive programming is about watching out for the other guy. For example, it is dangerous to assume that the arguments passed to a function will always be reasonable. Here is a very simple example of what I'm talking about:

```
float average(float *array, int size)
{
      float sum=0;
      int i;
      for(i=0;i<size;i++){ sum = sum + array[i]; }
      return(sum/((double)size));
}
```

The previous code does not check to see if the size argument is zero. The average() function could inadvertently be fed an argument whose value is zero and then attempt to divide by zero in the return statement.

Solving this problem is as simple as adding a line of code:

```
float average(float *array, int size)
{
      float sum=0;
      int i;
      if(size<=0){  throw(DIVIDE_BY_ZERO);  }
      for(i=0;i<size;i++){ sum = sum + array[i]; }
      return(sum/((double)size));
}
```

Types of Bad Arguments

All sorts of bad arguments can be passed to a function. The following list enumerates a few of the more common types:

- NULL pointers

- Dangling pointers

- Out-of-range values

- Incorrect data types

- Incorrect amount of data

NULL pointers can be dealt with easily; you just check to see if a pointer is equal to NULL. Dangling pointers are a little more problematic; the best way to deal with them is to be disciplined with how and when you allocate and free memory. In other words, there is no simple way to test for a dangling pointer (i.e., without getting platform specific or perhaps writing your own memory management service).

Incorrect data type arguments are a serious problem in C, a language that makes it very easy to allow one thing to look like another. Take a look at the following routine:

```
void casting()
{
    char *sPtr;

    sPtr = (FILE *)malloc(sizeof(FILE *));
    sPtr = (FILE *)fopen("file.txt","w");
    if(sPtr==NULL){ return; }

    printf("%lu\n",abs(sPtr));

    fputs("never sit with your back to the door\n",(FILE *)sPtr);
    fclose((FILE *)sPtr);
    return;
}
```

In the previous code you have a pointer, to a character value, storing the address of a FILE structure. This address can then be used as an integer argument to a function. The casting facilities of C allow a specific type of value to masquerade as something that has a completely different purpose. As with dangling pointers, incorrect data types are sometimes more of a semantic problem. You'll have to keep an eye out and review your code periodically for careless errors.

Buffer Overflows

A whole cottage industry of hacking tools has arisen from the existence of buffer overflow problems. A buffer overflow occurs when too much data is fed to a function as an argument. The argument ends up overwriting the activation record of the invoked function, and this can result in the execution of foreign code. Aleph One authored the canonical work on buffer overflows, "Smashing the Stack for Fun and Profit," in issue 49 of *Phrack* magazine. What I am going to give you is basically the executive summary of that article.

Let's take a closer look at how buffer overflows work. Examine the following code:

```c
/* BufferOverflow.c -----------------------------------------*/
#include<stdio.h>
#include<stdlib.h>
#include<string.h>
#define BUFFER_SIZE        4

void victim(char *str)
{
     char buffer[BUFFER_SIZE];
     strcpy(buffer,str);
     return;
}/*end victim-------------------------------------------------*/
void redirected()
{
     printf("\tYou've been redirected!\n");
     exit(0);
     return;
}/*end redirected--------------------------------------------*/
void main()
{
     char buffer[]=
     {
             '1','2','3','4',                  /*buffer[4 bytes]*/
             '5','6','7','8',                  /*EBP[4 bytes] */
             '\x0','\x0','\x0','\x0','\x0'     /*EIP[4 bytes]*/
     };
     void *fptr;
     unsigned long *lptr;

     printf("buffer = %s\n",buffer);
```

```
fptr = redirected;
lptr = (unsigned long*)(&buffer[8]);
*lptr = (unsigned long)fptr;

printf("main()\n");
victim(buffer);
printf("main()\n");      // the program will never make it to this code
return;
}/*end main------------------------------------------------------------*/
```

When this program is executed, the following output is streamed to standard output:

```
buffer = 12345678
main()
        You've been redirected!
```

The key to this technique is the activation record of the victim() function. The basic makeup of the activation record is displayed in Figure 1-1.

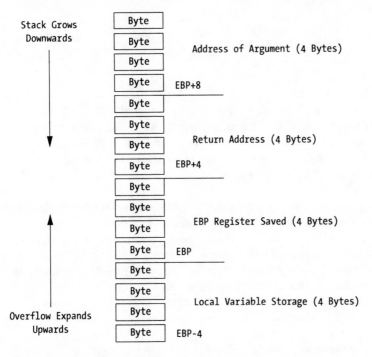

Figure 1-1. The activation record of victim()

The fun begins when you store the address of the redirected() function in the last few bytes of the buffer[] array, as shown in the following snippet. This will come in handy later on.

```
fptr = redirected;
lptr = (unsigned long*)(&buffer[8]);
*lptr = (unsigned long)fptr;
```

When the victim() function is invoked from main(), the first thing that happens is that the address of the array argument is pushed onto the stack. Next, the return address is pushed onto the stack.

```
lea eax, DWORD PTR _buffer$[ebp]
push eax
call _victim
```

Once execution has jumped to victim(), assuming you are working on Intel, the contents of the EBP register will be saved on the stack so that it can be used to refer to the contents of the activation record (activation record elements are specified in terms of an offset from EBP).[8] The current stack pointer is copied into EBP and storage for local variables is allocated.

```
push ebp          #save EBP
mov ebp, esp      #EBP now points to stack frame
push ecx          #make room for local variables
```

All told, the activation record for victim() is 16 bytes in size.

When the strcpy() routine is called, the buff[] array in victim() can only handle the first 4 bytes of the 13-byte argument. This means that a part of victim()'s activation frame will be overwritten (see Figure 1-2). Specifically, the old return address is adjusted to point to the address of redirected(). When the victim() function tries to return, it will cause execution to take a little detour.

What I just gave you was the featherweight version of the buffer overflow trick. When the big dogs do this trick, they embed instructions in the overflow and rewrite the function's return address so that it ends up executing these embedded instructions. If the application executing this foreign code is running as the root user, the hacker can very easily take over the machine. In other words, that hacker can sink your battleship.

Protecting yourself against this kind of attack is actually fairly simple. To defend against buffer overflows, you should always avoid functions like strcpy() and strcat(), which don't bounds check when they copy. Instead, use functions like strncpy() and strncat().

---

8. *Introduction to Assembly Language Programming* (Springer Verlag, 1998). ISBN: 0-387-98530-1)

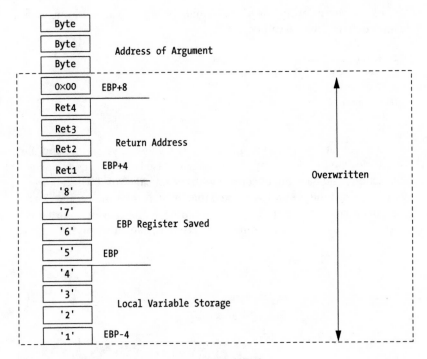

Figure 1-2. The activation record is modified.

Double-Checking Creates Code Bloat

There is a downside to all this double-checking code: it adds to the memory footprint of your application. Checking code translates into extra instructions in the final binary. One solution to this problem is to use macros that can be removed.

```
#ifdef DEBUG
#define CHECK(x)   if(x<=0){ throw(X_ERROR); }
#else
#define CHECK(x)
#endif
```

While the macro solution addresses the memory footprint issue, it does not improve code readability. The potential still exists for your code to have so many macro statements that you can't follow the logical flow of the code. In a worst-case scenario, every line of code would be accompanied by one or more lines of macro-based validation.

```
CHECK_DB_NAME(dbStr);
CHECK_DB_TABLE_NAME(dbTableStr);
dbHandle = openDB(dbStr,dbTableStr);
CHECK_DB(dbhandle);
```

Another solution would be to build a *firewall* between your code and the outside world. You can do this by placing macro-based checking code only in those functions that have direct contact with the outside world. This allows functions inside of the firewall to assume that all of the arguments that they receive will be sane (see Figure 1-3). Implementing a firewall works particularly well when a system has a limited interface to the outside world.

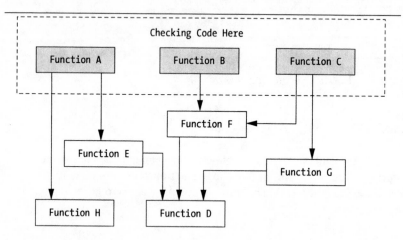

Figure 1-3. Selective software fortification

Fail Gracefully

If your program is going to crash, try to make it as graceful a crash as possible. I recommend adhering to the following guidelines:

- If the current program state can be corrected, do so.

- If corrections can't be made, try reverting to a default state.

- If you cannot revert to a default state, alert the user somehow.

- Give the user the opportunity to make adjustments, or to abort.

- If the user wants to abort, release resources/save state information.

In short, try to have an application *heal itself* if an error occurs (forget about using pixie dust). If the program is beyond healing, then kill it safely (i.e., close open files, shut down network connections, terminate other running threads, etc.) and preserve enough state information to facilitate forensic analysis.

Naturally, there are some events that an application cannot recover from. A good example of this is a kernel mode driver that has run amok. In this case, the kernel itself has gone haywire, and your application probably won't be given the opportunity to do anything of consequence before the machine spirals towards a fiery crash.

1.2.3 Data Scope

Global variables, particularly in a structured language like C, can sabotage the integrity of a program. Their presence may start off innocently, but the road to hell is paved with good intentions. Early languages like COBOL utilize a single code segment and a single data segment. Traditional COBOL applications don't have a stack or a heap. In other words, all of a program's variables and routines in COBOL are global. Everything can call everything else. There is no privacy. Local variables do not exist. Take a look at the following short COBOL program:

```
000010 @OPTIONS MAIN
000013 IDENTIFICATION DIVISION.
000020 PROGRAM-ID. GLOBALAPP.
000021*-------------------------------------------------
000022 ENVIRONMENT DIVISION.
000023 CONFIGURATION SECTION.
000026 INPUT-OUTPUT SECTION.
000027*-------------------------------------------------
000028 DATA DIVISION.
000029 WORKING-STORAGE SECTION.
000030 01 ASSETS PIC 9(3)V99  VALUE 000.00.
000031 01 DEBT   PIC 9(3)V99  VALUE 000.00.
000032 01 NET    PIC S9(3)V99 VALUE 000.00.
000033 01 PRINT  PIC ZZZ.ZZ.
000034*-------------------------------------------------
```

```
000035 PROCEDURE DIVISION.
000036 MAIN-CODE SECTION.
000037 MAIN.
000038 MOVE 121.34 TO ASSETS.
000039 MOVE 57.20  TO DEBT.
000040 PERFORM COMPUTE-NET.
000050 STOP RUN.
000060 SUBROUTINE SECTION.
000070 COMPUTE-NET.
000080 MOVE ASSETS TO NET.
000090 SUBTRACT DEBT FROM NET.
000091 MOVE NET TO PRINT.
000100 DISPLAY " NET: " PRINT.
```

Like all COBOL 85 programs, this one has a single DATA DIVISION and a single PROCEDURE DIVISION. When this program is loaded into memory, the data division will be loaded into the data memory segment and the procedure division will be loaded into the code memory segment. The elements in both memory segments are global.

While a system administrator may love this type of program, because it can't leak memory (i.e., it has no dynamic memory allocation), any programmer worth their salt would run away screaming and hide in the restroom.

But why? The previous COBOL program actually doesn't look that bad? It's only a few dozen lines of source code? Ah ha! You've fallen into the trap. Now imagine a 750,000-line monster in which everything is global, and local variables are "faked" using obscure naming conventions. To locate a subroutine's variables, you have to scroll up half a million lines and search through a list of several thousand declarations.

Global Variables Destroy Modularity

A *modular* program is one that can be decomposed into a set of stand-alone, reusable software components. In object-oriented languages, modularity is referred to as *encapsulation*. Each component in a modular program is basically a little black box that hides its implementation from the rest of the world. This allows the components to behave like Legos, which can painlessly be combined into different configurations. Hassle-free rearrangement facilitates both debugging and maintenance.

NOTE *In some engineering circles, a* component *denotes a software construct that has a certain set of attributes.[9] Specifically, a component must both conceal its implementation and offer an immutable interface. Encapsulation and reusability are the key features of a component. Microsoft supported component construction with the COM framework in the 1990s. Microsoft currently supports a new way of creating custom controls under the .NET Framework.[10]*

Global variables inhibit modularity by causing software components to depend on each other. In other words, global variables tie the implementation of an application's components together in a distinct fashion so that they can't be cleanly separated or reconfigured.

For example, if a program written in a structured language, like C, uses global variables, you can't be sure about what its functions do. The parameter lists give an incomplete view of what the functions use for input, and what they return as output. In the ideal case, you should be able to tell what a function does simply by looking at its type signature. Global variables don't let you do this. Hence, an engineer practicing defensive programming techniques will make a point to *minimize* the scope of variables rather than maximize their scope.

Global Variables Lead to Gruesome Side Effects

Global variables lead to all sorts of gruesome side effects. In a large system, if you change a global variable in one function, it can end up causing unexpected changes in a completely unrelated function. In order to successfully modify a global variable, you have to keep in mind all the other places in which the global variable is used; and the human mind really can only keep about seven items, plus or minus two, in its task list.[11]

In 1999, I was one of the world's struggling Y2K programmers. I slaved away for months in a vast cube farm whose reputation for claiming lives had spread throughout the Midwest. During my tenure, I saw variables named

---

9. Matt Nicholson, "Understanding Software Components," *DNJ Online,* September 1997

10. Duncan Mackenzie, "Developing Custom Windows Controls Using Visual Basic .NET," *MSDN,* May 2002

11. George A. Miller, "The Magical Number Seven, Plus or Minus Two," *Psychological Review,* 1956, vol. 63, pp. 81–97

after people's pets, most of whom were probably all dead considering that the COBOL I was fixing had been written in 1980. There were times when I would change a variable on line 0x00901376 and then see the effects of this change ripple across the system to lines 0x00110453 and 0x00485255.

Having to come to terms with this random behavior, people became superstitious. It was the only way to bring order out of chaos. One programmer I met, named Howie Ernesti, wouldn't check in his fixes unless he had his lucky tie on. Eventually, it got to the point were I was scared to touch anything at all. To compensate for my fear, I became an expert at making cosmetic changes. In November of 1999, when some brave soul stood up and screamed, "Man, we're going to have to rewrite all this freakin' code . . . it's just not maintainable!" we pretended to ignore him. However, as we hunched over our serial terminals, pretending to be deep in thought, we could not help but silently nod in agreement.

1.2.4 Logging

Logging is another tool for the defensive programmer. Logging application data generated at runtime has two basic uses:

- Capture important program events

- Trace program execution

System administrators are interested in the first type of logging. Maintenance engineers are interested in the second type of logging. Tracing program execution is a quick-and-dirty way to see what's going on underneath the hood. It's basically an expedient alternative to cranking up a debugger. In this section, I am going to present a simple logging framework so that you can see what type of issues are important.

Framework Outline

The logging framework that I implemented has three players. A LogMessage object generates log messages. The LogMessage object passes its log messages to a LogFilter object, which screens the messages according to some criterion. Messages that make it past the filter will be passed off to a LogHandler object, which is responsible for persisting the log message (see Figure 1-4).

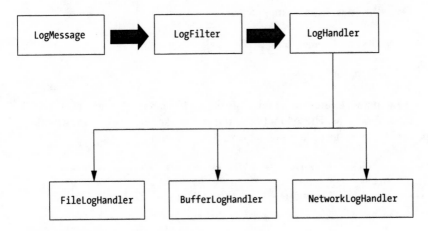

Figure 1-4. The logging framework

The LogFilter class is actually a virtual base class. Its purpose is to spell out an interface that will be implemented by various subclasses (i.e., FileLogHandler, NetworkLogHandler, BufferLogHandler, etc.). The idea is to allow different handlers to be available without the LogFilter having to know about them. All the LogFilter object sees is an array of LogHandler objects.

LogMessage

The LogMessage object generates messages. It is also a singleton object, such that at any time in an application there can be only one LogMessage instance. The general log message format is as follows:

```
[class.function][severity][payload]
```

For example:

```
[Employee.remove()][ERROR][employee does not exist]
```

The message specifies the class and member function that generated the log event. The severity field can be one of three values:

- ADMIN: For normal system events

- ERROR: For terminal faults

- TRACE: For debugging

Log messages are generated by invoking the admin(), trace(), and error() member functions. These functions, in turn, invoke the log() method, which passes the message on to the filter object for screening.

```cpp
/*++++++++++++++++++++++++++++++++++++++++++++++++++++++++++++++++++++++++
+ Declaration                                                            +
++++++++++++++++++++++++++++++++++++++++++++++++++++++++++++++++++++++++*/
class LogMessage
{
        private:
        static LogMessage *logMessage;
        static char *buffer;
        LogFilter *logFilter;
        LogMessage();
        void log
        (
                char *className,
                char *function,
                const char *level,
                char *message
        );

        public:
        const static int MAX_BUFFER_SIZE;
        const static char *ADMIN;
        const static char *ERROR;
        const static char *TRACE;
        static LogMessage* getInstance();
        void registerFilter(LogFilter *logFilter);
        void admin
        (
                char *className,
                char *function,
                char *message
        );
        void error
        (
                char *className,
                char *function,
                char *message
        );
```

```
    void trace
    (
            char *className,
            char *function,
            char *message
    );
};


/*++++++++++++++++++++++++++++++++++++++++++++++++++++++++++++++++++++++
+ Definitions                                                         +
++++++++++++++++++++++++++++++++++++++++++++++++++++++++++++++++++++++*/
const int LogMessage::MAX_BUFFER_SIZE = 1024;
char* LogMessage::buffer = new char[MAX_BUFFER_SIZE];
LogMessage* LogMessage::logMessage=NULL;
const char* LogMessage::ADMIN = "ADMIN";
const char* LogMessage::ERROR = "ERROR";
const char* LogMessage::TRACE = "TRACE";


LogMessage::LogMessage()
{
}/*end constructor-----------------------*/
LogMessage* LogMessage::getInstance()
{
    if(logMessage!=NULL)
    {
            return(logMessage);
    }
    logMessage = new LogMessage;
    return(logMessage);
}/*end LogMessage::getInstance()-----------------------------------*/
void LogMessage::registerFilter(LogFilter *logFilter)
{
    if(logFilter!=NULL)
    {
            (*this).logFilter = logFilter;
    }
}/*end LogMessage::registerFilter--------------------------------*/
void LogMessage::log
(
    char *className,
    char *function,
    const char *level,
    char *message
)
```

```
{
    int length;
    length = strlen(className)+
                    strlen(function)+
                    strlen(level)+
                    strlen(message);
    if(length>=MAX_BUFFER_SIZE){ return; }

    sprintf
    (
            buffer,
            "[%s.%s][%s][%s]\n",
            className,
            function,
            level,
            message
    );
    if(logFilter!=NULL)
    {
            (*logFilter).filter(buffer);
    }
}/*end LogMessage::log----------------------------------------------*/
void LogMessage::admin
(
    char *className,
    char *function,
    char *message
)
{
    (*this).log(className,function,ADMIN,message);
}/*end LogMessage::admin--------------------------------------------*/
void LogMessage::error
(
    char *className,
    char *function,
    char *message
)
{
    (*this).log(className,function,ERROR,message);
}/*end LogMessage::error--------------------------------------------*/
void LogMessage::trace
(
    char *className,
    char *function,
    char *message
)
{
    (*this).log(className,function,TRACE,message);
}/*end LogMessage::trace--------------------------------------------*/
```

LogFilter

The LogFilter object maintains a list of LogHandler objects and screening strings. When a log message is submitted to the LogFilter, via a call to filter(), the log message is compared against a series of filter strings. If no filter strings exist, then all of the messages are passed on to the handlers. Otherwise, LogFilter will only allow messages through that have text specified by at least one of the filters.

For example, let's assume you want to log the following messages:

```
[class.function()][TRACE][the truth is out there]
[class.function()][ERROR][trust no one]
[class.function()][ADMIN][I will not eat green eggs and ham]
[class.function()][ERROR][there are those who call me Tim]
```

Also assume the following four filter strings:

```
"ADMIN"
"test"
"trust"
"kilroy"
```

Only the second and third log messages will pass through the filter and be routed to the LogHandler. This is because the second and third log messages contain filter strings. If no filter strings were specified, then all four of the log messages would be routed to LogHandler.

Let's take a look at the source code for LogFilter:

```
/*++++++++++++++++++++++++++++++++++++++++++++++++++++++++++++++++++
+ Declaration                                                      +
++++++++++++++++++++++++++++++++++++++++++++++++++++++++++++++++++*/

#define MAX_HANDLERS    10
#define MAX_FILTERS     50

class LogFilter
{
    private:
    int nHandlers;
    int nFilters;
    LogHandler *handlerArray[MAX_HANDLERS];
    char *textFilters[MAX_FILTERS];
    char *screen(char *string);
```

```
    public:
    LogFilter();
    void addHandler(LogHandler *logHandler);
    void addFilter(char *string);
    void filter(char *string);
};


/*++++++++++++++++++++++++++++++++++++++++++++++++++++++++++++++++++++++++
+ Definitions                                                            +
++++++++++++++++++++++++++++++++++++++++++++++++++++++++++++++++++++++++*/

LogFilter::LogFilter()
{
    nHandlers = 0;
    nFilters  = 0;
}/*end constructor--------------------------------------------------*/
void LogFilter::addHandler(LogHandler *logHandler)
{
    if(nHandlers==MAX_HANDLERS){ return; }
    handlerArray[nHandlers]=logHandler;
    nHandlers++;
}/*end LogFilter::addHandler----------------------------------------*/
void LogFilter::addFilter(char *string)
{
    if(nFilters==MAX_FILTERS){ return; }
    textFilters[nFilters]=string;
    nFilters++;
}/*end LogFilter::addFilter-----------------------------------------*/
void LogFilter::filter(char *string)
{
    int i;
    if(nFilters==0)
    {
            for(i=0;i<nHandlers;i++)
            {
                    (*handlerArray[i]).persist(string);
            }
            return;
    }

    for(i=0;i<nHandlers;i++)
    {
            if(screen(string)!=NULL)
            {
                    (*handlerArray[i]).persist(string);
            }
    }
```

```
}/*end LogFilter::filter-------------------------------------------*/
char* LogFilter::screen(char *string)
{
    int i;
    for(i=0;i<nFilters;i++)
    {
            if(strstr(string,textFilters[i])!=NULL)
            {
                    return(string);
            }
    }
    return(NULL);
}/*end LogFilter::screen-------------------------------------------*/
```

LogHandler

The LogHandler is an abstract base class with a single pure virtual member function. The LogHandler exists to persist log messages to some type of storage. It also exists to serve as an interface that subclasses must implement.

```
class LogHandler
{
    public:
    virtual void persist(char *string)=0;
};
```

FileLogHandler

The FileLogHandler class extends the LogHandler base class. It takes log messages passed on to it by the filter and persists them to a file.

```
/*++++++++++++++++++++++++++++++++++++++++++++++++++++++++++++++++++
+ Declaration                                                      +
++++++++++++++++++++++++++++++++++++++++++++++++++++++++++++++++++*/

class FileLogHandler:public LogHandler
{
    private:
    FILE *filePtr;
    unsigned int maxMessageSize;

    public:
    FileLogHandler(unsigned int maxMessageSize, FILE *filePtr);
    ~FileLogHandler();
    void persist(char *string);
};
```

```
/*++++++++++++++++++++++++++++++++++++++++++++++++++++++++++++++++++++++++
+ Definitions                                                           +
++++++++++++++++++++++++++++++++++++++++++++++++++++++++++++++++++++++++*/

FileLogHandler::FileLogHandler
(
     unsigned int maxMessageSize,
     FILE *filePtr
)
{
     (*this).maxMessageSize = maxMessageSize;
     (*this).filePtr = filePtr;
}/*end constructor--------------------------------------------------*/
FileLogHandler::~FileLogHandler()
{
     fclose(filePtr);
}/*end destructor---------------------------------------------------*/
void FileLogHandler::persist(char *string)
{
     if(strlen(string)>=maxMessageSize)
     {
          fwrite(string,1,maxMessageSize,filePtr);
          return;
     }
     fputs(string,filePtr);
}/*end FileLogHandler::persist--------------------------------------*/
```

Testing the Logging Framework

The following driver code constructs three log messages and passes them through a filter into a file repository. This file repository just happens to be standard output, so that you can see the results of the driver code visually.

```
FileLogHandler logHandler(LogMessage::MAX_BUFFER_SIZE,stdout);

LogFilter logFilter = LogFilter();
logFilter.addHandler(&logHandler);

logFilter.addFilter((char*)LogMessage::TRACE);
logFilter.addFilter("error msg");

LogMessage *message = LogMessage::getInstance();
(*message).registerFilter(&logFilter);
(*message).admin("class","function","admin msg");
(*message).trace("class","function","trace msg");
(*message).error("class","function","error msg");
```

When this driver code is executed, the following output is streamed to stdout:

```
[class.function()][TRACE][trace msg]
[class.function()][ERROR][error msg]
```

Notice how the first message was not displayed. This is a result of the logging filters that were set.

Framework Extensions

There are several ways in which this framework can be improved. First, I hard coded the configuration of the logging code in my driver code. To make configuration a little more dynamic, I could have placed configuration parameters in a text file and then have an engine read the text file and set up the corresponding parameters.

```
#sample configuration file--------------------
LogHandler.FileLogHandler        = ON;
LogHandler.BufferLogHandler      = OFF;
LogHandler.NetworkLogHandler     = ON;

LogFilter.Filter    = "TRACE";
LogFilter.Filter    = "ERROR";
LogFilter.Filter    = "file not found";
LogFilter.Filter    = "bad password";
LogFilter.Filter    = "user does not exist";
```

Static configuration, via a configuration file, is the first step. The next step would be to build a GUI client that allowed you to change configuration parameters at runtime (see Figure 1-5). Naturally, this would also require changes to the logging framework.

There is one thing I have been quiet about: synchronization. Your application may have many threads running at the same time. If this is the case, then you will need to synchronize access to the LogMessage class so that only one thread is logging at a time. Because synchronizing threads tends to be platform specific, I decided to leave it out of my example. However, you should keep this issue in the back of your mind so that it doesn't sneak up on you in the future.

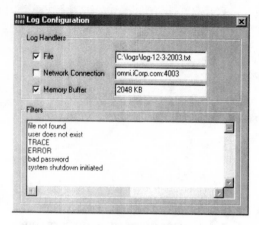

Figure 1-5. Logging GUI concept

1.2.5 Documentation

Incorrect documentation, too much documentation, and absent documentation all rank right up there with global variables in terms of negative impact. To be honest, I'm not sure which is worse.

Incorrect Documentation

Incorrect documentation is usually the result of historical forces. Here is the usual scenario: the original engineer, having a vestige of integrity, leaves comments in the code to describe what's going on in their small corner of the system. A few years down the line, a weary maintenance engineer comes wandering through this remote area, flashlight in hand, and decides to make a change to accommodate additional features. Unfortunately, being in such a rush, the maintenance engineer doesn't take the time to update the comments.

If this happens repeatedly, in enough places, the in-code documentation will become worthless. Fortunately, the solution is simple: keep documentation up to date. It takes nothing more than discipline. It's a behavioral problem, not an engineering problem. I don't buy the excuse "We didn't have time." Changing a comment to reflect a new change takes only a marginal amount of time, and the return is well worth the investment.

The bad news is that there are not many tools (short of frequent, and never-ending, code reviews) to force engineers to keep documentation current. At a start-up company, where people live according to Internet time, sacrificing documentation is the generally accepted practice. Things have to get out the door as soon as possible, and managers are willing to look the other way to get a beta released. This is why a number of engineers favor the approach of making source code as self-documenting as possible.

Too Much Documentation

This scenario can occur when some overzealous engineer decides that every single routine needs to be documented, even if it is a one-liner. Not only does too much documentation hurt readability, but it also tends to morph into incorrect documentation after a period of time.

Imagine having to deal with the following comments:

```
// This variable is used as a key element for the Monte Carlo
// approach to simulating the average severity of loss
// experienced over a single year in terms of amount paid
// per policy. It's a well known fact that obtaining anything
// but a pseudo-random number from well-published algorithms
// is a tenuous approach at best. To obtain true aperiodic
// random values I decided to used a combination of keyboard
// latency and standard library algorithms. The l_dwNbrFnl
// value is obtained from the routine on zeus.iCorp.com in
// /univ/7.05/src/gen/dict/src/include/common/stat.c. This
// algorithm uses Lehmer's ( 1951 ) linear congruential
// generator ( LCG ), such that l_wFirst is the seed of the
// simulation process. The l_dwNbrFnl value must also be
// subject to post-processing by the bnds.c routine in
// /univ/7.05/lib/src/shared/src/lib directory. Actual
// random data is obtained via a small memory resident
// application that intercepts CPU keyboard
// interrupts from the 80259 controller. Average time between
// keystrokes is averaged and placed in the volatile
// intvl variable. The presence of 'A' and 0x01 can be
// understood by recalling that the simulation software
// assumes a specific lower range value to prevent
// the numeric coprocessor from introducing rounding errors.
int l_wFirst = 0x01 + 'A' * l_dwNbrFnl % intvl;
```

Absent Documentation

I worked for a middleware company that had a source code base of over 16 million lines of C code. Back in the early 1980s, it took several days on a high-end Unix machine to compile the system. The person in charge of development discovered that the in-source comments were slowing down the compiler by almost 4 hours. To speed things up, he ordered a team of engineers to delete all the comments.

Twenty years later, there are still engineers who suffer from this decision. Those comments represented the mind share of dozens of programmers, most of whom had either left the company, been promoted, or suffer from amnesia. I can only guess at how much it has cost to regrow all that knowledge.

Record Intent

Documentation is somewhat of a religious topic. Some engineers believe that if you feel the need to document, then you should clean up your code until you do not need to document. Other engineers believe that compulsory documentation is the answer.

Both sides have valid reasons for their views. On the self-documenting side of the tracks, you have the cowboys who understand that production code gets changed so much, and so often, that it is easy for documentation to become out of date, or incorrect. On the other side of the tracks, you have old codgers who have worked with enough legacy code to appreciate the fact that it is not always possible to read the mind of the person who wrote the original code back in 1978. Doing your job can be a lot easier if you have some notion of what the original programmer was thinking about.

I prefer to travel down the middle of the road. I think that documentation should convey the *intent* of your code. In other words, do not tell *how* you do something, but instead tell *why* you do something. This cuts down on superficial comments and still allows vital information to persist.

Generate Documentation Automatically

Self-documenting code is still somewhat of a holy grail. I think that the Java SDK's *javadoc* tool is a step in the right direction. The idea behind javadoc is very powerful. A tool traverses source code and generates a well-organized HTML summary that includes hypertext cross-references and indices. These features make it very easy to find your way around a new Java API.

If you are not using Java, then you may have to build your own tool. This is really not as bad as it sounds (in fact, it can be very rewarding). As with javadoc, I would recommend generating a final deliverable that is

- Formatted in HTML

- Cross-referenced via hypertext

- Indexed

- Has options to exclude private routine descriptions

I recommend HTML because the browser is such a ubiquitous user interface. If you want to be really cutting edge, you could build a tool that generates documentation in XML. Having cross-referencing facilities built into the documentation, via hypertext, will help the reader navigate your API without having to pause to look for things. Anyone who has worked with a large system, like the Linux kernel, can appreciate the true power of this feature.[12]

If your documentation is going to be read by people who are merely going to use your code (as opposed to modify it), then you may want to add a feature so that documentation for private routines can be excluded. This will provide an interface description without exposing the internal operation of your code.

1.2.6 Design for Change

This is one of the hardest things for programmers to accept. The reality of software engineering is that a production system is never really "done." Ever.[13] A system is typically only "done" when it is put out of commission (and even then, it may get transformed into an open source project and a small group of die-hard programmers will keep it on life support indefinitely). A production system is more like Jason, from the *Friday the 13th* movie series. You think you finally beat him, you think that he's finally been conquered, and BAM . . . he's back from the dead.

A programmer in charge of maintaining a program cannot simply solve a problem and move on. The only people who ever get to move on are architectural consultants who bill by the hour. Instead, the average maintenance programmer will be faced with continually reworking variations of the same basic theme in an effort to accommodate new features. Fortunately, there are design techniques, which can be used during implementation, that facilitate later modification.

Target Interfaces

An *interface* is a contract that defines the services that the client code, referencing the interface, can expect to have access to. In C++, abstract base classes can be used to create interfaces. A properly designed interface will be complete, simple, and encourage efficient implementation. This is not as easy as it sounds given that these requirements are somewhat at odds with each other.

One way to accommodate change in a code base is to reference objects using an abstract interface instead of a specific class. This allows changes to

---

12. http://lxr.linux.no
13. http://www.openvms.org

be made to the underlying implementation without having to touch the client code that uses the interface. The idea is to commit only to an interface, so that you can backpedal, if you need to, without altering the client code.

For example, in the following C++ source code:

```
const int ARRAY_LENGTH = 6;
int array[ARRAY_LENGTH] = { 1, 2, 3, 4, 5, 6 };
LinkedList *linkedList = new LinkedList;
for(int i=0;i<ARRAY_LENGTH;i++)
{
    (*linkedList).add(array[i]);
}
delete(linkedList);
```

you could replace LinkedList with the more general List interface, and then assign a reference to the interface using an abstract factory design pattern:

```
const int ARRAY_LENGTH = 6;
int array[ARRAY_LENGTH] = { 1, 2, 3, 4, 5, 6 };
List *list = ListFactory.getList(ListFactory.LINKED_LIST);
for(int i=0;i<ARRAY_LENGTH;i++)
{
    (*list).add(array[i]);
}
delete(list);
```

This would offer the opportunity to use different list data structures, at runtime, by feeding different parameters to the factory. Interfaces were literally invented for the sake of making algorithms and data structures pluggable.

Avoid Hard Coding

In the perfect application, everything would be configurable. You should aspire to this ideal by specifying hard-coded values in one of three places:

- The shell environment

- The command line

- A configuration file

The shell environment can be used to specify a *small set* of values that will *not change* much during the development cycle.

```
C:\WINDOWS>set config=DebugConfig
C:\WINDOWS>set
PATH=C:\WINDOWS;C:\WINDOWS\COMMAND
PROMPT=$p$g
TEMP=C:\WINDOWS\TEMP
CONFIG=DebugConfig
```

If you have a *small set* of values that will *change frequently* during the development cycle, then you should pass them to the application on the command line:

```
C:\> OrderServer.exe –threads 5  -bufferSize  10KB
```

If your application uses a *large number* of configuration parameters, then it is best to place them in a configuration file. Most configuration files on Unix adhere to the convention of placing each configuration parameter on its own line. For example, the following text can be used to configure the init process:

```
# inittab for linux
id:1:initdefault:
rc::bootwait:/etc/rc
1:1:respawn:/etc/getty 9600 tty1
2:1:respawn:/etc/getty 9600 tty2
3:1:respawn:/etc/getty 9600 tty3
4:1:respawn:/etc/getty 9600 tty4
```

For situations in which your configuration data conforms to a hierarchy, an alternative would be to format the configuration file using XML.

```
<Logging>
    <ConsoleLogger/>
    <FileLogger>
            <name>server.log</name>
            <limit>2MB</limit>
    </FileLogger>
    <NetworkLogger>
            <address>10.0.0.8</address>
            <port>5100</port>
            <key>111-222-333-444-555</key>
    </NetworkLogger>
    <Filter>
            <levels>ADMIN</levels>
            <content>"file not found"</content>
    </Filter>
</Logging>
```

Separate Mechanism and Policy

It's a good idea to keep *how* you get something done separate from *what* you want done. Policy dictates what actions should be taken under different situations. Mechanism dictates how policy is actually implemented. Source code that distinguishes between the two is easier to modify and debug. This tactic can be realized through a judicious use of interfaces.

For example, assume you need to implement a dictionary that matches a value to a key. One way to implement a dictionary would be to use a hash table as the underlying data structure. Hash tables are useful in circumstances where the key space is small and memory is limited.

Another way to implement a dictionary would be to use a B-tree data structure. B-tree data structures are useful in circumstances where the key space is large and secondary storage is to be used. A dictionary implementation that kept mechanism and policy distinct would be flexible enough to use both data structures and have facilities to switch the underlying data structure being used at runtime.

1.2.7 Incremental Refinement

Source code is like plutonium: it represents a resource that has the potential to generate enormous value. Like plutonium, source code can be refined through an extended, iterative process that produces a final product that is relatively free of impurities. The more sophisticated the refinement process, the more pure (and valuable) the end result will be. The U.S. Department of Defense spends billions of dollars on manufacturing weapons-grade plutonium. Similarly, Microsoft spends billions of dollars on the development of Windows. You don't have to have a federal budget to build stable, fault-tolerant, software; you just need to incorporate a defensive mindset and place a premium on the detection of bugs.

No one ever catches all of an application's bugs during the first pass. There is always that one obscure combination of data and logic that you didn't plan for. In light of this, you should plan to make several passes of the same code, with the intention of making the code successively more stable. Old-timers used a primitive version of this technique known as *Code A Bit, Test A Bit* (CABTAB). But unlike CABTAB, this approach is backed up by a concrete set of techniques that you can follow to discourage the introduction of bugs into your software.

Revisit, Sleep, and Revisit Again

Hindsight is always 20-20. In other words, you can't really understand a problem until you have had firsthand experience with it. With regard to the ancient game of Wei Ch'i, the Chinese have a saying that translates to *"Hurry up and lose."*

Don't expect the first pass of a software component to be bug free. Think of it as an opportunity to better understand the problem that you're dealing with. When you feel like you are done with a specific component, go on to other problems. Then, after a day or so, go back and revisit your earlier solution. The time that you spent working on other parts of the application will give you an opportunity to see how the earlier component fits into the larger system. This contextual information will give you a better insight into how problems could arise.

Maintain a Checklist

After you are done with the first pass of development, sit down and enumerate all the potential refinements that could be implemented and then make another pass. This may sound sophomoric, but it is important. Or, to quote Murphy: *"If it's simple and it works, then it's not stupid."* The human brain can only keep seven, plus or minus two, active tasks in its process table. By using a list, you insure yourself against this inherent limitation.

The Refinement Checklist at the end of this chapter should serve as a starting point for your checklist. Literally go down the list and check items off as you address them. Don't expect to satisfy all of the list's criteria on the first pass. Some items on the list may only be resolved after the third or fourth pass. In essence, the list serves as a long-term roadmap that provides direction on how to fortify your source code over the course of multiple passes. By the time you have checked all the items on the list off, your code should be relatively stable.

1.3 Unit Testing

Mandatory and rigorous unit testing is an essential tool for eliminating bugs during implementation. Of all the preventative medicine that I can think of, unit testing is the most effective. An application that successfully passes its unit tests is very close to being inoculated against most types of bugs.

Unit Testing Is Not System Testing

There are different types of software testing. The engineers who do the actual coding perform *unit testing* during the implementation phase. *System testing* is performed by dedicated QA engineers, who work with the final deliverable produced by the implementation phase. Table 1-2 enumerates several types of system testing. System testing is a lengthy process that can takes weeks of effort. Unit testing a system, on the other hand, can typically be performed in a short period of time (i.e., less than a day).

Table 1-2. Types of System Testing

System Test	Purpose
Functional test	Determines if the application does what it's supposed to
Regression test	Verifies that previously fixed bugs have not reappeared
Stress test	Examines behavior under a large number of service requests
Performance test	Measures execution speed and memory footprint
Security test	Verifies that an application can withstand intrusion attempts
Installation test	Determines if the installation subsystem works
Usability test	Measures the ability of a user to interact with the application
Conformance test	Checks to see if the application conforms to a specified standard

1.3.1 Motivation Behind Automated Testing

One way to test an application is to run it with a custom-built driver and then read the tracing information that the logging code produces. This technique *does* work; it's just that it is time consuming.

```
[Config.process()][ADMIN][reading configuration file C:\src\config\cfig.xml]
[Config.parse()][ADMIN][parsing XML]
[Config.load()][ADMIN][loading configuration parameters]
[Config.load()][ERROR][database IP address not found, using default]
[order.run()][ADMIN][server initiated to receive orders]
[order.proc()][TRACE][customer order received (joe,Blow,192-345-11122)]
[order.Enter()][TRACE][customer order received (jack,smith,832-932-9483)]
[order.Enter()][ERROR][failed to authenticate (IP: 192.6.12.122)]
[order.Enter()][TRACE][ sending security alert to monitor]
[order.Enter()][TRACE][customer order received (Tim,Allen,234-433-4569)]
[System.reorg()][ADMIN][system reorg scheduled]...
```

Every time you make a change to your code and run the test driver, you will need to read through all of the tracing output.

Another problem with this approach is that the testing configuration is hard coded in the custom-built driver. Every time that you institute a change in the testing scenario, you will need to recompile the driver to implement the change. This makes configuration of the test part of the compile cycle and (depending on the size of your source base) also consumes time.

When an error finally does occur, it's mixed in with all of the other lower-priority messages. To find out if an error occurred, you will need to manually sift through the log output. Using a text search tool like grep can help, but you don't always know what you are looking for.

Unit Testing Requirements

An automated testing framework will solve the problems posed by the logging approach. Specifically, a successful testing framework will have the following set of features:

- Test results are validated programmatically, not visually.

- Screen output is limited to a short postmortem summary.

- Error information is redirected to a file or network connection.

- Configuration exists outside the compile cycle.

What you want to avoid is dealing with thousands of lines of text output, and then having to manually check the output by hand. You need something that automates the testing process. To this end, programmatic assertions should be used.

Instead of using the following:

```
printf("nAccounts=%ld\n",nAccounts);
```

you want something like this:

```
tester.assertEquals(nAccounts,100,"myClass","myFunction");
```

This function call will test to see if nAccounts is equal to 100, and if it is not, the function will log an error message to a file (or anything else that will save you from piping data to the console) and cause the current unit test to fail. If equality holds, the code will do nothing, such that you don't have to sift through an ASCII console dump just to verify correctness. No news is good news.

Another way to offer feedback to users without blinding them with printf() statements is to provide a short postmortem summary, indicating which tests failed and which tests succeeded. Failure details should be redirected to a file to avoid pushing the summary out of view.

```
Configuration File: C:\src\server\engine\test.tst
Tests Ran    15
Succeeded    13
Failed        2
Failed Tests:      (for details, see C:\src\server\engine\error.txt)
TestAddUser
TestDelUser
```

Finally, to make sure that configuration is not a part of the compile cycle, test run scenarios are specified in a configuration file. This allows changes to be made to the test without having to recompile everything.

Unit Testing Improves Your Confidence

The end result of disciplined unit testing is that it allows you to confidently implement changes. With log-based tracing, you can never be sure if your most recent change broke something without wading through a screen dump. With unit testing, the feedback is quicker and less ambiguous. This not only speeds up the development process, over the long run, but it also improves the stability of the final deliverable. The investment made in constructing the unit tests pays for itself many times over.

In this sense, unit tests are like scaffolding on a skyscraper. They are a fundamental part of the construction process, even though they are not a part of the completed structure. When construction is over, the scaffolding falls away and presents the user with a finished product.

Test for Requirements

In a perfect world you would be able to check every single execution path of the software being tested. If you cannot afford to be this thorough, then you should at least test each feature that the software is supposed to implement. See if you can force your code to crash. Try throwing data at the software that is incomplete or out of bounds. In other words, think like an attorney: *how is this program going to try to get out of its contract?*

Test As Much As You Code

There are some engineers who recommend that testing code should comprise up to 50 percent of the total amount of code that gets written.[14] In other words, you should write as much testing code as deployable code. This is not entirely unreasonable, given the benefits afforded by testing rigorously.

Whatever you do, don't skimp on testing code because of time constraints. This is a recipe for disaster that will inevitably backfire on you. If you are faced with time constraints, cut features instead of unit-testing code. This way you can at least be sure that the features that you do include will work correctly.

---

14. Frederick P. Brooks Jr., *The Mythical Man-Month* (Addison-Wesley, 1995. ISBN: 0-201-83595-9)

1.3.2 Steps Towards a Framework

For the sake of illustration, I am going to provide an example of how you can implement programmatic tests in C++. The following class, named Tester, can be used to construct the assertions that I mentioned earlier.

Before diving into the source code, I think it might help to see how the Tester class is used in practice. Let's start with the code that drives the test:

```
void main()
{
    try
    {
        performStringTest();
    }
    catch(TestException *exception)
    {
        const int size = 256;
        char buffer[size];
        Tester::getExceptionInfo(buffer,size,exception);
        printf("%s\n",buffer);
        delete((*exception).location);
        delete(exception);
    }
}
```

The code that actually performs the test is in performStringTest(). If the test fails, an exception will be thrown. The Tester class has a member function named getExceptionInfo(), which can be used to display a formatted text message about the exception.

The performStringTest() function sets up the necessary testing structures, and then compares two strings. This is where you see the assertEquals() function that I briefly mentioned earlier.

```
void peformStringTest()
{
    Location *location = new Location;
    (*location).className = "none";
    (*location).function = "performStringTest()";
    (*location).testName = "string test";

    TestException *testException = new TestException;
    (*testException).location = location;

    Tester::assertEquals(testException,"Texas","California");

    delete((*testException).location);
    delete(testException);
}
```

Naturally, this test should fail. When the program is run, the following output is displayed:

```
[string test][none.performStringTest()][Texas!=California]
```

The first field is the name of the unit test. The second field specifies the class and function where the test occurred. The last field details the values that were compared.

The Tester class uses polymorphism heavily to provide a uniform interface. If any of the assertEquals() functions fail, the assertFailed() function is invoked. The assertFailed() function consolidates exception data and throws a TestException object.

The implementation of the Tester class follows:

```
/* UnitTest.cpp --------------------------------------------------*/

#include<stdio.h>
#include<string.h>

#define BOOL          int
#define TRUE          (1==1)
#define FALSE         !TRUE

struct Location
{
    char *testName;
    char *className;
    char *function;
};

struct TestException
{
    Location *location;
    char *message;
};

/*++++++++++++++++++++++++++++++++++++++++++++++++++++++++++++++++++++
+ Declaration                                                       +
++++++++++++++++++++++++++++++++++++++++++++++++++++++++++++++++++++*/

#define TESTER_BUFFER_SIZE  256
class Tester
{
    private:
    static char *buffer;
    static void assertFailed
```

```
(
        TestException *testException,
        char *message
);

public:
static void assertEquals
(
        TestException *testException,
        char var1,
        char var2
);
static void assertEquals
(
        TestException *testException,
        short var1,
        short var2
);
static void assertEquals
(
        TestException *testException,
        int var1,
        int var2
);
static void assertEquals
(
        TestException *testException,
        long var1,
        long var2
);
static void assertEquals
(
        TestException *testException,
        float var1,
        float var2
);
static void assertEquals
(
        TestException *testException,
        double var1,
        double var2
);
static void assertEquals
(
        TestException *testException,
        char *var1,
        char *var2
);
```

```
        static void assertEquals
        (
                TestException *testException,
                void *var1,
                void *var2
        );
        static void getExceptionInfo
        (
                char *buffer,
                int bufferSize,
                TestException *testException
        );
};

/*+++++++++++++++++++++++++++++++++++++++++++++++++++++++++++++++++++++++++
+ Definitions                                                            +
+++++++++++++++++++++++++++++++++++++++++++++++++++++++++++++++++++++++++*/

char* Tester::buffer = new char[TESTER_BUFFER_SIZE];
void Tester::assertFailed
(
    TestException *testException,
    char *message
)
{
    (*testException).message = message;
    throw(testException);
}/*end Tester::assertFailed----------------------------------------*/
void Tester::assertEquals
(
    TestException *testException,
    char var1,
    char var2
)
{

    if(var1!=var2)
    {
            sprintf(Tester::buffer,"%c!=%c",var1,var2);
            Tester::assertFailed(testException,buffer);
    }
}/*end Tester::assertEquals----------------------------------------*/
void Tester::assertEquals
(
    TestException *testException,
    short var1,
    short var2
)
```

```
{
    if(var1!=var2)
    {
            sprintf(Tester::buffer,"%d!=%d",var1,var2);
            Tester::assertFailed(testException,buffer);
    }
}/*end Tester::assertEquals----------------------------------------*/
void Tester::assertEquals
(
    TestException *testException,
    int var1,
    int var2
)
{

    if(var1!=var2)
    {
            sprintf(Tester::buffer,"%d!=%d",var1,var2);
            Tester::assertFailed(testException,buffer);
    }
}/*end Tester::assertEquals----------------------------------------*/
void Tester::assertEquals
(
    TestException *testException,
    long var1,
    long var2
)
{

    if(var1!=var2)
    {
            sprintf(Tester::buffer,"%ld!=%ld",var1,var2);
            Tester::assertFailed(testException,buffer);
    }
}/*end Tester::assertEquals----------------------------------------*/
void Tester::assertEquals
(
    TestException *testException,
    float var1,
    float var2
)
{

    if(var1!=var2)
    {
            sprintf(Tester::buffer,"%f!=%f",var1,var2);
            Tester::assertFailed(testException,buffer);
    }
```

```
}/*end Tester::assertEquals-----------------------------------------*/
void Tester::assertEquals
(
    TestException *testException,
    double var1,
    double var2
)
{

    if(var1!=var2)
    {
            sprintf(Tester::buffer,"%e!=%e",var1,var2);
            Tester::assertFailed(testException,buffer);
    }
}/*end Tester::assertEquals----------------------------------------*/
void Tester::assertEquals
(
    TestException *testException,
    char *var1,
    char *var2
)
{

    if(strcmp(var1,var2))
    {
            unsigned int limit = TESTER_BUFFER_SIZE/2;
            if((strlen(var1)>=limit)||(strlen(var2)>=limit))
            {
                    sprintf(Tester::buffer,"strings not equal");
            }
            else
            {
                    sprintf(Tester::buffer,"%s!=%s",var1,var2);
            }
            Tester::assertFailed(testException,buffer);
    }
}/*end Tester::assertEquals----------------------------------------*/
void Tester::assertEquals
(
    TestException *testException,
    void *var1,
    void *var2
)
{

    if(var1!=var2)
    {
            sprintf(Tester::buffer,"objects not same instance");
            Tester::assertFailed(testException,buffer);
    }
}/*end Tester::assertEquals----------------------------------------*/
```

```
#define DELIMITERS    10
void Tester::getExceptionInfo
(
       char *buffer,
       int bufferSize,
       TestException *testException
)
{
       int length;

       length =        strlen((*(*testException).location).testName)+
               strlen((*(*testException).location).className)+
               strlen((*(*testException).location).function)+
               strlen((*testException).message)+
               DELIMITERS; //for extra formatting characters

       if(length>=bufferSize)
       {
               sprintf(buffer,"\0x0");
               return;
       }

       sprintf
       (
               buffer,
               "[%s][%s.%s][%s]",
               (*(*testException).location).testName,
               (*(*testException).location).className,
               (*(*testException).location).function,
               (*testException).message
       );
}/*end Tester::getExceptionInfo----------------------------------*/
```

To flesh out the remaining portion of the testing framework, you will need to construct an object that runs a series of tests and records which ones succeed and which ones fail (i.e., keeps track of which ones throw exceptions and which ones do not). In addition, you will need to implement a class that reads a configuration file and uses the file's parameters to configure the object that runs the tests.

1.3.3 Framework Extensions

I can think of a couple ways in which you could take my basic idea and push it a little further. For example, you could use XML to format the testing configuration file:

```
<testSuite>
    <test>
        <testName>Test Order Entry</testName>
        <testParameter>
            <name>inventoryID</name>
            <value>516-71123</value>
        </testParameter>
        <testParameter>
            <name>quantity</name>
            <value>1700</value>
        </testParameter>
    </test>
</testSuite>
```

This XML snippet specifies a test suite consisting of a single test. The test is identified by its name (i.e., "Test Order Entry"), and parameters that are needed to perform the test (i.e., inventoryID and quantity).

Performance Metrics

Performance metrics are another potential addition. It might be interesting to record the execution time of each test, so that you could see if recent modifications have affected performance. Most of the ANSI time routines deal with time in terms of seconds. The ANSI clock() routine is one of the few time routines that works with time on a finer granularity than seconds. However, I also discovered that support for it varies among platforms.

To measure smaller units of time, you will need to get platform specific. I had enough trouble on Windows that I thought I would help to provide sample code, to give Windows-oriented engineers a head start. On Windows, I discovered three different ways to measure small amounts of time:

- The ANSI clock() routine

- The GetTickCount() Win32 routine

- The QueryPerformanceCounter() Win32 routine

NOTE *Bear in mind that Windows is not a Real-Time Operating System (RTOS), and time measurements will always be a little sketchy down on the nanosecond level.*

The following program demonstrates how to use these three amigos:

```c
/* WindowsTime.c -------------------------------------------------*/
#include<stdio.h>
#include<time.h>
#include<math.h>
#include<windows.h>

#define LIMIT 25000

void doWork()
{
     double j=21.0;
     double k=3.0;

     double l=pow(j,k);     //expensive routine
     return;
}/*end doWork-----------------------------------------------------*/
void useANSIClock()
{
     clock_t start;
     clock_t finish;
     float diff;
     long int i=0;

     start = clock();
     for(i=0;i<LIMIT;i++)
     {
             doWork();
     }
     finish = clock();

     diff=((float)(finish-start))/((float)CLOCKS_PER_SEC);
     printf("seconds elapsed=%e\n",diff);
     return;
}/*end useANSIClock----------------------------------------------*/
void useGetTickCount()
{
     unsigned long ms_start;
     unsigned long ms_finish;
     unsigned long ms_diff;
     long int i=0;

     ms_start = GetTickCount();
     for(i=0;i<LIMIT;i++)
     {
             doWork();
     }
     ms_finish = GetTickCount();
```

```
        ms_diff=ms_finish-ms_start;
        printf("milliseconds elapsed=%lu\n",ms_diff);
        return;
}/*end useGetTickCount---------------------------------------------*/
void usePerformanceCounter()
{
        LARGE_INTEGER countStart;
        LARGE_INTEGER countFinish;
        LARGE_INTEGER countDiff;
        LARGE_INTEGER countFreq;
        float diff;
        long int i=0;

        if(QueryPerformanceCounter(&countStart))
        {
                for(i=0;i<LIMIT;i++)
                {
                        doWork();
                }
                QueryPerformanceCounter(&countFinish);

                countDiff.QuadPart = countFinish.QuadPart-countStart.QuadPart;
                QueryPerformanceFrequency(&countFreq);

                diff = ((float)countDiff.QuadPart)/
                        ((float)countFreq.QuadPart);

                printf("elasped ticks=%I64lu\n",countDiff.QuadPart);
                printf("elasped seconds=%e\n",diff);
        }
        else
        {
                printf("High-Performance Timer Not Functional");
        }
        return;
}/*end usePerformanceCounter----------------------------------------*/
void main()
{
        useANSIClock();
        useGetTickCount();
        usePerformanceCounter();
        return;
}/*end main--------------------------------------------------------*/
```

When I ran this code, I obtained the following results:

```
seconds elapsed=0.000000e-000
milliseconds elapsed=15
elapsed ticks=14469
elapsed seconds=1.212642e-002
```

Note how the ANSI `clock()` function doesn't work. In fact, it seems like it might be a dummy call that is not implemented.

Another improvement that could be made pertains to the test summary report. Instead of just streaming an ASCII text summary to the console, you could build a graphical interface that displayed the status of the testing in real time (see Figure 1-6).

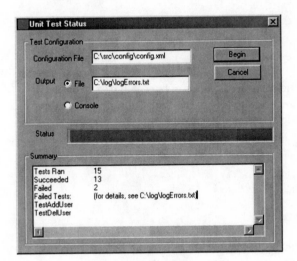

Figure 1-6. Unit test GUI concept

1.4 Tool Configuration

In this section, I present a few tips on how you can use your compiler to help keep bugs at bay. As with the other sections in this chapter, these tactics should be used before you deploy an application.

1.4.1 Use Compiler Warnings

A variety of bugs can creep up on a program. Syntax bugs normally crop up as the result of a careless error. Here is a classic example of a careless error:

```
if(nCount=5)
{
    doWork();
}
```

The following code will always evaluate to a true expression (i.e., the expression will evaluate to the integer 5). Not only that, it will assign the value 5 to nCount. The programmer who wrote this code probably meant to use the relational equals operator (i.e., = =) instead of just a plain old equals sign:

```
If(nCount==5)
{
    doWork();
}
```

Treat Warnings Like Errors

Syntax-related bugs are one of the few species of bugs that can be easily caught. Your compiler is the primary tool to this end. Compilers issue three basic types of statements to standard output while processing a file:

- Status messages

- Warnings

- Errors

A status message indicates to the user that the compiler is taking an action. The following types of status messages are displayed during a successful build:

```
Compiling...
UserData.cpp
orderClient.cpp
Linking...
orderClient.exe - 0 error(s), 0 warning(s)
```

A warning specifies a minor problem that will *not* prevent a program from running. Most compilers issue a warning and then go right back to building the program's executable.

```
warning: 'userName' : unreferenced local variable
```

An error specifies a problem that will cause the program to do something nonsensical. These tend to be statements that would cause the program to crash if they were executed. When a compiler encounters an error, it will refuse to complete the build.

```
error: '=' : cannot convert from 'const int' to 'int *'
```

The best way to locate and eliminate syntax-related bugs is to configure your compiler so that it has maximum sensitivity to warnings. In other words, configure the compiler so that it treats warnings like errors, and exits without building an executable. This tactic may be annoying, but it forces you to write code more defensively.

Don't Let Your Compiler Think for You

Although a compiler is capable of identifying syntax-related problems, you should not rely on it exclusively. The compiler is a tool that you can use to isolate bugs, but it is neither the best tool nor the only tool.

Back in the Iron Age, people used to obsess over their programs. They would trace the execution paths mentally, over and over again. They would show their code to other people and ask them to read it. There was a good reason for this: compiling a program meant submitting a job to the mainframe operator and waiting for a day or two. If an error existed, and the program did not function correctly, the programmer would have to go through the whole process all over again.

With the advent of the personal computer and 2 GHz processors, the waiting is over. With these changes has come a new attitude. Many software engineers now simply pound out code, tweak the code until there are no more compiler warnings, and then move on. The error in this approach is that it equates the absence of compiler warnings with the absence of programmatic errors. Don't ever beguile yourself into thinking that just because your program compiles it is bug free. You need to unit test as many execution paths as possible and have other people review your code.

1.4.2 Build Settings

Always make sure that you have a debug build available, even if you have deployed a release build to customers. This way, if a customer has a problem with their installation at 3:00 in the morning, you will have a corresponding build that you can debug. There is nothing more unnerving than having to deal with a problem that cannot be examined with a debugger. I know consultants who refused to work on projects because debuggers weren't available.

The Threat of Decompilers

The requirement for protecting intellectual property is often the justification for building without debug symbols. For instance, there are tools called *decompilers* that can take the debug build of a program and re-create the application's source code.

The symbol-rich file format of Java bytecode has made reverse engineering a serious threat to Java applications. The first well-known Java decompiler, named Mocha, was developed and released by Hanpeter van Vliet in 1996.[15] For all I know, there may have been some black-hat engineer who silently crafted their own in late 1995, but Vliet's was the first to be widely acknowledged. Vliet was deluged by e-mail from fellow engineers who were terrified that people were going to use Mocha to pirate software. To placate outraged developers, Vliet removed Mocha from his Web site.

During the week of the August 27, 1996, Vliet decided to take a democratic approach and allow the people who visited his site to vote on the fate of Mocha. The response overwhelmingly called for Mocha's return. The cat was out of the bag. Pandora's box had been opened, so rather than try to close the box again, smart developers directed their energy towards counteracting decompilers instead of stifling their distribution.

Decompiler Countertactics

If reverse engineering is a serious threat, then I can recommend two different measures:

- Obfuscation

- Strip the debugging symbols

An obfuscator is a tool belonging to the post-processor genus of the compiler family. An obfuscator is a tool that processes source code and compiles it into something that is more difficult to understand. In other words, it is the evil cousin of the beautifier, which is supposed to make code easier to read. Unix engineers may know obfuscation as *shrouding*. Obfuscators will remove white space, rename variables, add unnecessary instructions (this is known as *salting* code), and in extreme cases even try to sabotage decompilers.

Another tactic is to strip the debug symbols out of the executables that you send customers. The idea is to remove debugging information without otherwise altering the final executable. There are tools that will do this, like the strip utility on Unix, or John Robbin's privatestrip.exe utility for Windows.[16] This allows people, like sales engineers, to diagnose problems out in the field. They can arrive at a customer's site, insert the debug symbols, and diagnose the problems with all the added benefits of a debug build.

15. Thomas Gutschmidt, "Securing Java Code: Part 4," *developer.com*, June 6, 2001

16. John Robbins, *Debugging Applications* (Microsoft Press, 2000. ISBN: 0-7356-0886-5)

1.5 Machine Dependencies

The bugs resulting from machine dependencies are some of the subtlest that exist. Part of the reason for this is that people often don't think to suspect the hardware. Contemporary manufacturing has evolved to the point where if you buy a computer and it works for the first week, it will probably work without a hitch for the next ten years. Hardware problems just aren't usually much of an issue. Hence, forewarned is forearmed. In this section, I will bring certain platform-specific behavior to your attention so that you can become familiar with what the warning signs are.

1.5.1 Endianess

There are two different ways to store multibyte data values in memory: *big-endian* and *little-endian*. The big-endian convention dictates that the most significant byte of a value has the lowest address in memory. The little-endian convention is just the opposite: the least significant byte of a value must have the lowest address in memory.

Here's an example: let's say you have the multibyte value 0xABCDEF12 sitting somewhere in memory (for example, starting at a byte whose address is 24). The big- and little-endian representations of this value are displayed in Figure 1-7.

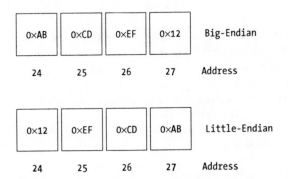

Figure 1-7. Big-endian versus little-endian

The storage method used will vary according to the hardware platform you're on. For example, the Intel family of 32-bit processors is a little-endian platform. If you own a PC that uses an Intel processor, you can prove this to yourself with the following program:

```
#include<stdio.h>
void main(int argc, char *argv[])
{
    unsigned long value = 0xABCDEF12;
    unsigned char *arr;
    arr = (unsigned char *)&value;
    printf("%X %X %X %X\n",arr[0],arr[1],arr[2],arr[3]);
    return;
}
```

If you are on a 32-bit 8x86 Intel-based platform, this program should print out the following:

```
12 EF CD AB
```

Arrays in C are always indexed from a low address to a high address. Thus, the first element of the array (i.e., arr[0]) also has the lowest address. The reason behind this is that arr[3] is the same as arr+3. In other words, the index is really an offset from the first element of the array.

Endianess is important because it makes transferring data between platforms difficult. Here is an example: suppose you are running an application that stores configuration data in a binary file. Also suppose that your current machine (an RS/6000 workstation) crashes and you are forced to take the source code of the application and build a new copy on a backup machine (an Intel laptop). The backup machine's endianness is different from that of the original computer.

It would be nice if you could recover the configuration of the old installation, so that you didn't have to spend several hours re-creating the old setup. However, you will not be able to because when you read in the binary data from the old configuration file, you will not be able to read in the values correctly. The integer value 0x11AA22BB persisted to file on one platform will get read in and look like 0xBB22AA11 on the new platform.

You could get around this by adding context-sensitive conversion functions to your code like the following:

```
#ifdef BIG_ENDIAN
value = convertToBigEndian(value);
#endif
```

But this can require a lot of extra effort, and mistakes can be frustrating.

1.5.2 Memory Alignment

Memory alignment is a characteristic of CPU design that requires certain data types to reside in memory, starting at an address that is a multiple of a specific integer value. For example, a 32-bit integer, on some platforms, must begin at an address that is a multiple of four. Another way of saying this is that the integer must be *aligned* on a 4-byte *boundary*.

Take the following structure declaration as an example:

```
struct Record
{
        int i;
        char ch;
};
```

On a platform where integers are 32 bits long and must begin on a 4-byte boundary, the Record structure will take up 8 bytes (4 bytes for the integer, a byte for the character, and 3 bytes of padding). If you have an array of such structures, this guarantees that the integer member of each structure in the array will begin at an address that is a multiple of four. See Figure 1-8 for an illustration of this.

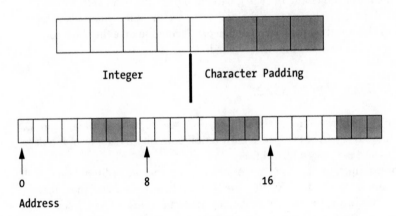

Figure 1-8. Memory alignment in action

Here is a snippet of code that I ran on a 32-bit Intel machine to verify this:

```
printf("sizeof(record)=%ld\n",sizeof(record));
```

When I executed the code, the following output was streamed to stdout:

```
sizeof(record)=8
```

In the past, I worked for a company that focused heavily on the portability of its product. It was written entirely in K&R C. To ensure portability, the structures in the source code used explicit padding.

For example:

```
struct FieldDef
{
      unsigned long   table;
      unsigned short  size;
      unsigned char   type;
      unsigned char   FILLER1;
};
```

Certain unnamed engineers every so often worked functionality into the padding. For example, padding was often used to store bit-wise flags. This was not done maliciously. The company had a sizeable customer base. Any changes to the structure definitions would impact everyone. To implement a modification, you would have to get the nod from the head architect. So, instead of having to go through the necessary architectural channels (which were formidable, trust me), some engineers decided to take the short route and just work with what they already had.

1.5.3 Data Type Sizes

The ANSI C specification has the final say with regard to what is and is not C. Unfortunately; the ANSI C spec is fairly ambiguous about the size of integer variables and memory addresses.

For example, under the auspices of DOS, integers and addresses are both 16-bit values. On Windows XP, they are 32-bit values. On an IRIX machine, with SGI hardware, they are 64-bit values. This makes life difficult because code written for one platform may need to be adjusted when it is ported to another platform.

For example, the function

```
void printSize()
{
      int i;
      int *ptr;
      printf("int size=%d ",sizeof(i));
      printf("addr size=%d\n",sizeof(ptr));
}
```

produces the following output under DOS:

```
int size=2 addr size=2
```

the following output under Windows XP:

```
int size=4 addr size=4
```

and the following output under IRIX:

```
int size=8 addr size=8
```

One way to irrevocably anchor a program to a specific platform is to persist information in the form of binary files. With binary files, data structures can be written directly to a file. There is no conversion. The bytes in memory are streamed straight to the disk. While this is a very fast way to commit information to storage, it also entails a significant caveat.

For example, let's say you open up a file in read/write binary mode and write the following type of structure to the file:

```
struct  BinaryDataStructure
{
      int field1;
      int field2;
      char field3;
};
```

On a platform that requires integers to be aligned on a 4-byte boundary, the structure will occupy 12 bytes in memory and 12 bytes will be written to disk.

```
FILE *fptr;
struct BinaryDataStructure data;
data.field1 =-45;
data.field2 =112;
data.field3 ='x';
fptr = fopen("file.bin","wb");
fwrite(((void*)&data),1,sizeof(data),fptr);
fclose(fptr);
```

If you copy the file.bin binary file to a platform that aligns its integers on an 8-byte boundary, you will be in deep trouble because the data for the first two integer fields will end up being treated like a single integer on the new platform (see Figure 1-9).

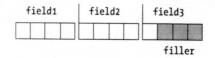

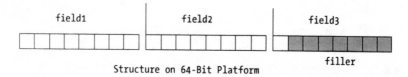

Figure 1-9. The danger of binary files

1.5.4 The Benefits of a Virtual Machine

To ease the pain of porting UNIX, Ken Thompson hacked a language named BCPL into a new language he named B. Soon afterwards, Dennis Ritchie and Brian Kernighan joined the project to transform B into C.

In 1980, another fellow from Bell Labs, named Bjarne Stroustrup (pronounced Be-ar-neh Strov-strup), invented C++. C++ is an object-oriented descendent of C. In fact, C++ programs were originally compiled into C by a tool named Cfront (as in *C front-end*).

The proliferation of various flavors of Unix, and their popularity with veteran developers, may make C/C++ seem like good multiplatform languages. In fact, every major operating system in the past 20 years has been written in C/C++.

Nevertheless, neither language is a good choice from the standpoint of writing code that resists hardware-related bugs. The problem is that C and C++ suffer from the three maladies I have just presented: endianess, memory alignment, and varying data type sizes. You might want to note that all of the examples in the previous three sections were written in C. Need I say more?

Virtual Machines Come of Age

Java began as a skunkworks project in the early 1990s. Scott McNealy, the current CEO, asked James Gosling to move his team to an unmarked building and prototype the next big thing (whatever that was). The engineers were originally focused on consumer appliances, and Java grew out of this almost by accident. The Java Virtual Machine (JVM) was originally implemented to support a programming language named Oak that was geared towards creating smart toasters. Sun released the Java SDK to the public in May of 1995.

Java attains its platform neutrality by compiling its programs to an instruction set that is executed by the JVM. The JVM is just a low-level interpreter that satisfies the requirements spelled out by the JVM specification. Anyone can build a JVM, using any development language, on any operating system, just as long as the specification is obeyed. Developers do not have to worry about endianess, memory alignment, or data sizes, because the binary-level composition of a Java program is defined completely by the specification. Java programs can be written on one platform and merely copied over to another. Porting is essentially a nonissue.

Other Virtual Machines

The JVM is not the only virtual machine on the market. The Parrot virtual machine, for example, executes bytecode compiled from Perl 6.[17] In days of yore, Pascal compilers often generated executables in p-code (as in *portable code*), which could be run on a p-code interpreter. There are also a number of COBOL vendors, like MicroFocus, that provide tools to compile COBOL to an intermediate code that can be executed by a special interpreter. Recently, Microsoft decided to make virtual machine technology an integral part of its .NET initiative (although if you mention p-code to Microsoft engineers, they will think you are talking about "packed-code," which is a code compression technology).

1.6 Summary

This chapter discussed steps that can be used during the implementation phase to reduce the opportunity for software bugs to appear. Suffice it to say that if you strictly followed the advice in this chapter, you wouldn't need to read the next two chapters. Unfortunately, not everyone who is confronted with maintenance work has had the honor of actually writing the original application (so perhaps Chapters 2 and 3 are still important).

The Bottom Line: Why Do Bugs Occur?

Bugs occur because people don't take the effort to eliminate them ahead of time. Table 1-3 lists a number of reasons why engineers don't make the initial investment.

---

17. http://www.parrotcode.org

Table 1-3. Core Software Problems

Core Problem	Solution
Unrealistic deadlines	Cut features to meet the deadline.
Scope creep	Obtain sign-off; associate a time expense with new features.
Ambiguous requirements	Formal clarification, backed up with a paper trail.
Complexity	See the Refinement Checklist and Chapter 3.
Laziness	Cappuccino.

Refinement Checklist: Proactive Bug Prevention

If you have decided to make the investment of time and effort necessary to proactively combat flaws, the following checklist can be used to iteratively refine source code so that it is more stable and fault tolerant:

- Do your functions and objects have strong cohesion?

- Are your functions free of unexpected side effects?

- Are your functions and objects loosely coupled?

- Do your procedures check for nonsensical conditions?

- Does your application fail gracefully if it is forced to crash?

- Have you eliminated global variables?

- Are important events being logged? Can you trace execution?

- Does the application's documentation describe intent?

- Does your code target interfaces instead of concrete classes?

- Have you eliminated all the hard-coded values?

- Does your code separate mechanism and policy?

- Did you construct a unit test for each component?

- Do your unit tests check every possible execution path?

- Do your unit tests check every requirement for each component?

- Have you configured your compiler to treat warnings like errors?

- Does your compiler build with debug symbols?

- Have you avoided endianess, alignment, data-type size problems?

- Have you been through this list more than four times?

CHAPTER 2

Debugging Tactics

Ordo ab chao

(Order out of chaos)

Don't Panic!

—Douglas Adams, *The Hitchhiker's Guide to the Galaxy*

The general predicament is as old as programming itself: an application is malfunctioning and it's your job to fix it. Naturally, the best person to fix an application is the original author. The majority of maintenance engineers, however, don't have this distinction. Typically, their boss hands them a program that someone else wrote three years ago, and they have to start from the very bottom of the learning curve.

There is, nonetheless, a general methodology that you can follow, from the time that the bug is reported until the time that the bug is resolved. In this

71

chapter, I will present a series of steps that you can walk through when you are faced with a bug. If you would like to get a preliminary snapshot of the entire process, a flowchart summary appears at the end of this chapter.

2.1 Initial Steps

The very first thing you should do is follow the quote stated at the beginning of this chapter. Above all, do not panic. I understand that being faced with what seems like mission impossible can be alarming, particularly when your job is at stake and you have to shoulder the load all by yourself. Once the general feeling of anxiety has subsided, you should sit down and try to follow the procedures outlined in this section.

2.1.1 Duplicate the Bug

Once the offending bug has been reported, try to see if you can duplicate the problem in your own environment. Request forensic evidence, if it is available, and make sure that you have the contact information of the person who reported the bug. In the event of an ambiguous description, nothing beats a real-time discussion. If you succeed in duplicating the bug, you can begin working on it in the privacy of your own cube, where you have all the amenities that make debugging easier (e.g., a debug build with symbols, source code, design documentation, your coworkers, etc.).

If you cannot duplicate the bug, then you may have to opt for the expensive option and visit the site where the bug has appeared. There are instances when this is unavoidable. For example, the bug may be tied to a 10-terabyte data set that you don't have the resources to duplicate. If at all possible, see if you can access the site remotely. If remote access is not available, for security reasons or because of a poor networking infrastructure, then you may have to pack your bags. I knew a financial consultant who worked for two years in Kazakhstan. The telecom service was so shaky there that even establishing a 12 kilobit-per-second dial-up connection was a losing proposition.

2.1.2 Bugs That Can't Be Duplicated

Certain classes of bugs are impossible to exactly duplicate. It is important to recognize them as early in the process as possible, because doing so can potentially save you days of frustration.

Here is a tentative list of well-known offenders:

- Dangling pointers

- Initialization errors

- Poorly synchronized threads

- Broken hardware

Dangling Pointers

A *dangling pointer* is a pointer variable that stores the address of a block of memory that has already been deallocated. The memory referenced by a dangling pointer may have been reallocated or may contain garbage. Between the time that the allocated memory was freed and the time that the dangling pointer is referenced, there is no guarantee that the value at the pointer's address will remain untouched. In fact, it is more likely that memory will be shuffled around, in an unpredictable manner, and you will not be able to make any solid conclusions about what the dangling pointer resolves to. This makes it hard to execute code with dangling pointers and get consistent results.

Examine the following source code:

```
#include<stdio.h>
#include<stdlib.h>
void dangling()
{
        int *ptr;
        ptr = (int*)malloc(sizeof(int));
        *ptr = 5;
        printf("%d\n",*ptr);
        free(ptr);
        //address is no longer valid
        printf("%d\n",*ptr);
}
```

When this code is executed, you will get console output that looks like this:

```
5
-572662307
```

As you can see, the memory manager frees the allocated memory and then modifies its contents. This example can be augmented to demonstrate, more clearly, how random behavior can place unpredictable values in deallocated memory.

```
/* dangling.c ---------------------------------------------------------*/
#include<math.h>
#include<stdio.h>
#include<stdlib.h>
#include<time.h>
void shuffleMemory(int *iptr)
{
        srand((unsigned)time( NULL ));
        *iptr = rand();
        return;
}/*end shuffleMemory----------------------------------------------------*/
void dangling()
{
        int *ptr;
        ptr = (int*)malloc(sizeof(int));
        *ptr = 5;
        printf("*ptr = %d\n",*ptr);
        free(ptr);
        shuffleMemory(ptr);
        printf("*ptr = %d\n",*ptr);
        return;
}/*end dangling--------------------------------------------------------*/
void main()
{
        dangling();
        return;
}/*end main------------------------------------------------------------*/
```

I ran this code repeatedly and got different results each time:

```
*ptr2 = 5
*ptr2 = 25070

*ptr2 = 5
*ptr2 = 25204
```

Naturally, my example is a little bit forced. Try to think of my code as a simulation rather than a concrete example. In an actual incident, the memory manager would reclaim the freed space for a new variable, and then overwrite the old value with the new variable's value.

Initialization Errors

When the operating system loads a program into memory, it doesn't necessarily wipe the slate clean for the new program. Vast swaths of RAM may have garbage remaining from the previous application that resided there. For the sake of performance, the operating system may neglect to initialize an area of memory before it is allocated to a process.

If you fail to explicitly initialize a variable, it will probably contain junk from somewhere else. In a real-life situation, this junk is often random. This makes it hard to duplicate behavior that is based on a variable that hasn't been initialized.

Here is an example:

```
/* stackGarbage.c ------------------------------------------------*/
#include<stdio.h>
void firstCall()
{
        char array[] = {'a','b','c','d','e','f','g','h'};
}/*end firstCall-------------------------------------------------*/
void secondCall()
{
        char ch1;
        char ch2;
        printf("%c\n",ch1);
        printf("%c\n",ch2);
}/*end secondCall-----------------------------------------------*/
char thirdCall()
{
        char ch3;
        return(ch3);
}/*end thirdCall------------------------------------------------*/
void garbageInit()
{
        firstCall();
        secondCall();
        printf("%c\n",thirdCall());
}/*end garbageInit---------------------------------------------*/
```

When garbageInit() is executed, the following output will be generated:

```
e
a
p
```

The firstCall() invocation places a series of letters on the stack that are picked up by the following calls. Because the next two calls (i.e., secondCall() and thirdCall()) do not initialize their variables, they contain garbage that is left over from firstCall().

Poorly Synchronized Threads

Synchronization problems are one reason why I am distrustful of people who multithread with abandon. Thread behavior can be next to impossible to duplicate from one run to the next. This is partially due to the thread scheduler, whose underlying algorithm tends to be, as you might expect, context sensitive. If multiple threads share a region of memory, it can be very difficult to reproduce the stream of values stored in that region of memory.

> **NOTE** *Threads are often used with the intention of making an application faster, the justification being that switching between threads involves much less overhead than switching between processes. The problem with this mindset is that most threads end up sharing resources, and this requires the resources to be synchronized. The mutual exclusion primitives used to synchronize a resource can consume an enormous amount of processor time (potentially eliminating any performance gain—see Chapter 6 for the gory details). Not only that, but the time required to debug a multithreaded application can be disproportionate.*

The SecureRandom class in the java.security package of the Java SDK represents a cryptographically strong Pseudo-Random Number Generator (PRNG). In other words, it generates random values that are nondeterministic. To implement this requirement, the default service provider from Sun creates a set of threads and has them request garbage collection (i.e., via the System.gc() call). Although the nuts and bolts of the implementation are proprietary, the fact that Sun uses this approach does hint at just how difficult it can be to duplicate thread-based interaction.

Broken Hardware

In the book *CYBERPUNK*,[1] Clifford Stoll recalls how he disconnected malicious hackers from a server at a California laboratory by dangling his keys near the network interface. Although the electrical interference was being faked, in Clifford's story, it is a real threat in situations where you have lots of

---

1. Katie Hafner, *CYBERPUNK: Outlaws and Hackers on the Computer Frontier* (Touchstone Books, 1995. ISBN: 0-684-81862-0)

electronic equipment and cable in close proximity. Interference is a truly random occurrence, and if a bug is somehow related to it, you can expect the bug to also behave sporadically.

Sometimes a bug even slips into mass-produced processors. For example, in July of 1994, a professional mathematician named Dr. Thomas Nicely[2] announced that he had found defects in the Intel Pentium processor. Shortly thereafter, Intel contacted Nicely and convinced him to enter into a nondisclosure agreement. Personally, with billions of dollars at stake, I'm surprised Dr. Nicely didn't disappear mysteriously (it happens in the oil industry). Eventually, the truth came out and by December the media had started covering the story. Anyone using the flawed Pentium CPU to run computationally intensive software was at risk for intermittent errors.

Finally, some machines just have demons in them. If you're faced with a bug that appears and vanishes, one thing you might want to think about is moving the application to another machine. Reinstall the operating system from scratch, with all of the current patches, on this new machine so that you're sure that you're starting with a clean slate. If the error still crops up, and your software is portable enough, you can then move the application to a different hardware platform to see what happens.

2.1.3 Verify the Bug Is Genuine

Once you have been able to duplicate a bug, or at least see it occur with your own eyes, it is a good idea to check that the bug is genuine and not some weird user error. Catching a user error, camouflaged as a bug, could potentially save you a lot of time and aggravation.

During high school I worked with a man who repaired furnaces. Like kernel engineers, we spent our days mucking around in the obscure recesses of large structures. One day we visited an apartment building where the landlord complained that the heat had mysteriously gone off. Under normal circumstances, this would mean that there had been a fundamental system failure. Getting the heat back on could entail days of work and replacing a bunch of expensive parts. My boss began by asking the standard set of questions: "Have you been leaving doors or windows open? Is at least one of your rooms getting heat?"

The landlord replied, "No, yesterday it suddenly got cold and the damn thing wouldn't respond when I turned up the thermostat."

When we lugged our tools down to the basement of the building to examine the furnace, we discovered that someone had turned off the furnace

---

2.   http://www.trnicely.net/

manually. There was a little fuel knob that supplied the whole show, and someone had simply turned it to the "closed" position. The landlord later found out that one of his children had been playing down in the basement and had fiddled with the furnace knobs.

2.2 Resolving the Bug: Quick Fixes

Most of the time, resolving a bug will entail a deliberate and measured approach. However, there may also be instances in which you can sidestep all the formality and resolve a bug quickly. In this section I am going to present a collection of practical tricks that you can use to shoot from the hip. Just don't expect to get a bull's-eye every time.

2.2.1 Examine Recent Changes

If the source code you're working on suddenly doesn't function, the first thing you should do is see if someone has recently made changes to the source tree. If it's not you, then it has to be someone else. For example, people have been known to check in source code that fails to compile, or that contains logical errors. This is just one of those things that happens when several people work on the same project. Think of it like the software industry's version of the Law of Large Numbers: the more people that work on the project, the higher the probability that an error will occur.

Ninety percent of the time, these kind of spontaneous problems occur when you check out a new build. If your build fails to compile, or function correctly, immediately look at the history of the offending files. In this sense, revision control systems are particularly handy in that they provide a paper trail of responsibility. It is difficult for people to hide in this environment (unless they literally check in code as someone else). If something blows up, then the guilty party's name will appear as the most recent entry in the history of the related source files.

> **NOTE** *Some revision control products have an automatic build feature, such that, after you check in a file, a build will be performed to validate the changes. Build results can then be posted to a Web site for everyone to see. In addition to assigning irrefutable culpability, this type of immediate feedback can save both time and headaches.*

How do you oblige people to check in code only after they are sure that it will build? One engineer told me his company maintained a hug pile of bricks, and it fell on anyone who happened to violate the protocol.

2.2.2 Use Tracing Information

Sometimes you can lay a bead on a problem just by looking at log messages. This is why I recommend logging in the previous chapter as a type of preventative medicine. If your tracing infrastructure is solid, you may never have to fire up a debugger. Instead, you will see a message like the following:

```
[Error][Order.addEntry()][database "order.db" does not exist]
```

And you will know immediately where (and what) the problem is. Granted, most of the time this only works well if you know what to look for, which is to say that you are the one who implemented the code originally. Nevertheless, you should make a cursory pass of your logs to see if anything obvious stands out.

2.2.3 Déjà Vu

There may be bugs that give you a sense of déjà vu. In other words, the bug may be similar to a problem that you've already encountered. Always take a moment to examine your bug to see if you may have already solved it somewhere else. Although tight cohesion is what all functions should aspire too, sometimes cut-and-paste programming can creep into a code base. This can result in a set of bugs that resemble each other.

The only way to detect related problems is through experience. Unfortunately, the people who possess this kind of recognition the most are the original authors. If you are a maintenance engineer, then it's probably a good idea to reinforce the experience you get by keeping notes of the problems that you encounter. Leverage every bit of information that you have.

If you don't have *any* experience, then at least try to take advantage of someone else's. If you still have access to the original author, see if you can pick that person's brain. Some people intentionally develop a case of amnesia after they have been promoted or moved on to another project. They may feel that the old project is a like a cement block hanging around their neck that keeps them from moving on to bigger and better things. If you ever get the feeling like someone is stonewalling you, send them your questions via e-mail and then send copies of the e-mail to your superiors and their superiors.

I was involved on a project once where a few senior people stonewalled a group of consultants. For political reasons, they decided to build a vast invisible wall between their little kingdom and the horde of billable-hour invaders. I was situated in the cube next to the consultant who was managing the project. One afternoon, one of the other consultants stopped by his cube. The other consultant claimed that he couldn't get anything done because none of the full-timers would explain anything to him. The managing consultant told him, "OK, Carter, save your e-mails. We'll need them for court when they try to sue us for not delivering."

Remember what I said about establishing a paper trail?

2.2.4 Know When to Quit

When I was in high school, there were always a couple of students who spent their time thinking of creative ways to cheat on final exams. Some things never change. For example, this one really weird guy, named Bill, would write answers on a small sheet of paper and then attach the paper to a string, which he would thread up his shirtsleeve and down his torso. Whenever he saw his social studies teacher, Mr. Longo, walking towards him, he would use his free hand to pull on the string and conceal the cheat sheet.

He never got busted, although if he had been caught he probably would have been expelled. That's an awfully big risk to take for a B+ grade.

You might be thinking to yourself, "Man, that's a lot of work just to cheat. Wouldn't it have been easier if he just studied for the exam?" If you are thinking this, you are correct. The hours that Bill spent jerry rigging up his elaborate cheating contraption took more time than it would have if he had just sat down and studied.

Debugging can also be like this. You can spend so much time looking for a quick fix that you spend more time than you would have if you had just done it the hard way. If you are going to use any of the tricks in this section, always place a time limit on yourself. After a certain period of time, admit defeat and move on to the methodology spelled out in the next section.

2.3 Resolving the Bug: The Scientific Method

In the previous section, I discussed a set of heuristics that could be used to resolve a bug expeditiously, with little or no preparation. In serious cases, none of them will work; you will be forced to fall back on a formal methodology that, although it may be time consuming, will always yield results if applied properly. In this section, I demonstrate how to utilize the scientific method to isolate bugs and offer a couple of minor variations of its usage.

2.3.1 General Approach

The scientific method is not just used by people at NASA. It is a way of inventing postulates and testing their validity, using hard data, with the long-term goal of building a *theory* that makes accurate predictions.

The following is a crude outline of the scientific method:

- Collect pertinent data.

- Form a tentative hypothesis based on the data.

- Make a prediction, based on the hypothesis.

- Test the prediction with an experiment.

- If the prediction and experimental results differ, start over.

This section is focused on using the scientific method to locate bugs. So these steps must be recast, and elaborated upon, in terms of isolating program flaws.

Collect Pertinent Data

Get your hands on as much forensic evidence as you can. This includes the bug report, e-mails, log files, and even screen shots. If you can duplicate the bug, you can also create your own data sets using a variety of diagnostic tools. Later in the chapter, I will enumerate the different types of diagnostic tools you can use and explain their usage.

Like any good detective, you should store your data in a safe place and protect it from being contaminated. Normally, this would mean changing data file permissions to read-only. In extreme scenarios, where big money is hanging in the balance, protecting your evidence could mean burning a CD and storing it in a locked cabinet.

Form a Hypothesis

A hypothesis is an educated guess that is consistent with existing data. In other words, take the data you collected in the first step and then speculate on what is causing the bug. Coming up with a decent hypothesis is an exercise in data analysis and creativity. If you have the time, brainstorm and come up with as many alternative hypotheses as you can. There are literally books, like Edward De Bono's, that have been written on how to devise competing postulates.[3] One thing to watch out for during this process is a dangerously sharp principle known as *Ockham's razor*. A wise old man named William of Ockham proposed it in the fourteenth century. In old English, Ockham's razor states that *"Entities should not be multiplied unnecessarily."* Or, in contemporary English: "What can be done with fewer assumptions is done in vain with more."

---

3. Edward De Bono, *Lateral Thinking: Creativity Step-by-Step* (HarperCollins, 1990). ISBN: 0-060-90325-2)

Perform an Experiment

The goal of an experiment is to test a hypothesis against a new scenario. If your hypothesis has merit, eventually it will morph into a theory. A theory is a conceptual framework that offers both an explanation and facilitates predictions. *The success of a theory is measured by its ability to predict accurate results.* Theories that only accommodate historical data are meaningless.

If you have a hypothesis that seems to make sense, you should use the hypothesis to make a prediction. Once you've made a prediction, you should perform an experiment and compare the results of the experiment against your prediction. If the results of the experiment are not consistent with your prediction, you need to either modify your hypothesis or construct an entirely new one. However, if the experimental results are consistent with your prediction, to within some predefined degree of sensitivity, your hypothesis is on its way to becoming a theory.

In the case of software debugging, the general format of your prediction will depend on the experimental design that you use. With regard to initially locating the source of the bug, two common experimental procedures are

- Incremental integration

- Binary search

I will spend the next two subsections discussing each of these in turn.

With regard to actually fixing the bug, once you have found it, there are no predetermined experimental designs. Which is to say that the experiments that you perform will depend upon the requirements that the application is supposed to implement. I can't give you any general advice other than to place a heavy emphasis on understanding the nature of the problem.

2.3.2 Locating the Bug: Incremental Integration

In the case of incremental integration, a program is decomposed into a finite set of distinct modules (see Figure 2-1). The experimenter then speculates about which module contains the bug. Thus, a generic prediction will have the form "The bug is in the nth module."

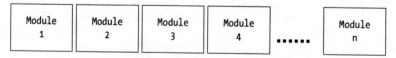

Figure 2-1. Program decomposition

Incremental integration begins by executing one module and then check-ing to see if the bug exists in that module. If the bug does not exist in the first module, then the next module is added and the experiment is repeated. This process continues, and modules are successively added, until the bug mani-fests itself.

In so many words, you keep adding program logic until something goes wrong, and this allows you to narrow down the bug to the most recently inte-grated module of code (see Figure 2-2). The only difficult part of this approach is finding a way to break up an application into modules that can be tested cumulatively. Not every program can be easily decomposed into little bite-sized modules. In addition, the test that you run for one module may differ from the test that you run for two modules. This may require the creation of "n" different tests for a program that has been broken up into "n" modules.

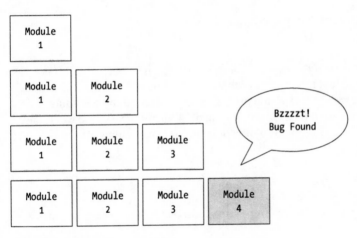

Figure 2-2. Increment integration procedure

2.3.3 Locating the Bug: Binary Search

The incremental integration procedure is sequential. In a worst-case scenario, it could require "n" different test runs. It's like searching an array by succes-sively traversing each element (i.e., this is an *order n* algorithm, or *O(n)*). For a large program, this is a very resource-intensive way to locate a bug. You need a technique that has superior worst-case performance.

One way to speed up the process of locating a bug is to switch to a recur-sive experimental design that utilizes the binary search procedure. In a binary search experiment, a program is conceptually divided in half (see Figure 2-3). The experimenter then makes a prediction as to which half the bug resides in.

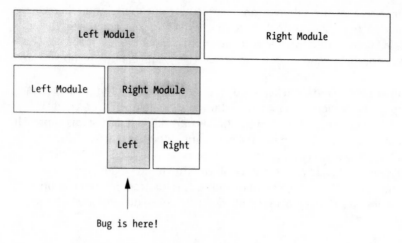

Bug is here!

Figure 2-3. Binary search procedure

The outcome of the experiment will indicate which half actually contains the bug. The half of the program containing the bug is then itself conceptually broken into two halves, and the process is repeated until the offending code is located exactly. For a program consisting of "n" distinct parts, the worst-case expense of a binary search is on the order of $\log_2 n$ (i.e., $O(\log_2 n)$).[4]

2.3.4 Understand the Problem

How do you make money in the stock market? It's easy: you buy low and sell high . . .

—Anonymous stock broker

Once you have located the bug, you need to correct it. How do you fix a bug? It's easy: you have to understand the problem. In order to use the scientific method to correct malfunctioning software, your hypotheses have to be plausible and well grounded. The only way to build a solid hypothesis is to have an insight into what is actually going on.

Understanding the problem is the number one most difficult part of debugging and maintenance. It may sound very simple and straightforward but, like turning a profit on Wall Street, it is rarely easy to do in practice.

---

4.   Donald Knuth, *The Art of Computer Programming, Volume 3: Sorting and Searching, Second Edition* (Addison-Wesley, 1998. ISBN: 0-201-89685-0)

What Is Understanding the Problem?

Understanding the problem involves performing two related activities:

- Identifying requirements

- Identifying how the requirements are implemented

In other words, you need to understand what the program is supposed to do, and how it goes about its business. You can use all the other debugging tactics like an expert, but if you don't understand the requirements, and how the program implements them, then you are sunk. Period.

Having an insight into what a software application is supposed to do will give you an intuitive feel for what should transpire when the program actually runs. Specifically, you will be able to recognize when the program is doing something that doesn't make sense. In order to locate a bug, you must be able to separate normal behavior from abnormal behavior. Once you have located the bug, if you understand how the program operates, you will be able to track down the underlying cause of the bug more efficiently.

The Original Author Is Leveraged

An unfortunate fact of life is that, usually, the original author will be the only person who possesses a complete understanding of a program's charter and blueprints. Heck, what do you expect, they wrote the damn thing. To add insult to injury, there is no easy way to regrow this type of knowledge if it has not been persisted somehow. This is why I placed such a heavy emphasis on documenting intent in the first chapter.

I knew a consultant who implemented an indexing scheme for a company in the data storage business. The underlying data structure had been "invented" by a fellow from overseas. It was not a B-tree, or B$^+$-tree, or B*-tree, or any variation thereof. It was a strange new hybrid, using Patricia Tries, that offered certain speed advantages in exchange for a healthy dose of complexity. The technical documentation needed to describe this data structure was close to 100 pages (and even then it was still somewhat incomplete). He was directed to implement the data structure in Java and was left alone for seven months.

Seven months later, he had a working prototype. This prototype was to become the core component of all the company's products; their very business model depended upon it. Occasionally, a bug would crop up. The people who were using the indexing code would go running to the consultant and present him with the error messages. He would look at the log traces for a few moments, then his face would light up and he would say, "Ah, I think I know what's doing that." Ten minutes later, the bug would be fixed and he would check in his changes.

The day finally came when the consultant had to leave for his next job. He was asked to pass on his code to a new hire, a freshly minted PhD from China. They spent three weeks, pulling ten hours a day, in the consultant's cube.

It didn't help. The recently hired PhD just couldn't seem to grasp how things operated. There was simply too much code. Although the existing technical documentation spelled out how things were supposed to work, nothing explained how the indexing scheme was actually implemented. The consultant had neglected to comment his code or leave design artifacts. Everything was in his head: all the little special cases, idiosyncrasies, and booby traps. The company ended up rehiring the consultant at double his old rate.

This is why telling someone to just "understand the problem" sounds a whole lot easier than it really is. Large and complicated programs make "understanding" a difficult task for even the most zealous maintenance programmer. High levels of complexity engender a learning curve that there is no simple way to climb. The only way to gain enlightenment is to forge straight ahead and put in the time. In Chapter 3, I will investigate this process rigorously. In this section I told you *why* understanding the problem is important. In Chapter 3, I will explain *how* to understand the problem.

2.3.5 Preventing Careless Errors

We are ready for any unforeseen event that may or may not occur.

—Vice President Dan Quayle, 9/22/90

We are sometimes are own worst enemies, whether speaking in public or spelling the word "potatoe." Likewise, during the debugging process, there are steps you can take to prevent yourself from sabotaging the scientific method.

Do Not Perform Experiments Concurrently

This is somewhat of a no-brainer. It is strictly a matter of discipline more than anything else. Whenever you're instituting changes to a software component, only make one change at a time. The reasoning behind this is simple: if your change doesn't fix the bug, or makes things worse by introducing new bugs, then you are able to narrow down the offending code very quickly. If, however, you institute a bunch of changes at the same time, you will have more than one potential suspect to interrogate.

The combinatorial possibilities can get very ugly. For example, let's assume that you have made three different changes to a program's source code (A, B, and C). If an error suddenly appears, it could be caused by only one of the three changes. Or, the error could be caused by an interaction between two of the changes (i.e., AB, BC, AC). Or, it could be caused by a combination of all three changes together (i.e., ABC). Thus, instead of a single suspect, you will have seven distinct scenarios to examine (i.e., A, B, C, AB, BC, AC, ABC).

Test the Fix

Once you have implemented a bug fix, you should stop. Don't check the bug back into revision control. Don't move on to the next action item. Go back to your code and test it. Specifically, you should perform three types of tests:

- Perform relevant unit tests.

- Remove the fix and then reinsert it.

- Perform a system-wide regression test.

The fact that your code compiles does not give you license to check it in. Always barrage a repaired software component with unit tests before you check it back into the source repository. This may involve amending the old unit tests or writing new ones; don't be scared to invest a little extra effort on unit testing.

Another tactic that you can use is to remove the fix, to see if the bug reappears. If the bug reappears, reinsert the fix to see if it solves the problem. This way you can verify that your new code is having an impact.

Your bug fix might actually have too much of an impact, which is to say that it might introduce side effects in other remote areas of the application. To protect against this type of subtle problem, you should consider running a system-wide regression test.

> **NOTE** A regression test *consists of a collection of testing scenarios that generate a specific, known output. When a software application has been altered, it can be run through these testing scenarios to see if the changes have introduced defects. The final analysis is performed by comparing the output generated by the most recent code against the output generated by the old code. If the outputs are dissimilar, then defects have crept in and the application has "regressed" to an inferior state. As with unit testing, regression testing is usually automated. Larger software companies will typically have a dedicated collection of QA engineers who perform regression tests.*

Make Backups

Always make sure you have performed backups before you begin surgery on a malfunctioning program. Murphy has a way of reminding the unprepared about his Law. Your patch may end up making the patient worse instead of better. Or, a power surge might kill your machine and leave you with a corrupted hard drive. In most cases, a daily backup of the revision control repository is all that is needed. Remote backups are useful when you wish to diminish risk by distributing the backup medium geographically.

Making backups is just a small part of a typical disaster recovery plan. A *disaster recovery plan* consists of a sequence of specific actions that must be performed if an emergency occurs (e.g., civil war, a tornado, an earthquake, a terrorist attack, etc.). It's like a movie script. Different staff members have different roles that they must play in order to continue business operations.

For administrators who want to keep their machines running, even in the event of a nuclear first strike, there is The Bunker. This is a site that you have to see to believe.[5] The Bunker is located in Kent, England. It was built during the cold war to serve as a fortified communications station. As such, it is immune to electromagnetic attacks from HERF weapons, EMP pulses, and TEMPEST equipment. In other words, the entire compound is bug proof. Armed guards patrol the grounds surrounding The Bunker. The Bunker itself is sealed behind two-ton blast proof doors. This is one hell of a collocation site.

2.3.6 Diagnostic Tools

The goal of an experiment is to produce an empirical result that can be used to confirm or deny a prediction. As a maintenance engineer, you have tools at your disposal to help you conduct experiments and gather empirical evidence. These tools include

- Tracing APIs

- Memory leak detectors

- Memory bounds checkers

- Performance profilers

- Debuggers

Tracing APIs

In the last chapter I presented an example of a logging API that could be used to trace execution. Tracing allows you to log what's happening in a program on a very fine level of granularity. The output generated by tracing code can be used to take shortcuts in terms of locating a bug. However, the benefits afforded by tracing do not come without a price. Tracing not only incurs

---

5.   http://www.thebunker.net

a performance hit, but it also requires significant modification of your source code. Source code with tracing statements is usually more difficult to follow than source code that does not contain tracing statements.

Memory Leak Detectors

Memory leak detectors, like Rational Software's Purify product,[6] can be used to track allocated memory that has not been freed. The Boehm-Demers-Weiser (BDW) conservative garbage collector[7] is a drop-in replacement for malloc(), which also doubles as a memory leak detector.

The BDW garbage collector is distributed in source code form and must be built with a compiler. On Windows, I had to tweak the make file a little in order to get what I needed. Specifically, to build a static, single-threaded library (i.e., gc.lib) that can be linked with generic ANSI C code, you need to delete gc_cpp.obj from the OBJS list. Once this fix has been implemented, you can compile the static library via the following command line:

```
C:\src\bdw\gc6.1>nmake /F NT_MAKEFILE
```

This will build both gc.lib and gctest.exe. You can run the gctest.exe binary to test gc.lib. The gctest.exe binary generates a log file named gc.log.

The following source code creates a memory leak and uses the BDW garbage collector to track the leak:

```
/* testBDW.c--------------------------------------------------------*/
#include<stdio.h>
#define GC_NOT_DLL
#define GC_DEBUG
#include<gc.h>

#define KB 1024
unsigned long freeBytes=0;
void printStatus()
{
        unsigned long currentBytes;
        currentBytes = GC_get_free_bytes();
        printf("heap size=%7lu\t",GC_get_heap_size());
        printf("free size=%7lu\t",currentBytes);
        if(freeBytes!=0)
        {
                printf("diff=%ld",(freeBytes-currentBytes));
        }
        printf("\n");
```

---

6. http://www.rational.com/products/purify_nt/index.jsp

7. http://www.hpl.hp.com/personal/Hans_Boehm/gc/

```
        freeBytes = currentBytes;
        return;
}/*end printStatus-------------------------------------------------*/
void main()
{
        int j;
        int i;
        int limit = 10;
        GC_find_leak = 1;
        for(j=0;j<limit;j++)
        {
                unsigned char *pointer;
                pointer = GC_malloc(10*KB);
                for(i=0;i<KB;i++){ pointer[i]=0x01; }
                printStatus();
        }
        printf("\n--explicit collection--\n");
        GC_gcollect();
        printStatus();
        return;
}/*end main---------------------------------------------------------*/
```

> **TIP** *You will need to make sure that your build environment has been set up via the* VCVARS32.bat *batch file that comes with Visual C++. Also, you will need to make sure you link with the* gc.lib *static library, and that the BDW* gc.h *header file is in your include path.*

This code allocates 10 kilobytes repeatedly, without freeing it, and generates the following output:

```
heap size= 65536      free size= 53248
heap size= 65536      free size= 40960      diff=12288
heap size= 65536      free size= 28672      diff=12288
heap size= 65536      free size= 16384      diff=12288
heap size= 65536      free size=  4096      diff=12288
heap size= 131072     free size= 57344      diff=-53248
heap size= 131072     free size= 45056      diff=12288
heap size= 131072     free size= 32768      diff=12288
heap size= 131072     free size= 20480      diff=12288
heap size= 131072     free size=  8192      diff=12288

--explicit collection--
heap size= 131072     free size= 118784     diff=-110592
```

As you can see, the heap size does *not* go monotonically downwards. This is because the garbage collector implicitly frees memory at runtime.

The final call to GC_gcollect() initiates a search for memory leaks. A log file named gc.log will be created in the current working directory that details these leaks. The contents of this file will look something like the following:

```
Leaked composite object at start: 0xbf9000, appr. length: 10244
Leaked composite object at start: 0xbf6000, appr. length: 10244
Leaked composite object at start: 0xbf3000, appr. length: 10244
Leaked composite object at start: 0xbf0000, appr. length: 10244
Leaked composite object at start: 0xbbc000, appr. length: 10244
Leaked composite object at start: 0xbb9000, appr. length: 10244
Leaked composite object at start: 0xbb6000, appr. length: 10244
Leaked composite object at start: 0xbb3000, appr. length: 10244
Leaked composite object at start: 0xbb0000, appr. length: 10244
```

Memory Bounds Checker

A memory bounds checker ensures that a program does not trespass into areas of memory where it should not be. For example, Bruce Peren's Electric Fence utility can be used to determine if a program is overrunning the boundaries of its malloc() buffer.

There are also stack checkers, which defend against stack smashing attacks. When it comes to checking the stack, the optimal approach is to insert checking code statically at build time via the compiler. The StackGuard compiler is a good example.[8] The alternative is to implement a platform-specific kludge with macros:

```
/*checkStack.c -------------------------------------------------*/
#include<stdio.h>
#include<stdlib.h>
#define SIG_VAL        0x11223344
#define SIGNATURE      int sig = SIG_VAL
#define RETURN         check(sig); return
void check(int sig)
{
        printf("signature=%x\n",sig);
        if(sig==SIG_VAL){ return; }
        printf("Stack has been corupted!\n");
        exit(1);
}/*end check-------------------------------------------------*/
void corruptStack(char *str,int limit)
{
        int i;
        for(i=0;i<limit;i++){ str[i]='a'+i; }
}/*end corruptStack-------------------------------------------*/
```

---

8.   Crispen Cowen et al., "Automatic Detection and Prevention of Buffer-Overflow Attacks." Paper presented at the 7th USENIX Security Symposium, San Antonio, TX, January 1998.

```
void testCall(int limit)
{
        SIGNATURE;
        char array[4];
        printf("limit=%d ",limit);
        corruptStack(array,limit);
        RETURN;
}/*end testCall-----------------------------------------------------*/
void main()
{
        testCall(1);
        testCall(2);
        testCall(3);
        testCall(4);
        testCall(5);
        testCall(6);
        testCall(7);
        return;
}/*end main-------------------------------------------------------*/
```

The key to my implementation is the signature integer (i.e., 0x11223344), which I place at the top of the local variable region in the stack frame. If the stack gets corrupted, this signature variable is overwritten (see Figure 2-4). By checking its value, I can see if a problem has occurred.

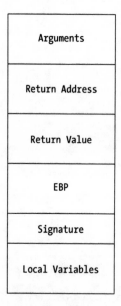

Figure 2-4. Placement of the signature

The reason why it's better to build this functionality into the compiler is that it's easy to forget to place in the macros, not to mention that my technique is not portable. The structure of a function's stack frame can vary from one compiler to the next.

When this code is built with Visual C++ and run on a 32-bit Intel machine, the following output is produced:

```
limit=1 signature=11223344
limit=2 signature=11223344
limit=3 signature=11223344
limit=4 signature=11223344
limit=5 signature=11223365
Stack has been corupted!
```

Unlike the heap and the stack, the data segment of an application is typically well protected by the native operating system, which is to say that you don't need a utility to protect against overruns. Any contemporary operating system will have hardware-based mechanisms to catch a program that attempts to move outside of its data segment.

For example, if the following program is executed:

```c
#include<stdio.h>
char array[20];
void main()
{
        int i;
        for(i=0;i<1024;i++){array[i]=0x7;}
}
```

the user will be greeted by a warning from the native operating system, as shown in Figure 2-5.

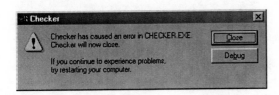

Figure 2-5. Native OS bounds checking

Profilers

Profilers are used to display how much time the different components of an application consume. Profilers are useful for identifying performance bottlenecks. They also provide frequency counts and call graphs so that you know how often (and by whom) a particular function is being invoked.

The GNU C compiler (i.e., gcc) has options so that you can insert profiling code into your program. This way, when your program runs, it keeps track of its own performance metrics. To persist these metrics, the profiling data is stored in a binary file named gmon.out. The GNU profiler processes this file and generates a human-readable summary.

> **NOTE** *The profiler does not actually run the application, as you might suspect. Instead the GNU profiler is merely a type of translator that takes the profiling data generated by the application itself and translates it into something you can read.*

Take the following simple program:

```
/* testProfiler.c --------------------------------------------------*/
#include<stdio.h>
#include<math.h>
void doWork()
{
        double var = 12.033/34.00032;
}/*end doWork---------------------------------------------------------*/
void doMoreWork()
{
        long var = 0x12345678 && 0x99887766;
}/*end doMoreWork-----------------------------------------------------*/
void longLoop()
{
        unsigned long int i;
        unsigned long begin;
        unsigned long end;
        begin = time();
        for(i=0;i<100000000;i++)
        {
                double retVal;
                if(i%2==0){ doWork(); }
                else{ doMoreWork(); }
        }
        end = time();
        printf("loop took %d seconds\n",(end-begin));
}/*end longLoop-------------------------------------------------------*/
int main()
{
        longLoop();
        return(0);
}/*end main-----------------------------------------------------------*/
```

This program can be compiled to include profiling code, using the -pg option.

```
C:\src>gcc -o testprof sourceCode.c -pg
```

When this program runs, it generates a gmon.out file.

```
C:\src>testprof.exe
loop took 6 seconds
```

You can process gmon.out with gprof to obtain a self-documenting, human-readable summary.

```
Each sample counts as 0.0555556 seconds.
```

% time	cumulative seconds	self seconds	calls	self s/call	total s/call	name
51.69	2.56	2.56				mcount
25.84	3.83	1.28	1	1.28	2.39	longLoop
14.61	4.56	0.72	50000000	0.00	0.00	doMoreWork
7.87	4.94	0.39	50000000	0.00	0.00	doWork
0.00	4.94	0.00	1	0.00	2.39	main

This summary has seven columns. It is followed by a cursory explanation of each column:

```
% time
The percentage of the total running time of the program used by this function.

cumulative seconds
A running sum of the number of seconds accounted for by this function
and those listed above it.

self seconds
The number of seconds accounted for by this function alone.
This is the major sort for this listing.

calls
The number of times this function was invoked,
if this function is profiled, else blank.

self s/call
The average number of milliseconds spent in this function per call,
if this function is profiled, else blank.
```

```
total s/call
The average number of milliseconds spent in this function
and its descendents per call, if this function is profiled, else blank.

name
The name of the function.
```

You may be wondering to yourself, "What in the heck is mcount? He didn't code anything with that name." As I mentioned earlier, the -pg option causes the compiler to insert special profiling routines into the executable. The function named mcount is a special profiling routine. As you can see from the summary, a definite overhead is associated with profiling.

In addition to a time-based summary, gprof also generates a call graph that will tell you who is invoking a certain function and how many times. As with the previous summary, it is also self-documented.

```
Call graph (explanation follows)

granularity: each sample hit covers 4 byte(s) for 2.33% of 2.39 seconds
```

index	% time	self	children	called	name
		1.28	1.11	1/1	main [2]
[1]	100.0	1.28	1.11	1	longLoop [1]
		0.72	0.00	50000000/50000000	doMoreWork [4]
		0.39	0.00	50000000/50000000	doWork [5]
		------	------	------	------
		0.00	2.39	1/1	__crt1_startup [3]
[2]	100.0	0.00	2.39	1	main [2]
		1.28	1.11	1/1	longLoop [1]
		------	------	------	------
					<spontaneous>
[3]	100.0	0.00	2.39		__crt1_startup [3]
		0.00	2.39	1/1	main [2]
		------	------	------	------
		0.72	0.00	50000000/50000000	longLoop [1]
[4]	30.2	0.72	0.00	50000000	doMoreWork [4]
		------	------	------	------
		0.39	0.00	50000000/50000000	longLoop [1]
[5]	16.3	0.39	0.00	50000000	doWork [5]
		------	------	------	------

```
This table describes the call tree of the program, and was sorted by
the total amount of time spent in each function and its children.

Each entry in this table consists of several lines.  The line with the
index number at the left hand margin lists the current function.
The lines above it list the functions that called this function,
and the lines below it list the functions this one called.
```

This line lists:

index   A unique number given to each element of the table.
             Index numbers are sorted numerically.
             The index number is printed next to every function name so
             it is easier to look up where the function is in the table.

% time   This is the percentage of the 'total' time that was spent
             in this function and its children. Note that due to
             different viewpoints, functions excluded by options, etc,
             these numbers will NOT add up to 100%.

self   This is the total amount of time spent in this function.

children   This is the total amount of time propagated into this
             function by its children.

called   This is the number of times the function was called.
             If the function called itself recursively, the number
             only includes non-recursive calls, and is followed by
             a '+' and the number of recursive calls.

name   The name of the current function. The index number is
             printed after it. If the function is a member of a
             cycle, the cycle number is printed between the
             function's name and the index number.

If you wanted to, you could probably write your own modest profiling framework. The hardest part would be dealing with all of the little accounting invocations that you would need to insert and delete from the source code. Implementing this with preprocessor macros would probably be your best bet.

```
int doWork()
{
        START_TIMER(DO_WORK);
        //do some work
        END_TIMER(DO_WORK);
}
```

If you wanted to get snazzy, you could have your profiling framework output the performance summary and call graph in XML.

```
<profile>
        <total run time>4.0000 seconds</total run time>
        <routineList>
                <routine>
                        <name>doWork</name>
                        <time used>.072</time used>
                        <percent total time>14.61</percent total time>
                        <times invoked>50000000</times invoked>
                        <ms per call>0.00</ms per call>
                </routine>
                <routine>
                        <name>doMoreWork</name>
                        <time used>.039</time used>
                        <percent total time>7.87</percent total time>
                        <times invoked>50000000</times invoked>
                        <ms per call>0.00</ms per call>
                </routine>
        </routineList>
</profile>
```

2.3.7 Basic Debugger Operation

A number of diagnostic tools can help you gather experimental data, but in terms of locating bugs, the debugger is the most powerful. In some instances, a debugger is the only diagnostic tool that makes sense. Large corporations that have a significant amount of legacy code typically don't maintain extensive design documentation or even consistent logging conventions (it's Murphy's Law in action). Sometimes the only way to understand what's going on is to fire up a debugger and start making your way through application logic.

The Advantages of Debugging

A debugger creates a controlled environment in which you can safely execute a program and examine its internal operation. It's sort of like having a VCR remote control. While a program is executing, you can freeze everything and peek at the running program's internal state. Or, if you want to see something happen in slow motion, you can slow things down and execute one statement at a time.

> **DEBUGGER**   *A tool that allows the execution path of a process to be temporarily paused such that the state of the process may be inspected and modified*

The laws of quantum mechanics (i.e., Heisenberg's Uncertainty Principle) dictate that the very act of observing will have an impact on the outcome of an experiment. Back in the 1920s, physicists discovered that a person performing a quantum-level experiment couldn't be objectively separated from the events that they were measuring. In other words, you are a part of your experiment and your very presence influences the metrics that you record. Such is life on the subatomic level.

Computer scientists are not subject to this principle. By using a debugger, an engineer can attain a completely neutral frame of reference and make observations without becoming a part of the experiment.

Most debuggers use three basic mechanisms to provide a neutral frame of reference:

- Breakpoints

- Watchpoints

- Single-step execution

Breakpoints

A *breakpoint* is a reserved, low-level instruction that is inserted among normal instructions in a routine. Breakpoints can be inserted while you are editing source code, such that they are compiled into the final executable. Breakpoints can also be inserted dynamically into a program's memory image at runtime by the debugger itself. Regardless of how it is inserted, a breakpoint causes the processor to stop the currently executing task and give control over to dedicated debugging routines that have been registered for this very purpose. This allows a debugger to step outside of the current task and assume an external frame of reference.

The GNU debugger (gdb) is a mature and sophisticated debugger. It has been ported to a number of Unix flavors, including Linux. Because of its accessibility and consistent interface, I will be using it to help illustrate debugging concepts.

To debug an application built with gcc, you will need to specify the -g option when you compile.

```
C:\src\dbg>gcc -o program src.c -g
```

To crank up the debugger and examine the program executable, which you saw in the discussion on profiling, simply type in the following:

```
C:\src\dbg>gdb program
```

To set a breakpoint at the entry point of the longLoop() function, use the break command.

```
(gdb) break longLoop
Breakpoint 1 at 0x1711: file src.c, line 13.
```

To set a breakpoint on line 17 in src.c, use the following variation of the previous command:

```
(gdb) break src.c:17
Breakpoint 2 at 0x172b: file src.c, line 17.
```

To see a summary of the current breakpoints set, use the info break-point command.

```
(gdb) info break
Num Type           Disp Enb Address    What
1   breakpoint     keep y   0x00001711 in longLoop at src.c:13
2   breakpoint     keep y   0x0000172b in longLoop at src.c:17
```

Once you have set a few breakpoints, you can initiate execution with the run command, and the debugger will run the application until it encounters the first breakpoint.

```
(gdb) run
Starting program: c:/_docs/code/docs/bookIdea/ch2/src/prof/program

Breakpoint 1, longLoop () at src.c:13
13              begin = time();
```

To continue executing, once a breakpoint has been encountered, use the continue command.

```
(gdb) c
Continuing.
```

To temporarily disable a breakpoint, use the disable command and refer to the breakpoint by its numeric equivalent displayed in the previous summary.

```
(gdb) disable  2
```

To reenable the breakpoint, use the enable command and specify the breakpoint by its numeric identifier (you can use the info breakpoint command, described previously, to see what the breakpoint-number mapping is).

```
(gdb) enable  2
```

To delete a breakpoint, use the delete command.

```
(gdb) delete  2
```

To exit the debugger, enter the quit command.

```
(gdb) quit
```

Watchpoints

A *watchpoint* is not attached to a particular location, like a breakpoint is. Instead, a watchpoint halts program execution when the value of a given expression changes. This is useful when you don't know where something is occurring, but you want to catch it when it does. Watchpoints tend to be much slower than breakpoints, but usually the benefits outweigh the costs when you don't know where an event is occurring.

To set a watchpoint during a gdb session, use the watch command.

```
(gdb) watch i
Hardware watchpoint 2: i
```

This sets a watchpoint on the index variable i. Once you issue the continue command, the program will execute until the variable changes in value.

```
(gdb) c
Continuing.
Hardware watchpoint 2: i

Old value = 3
New value = 0
0x00001720 in longLoop () at src.c:14
14                  for(i=0;i<100000000;i++)
```

To view a summary of the watchpoints during a debugging session, invoke the info watchpoint command.

```
(gdb) info watchpoint
Num Type           Disp Enb Address    What
1   breakpoint     keep y   0x00001711 in longLoop at src.c:13
        breakpoint already hit 1 time
2   hw watchpoint  keep y              i
```

Single-Step Execution

In *single-step execution*, the processor will execute a single statement and then return program control to the debugger. Single-step execution is used to trace a program's actions one instruction at a time.

Normally, a user will set a breakpoint, or watchpoint, in a region of code that they are interested in. When the path of execution halts, the user will then single-step through the code in question to see what's going on. Like I said before, it's similar to a using a VCR remote. You can fast-forward to the good part, and then inch forward, frame by frame, to delineate every little detail of your favorite scene. I've done this while watching the movie *The Usual Suspects,* to see if I could catch a glimpse of Keyser Soze.

The GNU debugger uses the step command (s) to single-step through code. Every time you step, the debugger shows you the source code of the instruction that it just executed.

```
Breakpoint 1, longLoop () at src.c:13
13                   begin = time();
(gdb) s
14                   for(i=0;i<100000000;i++)
(gdb) s
17                         if(i%2==0){ doWork(); }
(gdb) s
doWork () at src.c:4
4        void doWork(){ double var = 12.033/34.00032; }
(gdb) s
longLoop () at src.c:14
14                   for(i=0;i<100000000;i++)
```

Officially, there are three types of single stepping behavior (i.e., step into, step over, and step out of). What you have just witnessed was the "step into" version of single stepping. I will show you these three variations, and the differences between them, later on in Chapter 4.

Looking Around

Once you've stepped into a region of code with gdb, you can use the print command to display the current values of different variables:

```
(gdb) s
17                         if(i%2==0){ doWork(); }
(gdb) print i
$6 = 6
(gdb) print begin
$7 = 1049932788
```

If you'd like to see some of the surrounding source code, as opposed to just the source code of the statement being executed, then you can issue the `list` command.

```
(gdb) s
longLoop () at src.c:14
14              for(i=0;i<100000000;i++)
(gdb) s
17                      if(i%2==0){ doWork(); }
(gdb) list
12              unsigned long end;
13              begin = time();
14              for(i=0;i<100000000;i++)
15              {
16                      double retVal;
17                      if(i%2==0){ doWork(); }
18                      else{ doMoreWork(); }
19              }
20              end = time();
21              printf("loop took %d seconds\n",(end-begin));
(gdb)
```

If you specify the name of function after the `list` command, the debugger will give you the source code in the immediate vicinity of that function.

```
(gdb) list longLoop
4       void doWork(){ double var = 12.033/34.00032; }
5
6       void doMoreWork(){  long var = 0x12345678 && 0x99887766; }
7
8       void longLoop()
9       {
10              unsigned long int i;
11              unsigned long begin;
12              unsigned long end;
13              begin = time();
```

If you want to scroll the source code up or down, issue the list+ or list- commands.

```
(gdb) list+
14              for(i=0;i<100000000;i++)
15              {
16                      double retVal;
17                      if(i%2==0){ doWork(); }
18                      else{ doMoreWork(); }
19              }
```

```
20              end = time();
21              printf("loop took %d seconds\n",(end-begin));
22      }
23
```

NOTE *There are literally dozens of different production-quality debuggers available. The GNU debugger is one of the last remaining command-line debuggers still in use. The current generation of debuggers sold by Microsoft or Borland come as part of an integrated development environment (IDE) and have a GUI front-end. Nevertheless, the GNU debugger is still a powerful tool that has a consistent interface across multiple platforms. Hence, there are advantages to investing the time to become familiar with it. If you want to be old school and learn more about how to use the GNU debugger, extensive documentation is available both online[9] and in book form.[10]*

Debuggers Are Dangerous

Most computer science people have an innate curiosity when it comes to seeing how things work behind the scenes. There is nothing more tantalizing to us than discovering a little-known bit of information that other people do not know. This makes certain people good maintenance engineers, and other people good crackers. Curiosity is a sword that cuts both ways.

To an extent, this is why debuggers are dangerous. They allow us to dissect applications and discover the truth. The truth yields power, which can be abused.

The first debugger that I worked with was a tool named debug, which was shipped with Microsoft's DOS operating system. I first heard of debug in the mid 1980s. I was in the Cleveland Public Library looking for a book on BASIC when I encountered two older geeks huddled together at a table near the computer technology section. Sitting there with their thick, wide-rimmed glasses and their HP RPN calculators, they spoke in hushed reverence of debug's ability to patch binaries and disassemble BIOS interrupts. They whispered about debug like they had found a skeleton key to Fort Knox. I was in awe.

Later, when I looked up debug in a DOS user's manual, I read that because debug is a potentially dangerous command, it should be used only by technically experienced users.

Dangerous? Dangerous! It was like giving me a firecracker and telling me not to light it. The first chance I got, I visited a neighbor who owned an IBM

---

9.   http://www.cs.utah.edu/dept/old/texinfo/gdb/gdb_toc.html

10.   Richard Stallman et al., *Debugging with GDB: The GNU Source-Level Debugger* (Free Software Foundation, 2002. ISBN: 1-882-11488-4)

8088 PC. After entering the debug command, I was rewarded with debug's mysterious command prompt. For the next two hours, I flayed about like a beetle stuck on its back.

This initial paralysis was actually a good thing. It spurred my curiosity. My burning desire to master the debug command forced me to use several months of lawn-mowing money to buy Dan Rollin's book on 8088 Macro Assembly.[11] I read the book until the pages started to fall out.

How did I use my newfound knowledge? Well, my favorite trick was to hijack the interrupt table on a PC at the public library. Next, I would disable the keyboard and cause the machine to emit annoying high-pitched beeps every 30 seconds. Power corrupts.

2.4 Record Keeping

After you have successfully repaired a bug, it's a good idea to record your findings so that the investment of time and energy is not lost.

2.4.1 Individual Record Keeping

As a software engineer, performing your own assigned duties, there are steps that you can take to persist the knowledge that you have uncovered during the debugging process. This includes amending, or even augmenting, existing source code documentation and tracking frequently occurring problems.

Update Documentation

It's the old, tired excuse: "We didn't have time to document." People like this probably also neglect to pull their pants down in the restroom (it takes too much time). The truth is that the time needed to update comments is marginal at worst. Make sure to convey intent in your comments. Tell *why* the code does something, not just *how.* Comments that described "how" the corresponding source code works make the documentation into a worthless verbal rehash.

Finally, always be sure to look out for units of measure (e.g., milliseconds or seconds), assumed range limitations, and unexpected surprises (e.g., global data manipulation). If the original author has not documented these types of things, then you have the opportunity to help the next person who encounters the code.

---

11. Dan Rollins, *IBM-PC: 8088 MacRo Assembler Programming* (MacMillan, 1985). ISBN: 0-024-03210-7)

Personal Journal

Keep an informal log of the type of bugs that you've encountered. The more frequently you come across them, the more important it is for you to record them. For example, I have a habit of trying to access pointer information without using the indirection operator.

```
int *pointer;
*pointer = 5;
printf("value at address=%ld\n",pointer);   //whoops!
```

Some people take things to the extreme and keep a log of modifications while they are actually changing the code they are working on. This way, if they have lost track of the changes that they have made, they can go back to their log.

2.4.2 Collaborative Record Keeping

In order for a team of software engineers to work effectively, mechanisms have to be in place to facilitate concurrent project development and easy communication. Revision control systems and problem tracking systems are the two most common tools to this end.

Revision Control System

A *revision control system* basically tracks changes in a software program and allows geographically separated engineers to collaborate. Revision control is used to perform two basic functions:

- Manage multiple versions of the same source code.

- Manage access to source code by multiple engineers.

As updates are made to a software application, different versions of the same application will result. As time passes, bugs will arise that are specific to a particular version. This is because either a bug was fixed by a subsequent update or the update itself introduced new bugs. To address outstanding issues like bugs, it is crucial that a maintenance programmer have the ability to access source code that is specific to a particular version.

Revision control systems also implement controls so that developers can work on the same application (see Figure 2-6). For example, if two engineers are working on the same source file, there is a danger that they will end up overwriting each other's work. One technique that some systems use is to allow one engineer to lock a file while they work on it, so that other engineers cannot make changes. Other systems attempt to merge concurrent changes to the same file, just as long as none of the developers tried to modify the same line of code.

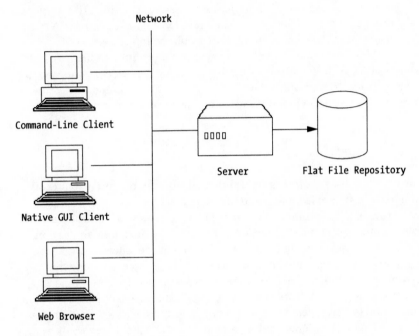

Figure 2-6. Revision control system design

Revision control systems are typically based on a client-server model. The server component maintains the different versions of the source code. The client allows an engineer to access a specific version of the source code, make modifications, and then commit those modifications. Most servers implement their own proprietary database as an alternative to relying on an external RDBMS. To efficiently store different versions of the same file, revision control systems tend to store only the differences between the consecutive versions of the same file.

There are a number of commercial revision control systems on the market. Microsoft sells one called Visual SourceSafe.[12] At the time of this book's

---

12. http://msdn.microsoft.com/ssafe/

writing, its retail cost is roughly $549 per user. Perforce Software[13] sells a revision control package that, unlike Microsoft's, runs on over 50 different operating systems and offers a multitude of different interfaces (e.g., Windows GUI, Web browser, or command line). Perforce refers to their product as a Software Configuration Management (SCM) system, because it offers features outside of version control. At the time of this book's writing, Perforce sells a 20-user license for $750 per user.

Freeware revision control systems are available, in addition to commercial packages. The most popular freeware revision control system is GNU CVS[14] (Concurrent Versions System). CVS is built on top of GNU RCS[15] (Revision Control System), which manages revision control for files. CVS extends RCS so that entire software projects can be managed, as opposed to just files. Walter Tichy implemented RCS in the 1980s at Purdue University. Later on, in 1989, Brian Berliner started on the current incarnation of CVS.

Problem Tracking System

A *problem tracking system* is a repository that stores information about software bugs, customer feedback, and salient QA incidents. As with a revision control system, it is meant to allow developers to collaborate and address problems that occur once a software application has gone into production.

Problem tracking systems are characterized by the following workflow: bug information is entered into a report that is then persisted to the tracking repository. Developers can then query the repository to see if new reports have been assigned to them. Some systems will automatically send an e-mail notification to developers when a new bug report has been assigned to them. Once the engineer assigned to the problem has made the necessary fixes, they can mark the report as "resolved." In some instances, a QA engineer will then test the fix and mark the report as "closed," or reopen the report and send it back for more fixing.

Defect tracking systems are based on a client-server model. The clients typically offer features so that a repository can be queried, and reports can be edited. The server manages concurrent access to reports by acting as an intermediary between the repository and the client components. Most bug tracking systems rely on an external database, like MySQL or PostgreSql, to store the report information (see Figure 2-7) because it tends to proliferate quickly. Contemporary systems often provide a Web-based client interface so that no additional software, other than a Web browser, needs to be installed.

---

13. http://www.perforce.com/

14. http://www.gnu.org/software/cvs/

15. http://www.cs.purdue.edu/homes/trinkle/RCS/

Network

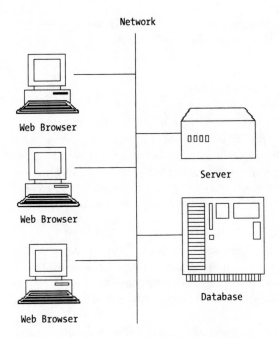

Web Browser

Server

Web Browser

Database

Web Browser

Figure 2-7. Problem tracking system design

There are number of Web-based commercial bug tracking systems. For example, IBM sells a product named ClearQuest.[16] They acquired this product when they bought Rational Software at the end of 2002. ClearQuest is designed to interoperate with Rational's ClearCase SCM tool (so that they can sell you two products instead of one). ClearQuest supports both Web-based clients and platform-specific GUI clients (Windows, AIX, and Linux). The Web server requires Microsoft IIS, so to a degree this ties the deployment to Windows if you want to service Web clients. ClearQuest stores its reports in a relational database like DB2, Oracle, or SQL Server. Price information is not forthcoming on the product's Web page, so you can expect ClearQuest to be an expensive product.

There are also a couple of battle-tested freeware bug tracking systems available. The most powerful of these is Bugzilla.[17] Terry Weissman first conceived Bugzilla while he was at Netscape. He wrote the first version in TCL. To broaden the appeal of Bugzilla, he ported his TCL code to Perl. When mozilla.org went online for the first time, in 1998, Bugzilla was released as an open source project. Bugzilla supports Web clients very nicely.[18] The current

16. http://www.rational.com/products/clearquest/

17. http://www.bugzilla.org/

18. http://bugzilla.mozilla.org/

stable version of Bugzilla requires Perl, MySQL, and a Web server (preferably Apache). It has been successfully installed on Solaris, Linux, and Windows.

Which Tracking Tools Are the Best?

Once I asked an Army Ranger which firearm he thought was the most effective on the battlefield. His answer was, "Whichever one you use the best." In other words, don't pick a tool because it's fashionable or because you think it looks good on your resume. If your project fails because you emphasized technology over engineering, the lengthy verbal diatribe that your old supervisor gives to potential future employers will easily annul that good-looking resume.

When you are under enemy fire, you have to stick to simple things that you know how to use. When the bullets start whizzing past your head, you won't have the calm state of mind necessary to effectively deploy the latest whiz-bang technology. Learning to use a new tool, or new programming language, can eat up valuable time. If you decide that you need to be on the cutting edge, then at least make sure you take training time into account when you draw up the schedule.

Price can be a significant issue, especially if you are low on the corporate food chain and in a department constrained by a tight budget. This can be the big equalizer for tools like CVS and Bugzilla. Most of the companies I have worked for seemed to intentionally make purchase order requisitions a long, drawn-out process. The goal is to make the ordeal so much work that you won't do it very often. Some managers simply avoid the topic, with the guarded expectation that you will find a way to make do with what you have. "OK, kid, here's your cube and your 486 workstation. I'll be down the hall in my office . . ."

> **NOTE** *To give you an example of what some people are up against: I once worked for a software vendor that was so tightfisted that you had to make a formal, written request to get a new ballpoint pen. There is a problem with this scheme. What if you are requesting a pen because you don't have one? How are you supposed to fill out the form to get a pen if you don't have one to begin with?*

2.5 Summary

A bug begins its life cycle (see Figure 2-8) when it is discovered by a customer and subsequently entered into a problem tracking system. This report is then assigned to you, the maintenance engineer. You can start by attempting to duplicate the bug and then ascertaining if the bug is actually a genuine problem (i.e., not some user error). If the bug is genuine, you can utilize a number of expedient measures to see if the bug can be resolved quickly (e.g., examining recent changes to the source tree, glancing through log files, or looking for similar past bugs).

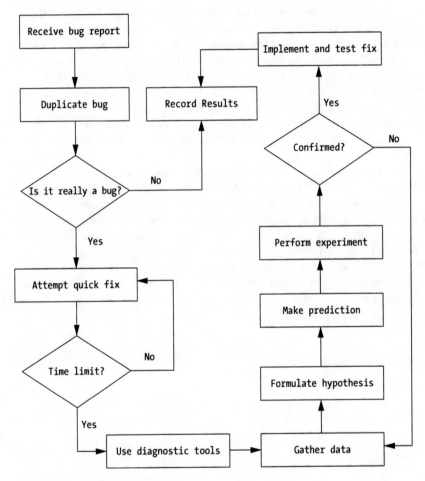

Figure 2-8. Debugging life cycle

If you are not able to resolve the bug with shoot-from-the-hip tactics, you should move on to more substantial measures after a predetermined time limit. Use your diagnostic tools to collect as much data as you can. The scientific method can then be applied to locate and fix the bug. Both the incremental integration and binary search procedures can be used to locate the bug. Fixing the bug requires an in-depth understanding of the program's requirements and implementation. Insight is the key, and this is a commodity that is not easily obtained.

Once you think you've fixed the problem, you should test your fix. If you still feel confident after this point, you should record your work. This includes updating documentation, adding entries into your own working journal, checking in source code to revision control, and marking the bug as "resolved" in the problem tracking system.

Having said all this, I would like to conclude the chapter by stating that writing about the debugging process is a hell of a lot easier than actually doing it. Most maintenance engineers are constantly put in a position where they are in a complete state of ignorance. The investment deity Warren Buffet once said that if you don't know who the fool in the market is, it's probably you. Please don't take this the wrong way, but most maintenance programmers are the "fools" in the market, which is to say that they are typically introduced into a project as outsiders with little or no understanding of the code that has been literally thrown in their lap. They are out of the loop, and this is not a good place to be.

I can sympathize with the trepidation and anxiety that such engineers suffer from. I have been there myself. The insider who originally wrote the code has either left for a better job, or moved on to another project. In my experience, the original authors will usually have very little to say about their code. Instead, they tend to quietly smirk, and then mumble to themselves, "Boy, am I glad I'm not that new guy. The source code for that program is a mess. It's a good thing I deleted my name from all those files."

It would be negligent to pretend that I could tell you how to quickly scale the learning curve in every case. However, I do have a few ideas that I can pass on to you. This leads us to the next chapter.

CHAPTER 3

Understand
the Problem

```
/*
You are not expected to understand this
*/
```

—Comment preceding the task-switching code in UNIX

In order to fix a bug in a program, you have to "understand the problem." This is another way of saying that you need to understand

- The program's requirements

- How the program implements those requirements

In general, establishing the requirements of an application is an issue only for the engineers who implement the first cut. Maintenance engineers rarely face this problem because they work exclusively on code that has already been deployed, and such code usually has the requirements spelled out in some form or another.

In the best-case scenario, a maintenance engineer will have access to a user manual, design documentation (e.g., UML class diagrams), and a formal requirements document. In the worst-case scenario, the application itself spells out the requirements in terms of existing functionality. In light of this, I am going to focus on how to deal with the second half of the problem: understanding how an application implements its requirements.

Unfortunately, this is easier said than done. A number of barriers stand in the way. Some of them are technical, others are sociological, and some are even cultural. In this chapter, I will discuss the hurdles that impede the analysis of a program's internals and then offer advice on how you can jump over them.

3.1 How Knowledge Is Lost

As I mentioned earlier in the book, the decision making process in business is not always based on pure logic. For example, it is not uncommon for a company to be infested by managers whose personal objectives do not match those of the company. Lou Gerstner faced an army of such people when he took over as CEO of IBM in 1993.[1] If this were not the case, most corporations would resemble the Borg: a biological machine made up of people acting under the direction of a vast global mind. Much to the contrary, the business world is populated by a large collection of self-governing individuals. This translates into politics, rivalry, and intrigue. And you thought Scott Adams was joking . . .

In large organizations, knowledge about a particular application may disappear as a result of organizational behavior. In other words, information is lost as a result of all the seemingly illogical things that happen when humans work together in groups. For maintenance engineers, this can make life very difficult because they rely heavily on other people, directly or indirectly, to decrypt old code.

---

1. Lou V. Gerstner Jr., *Who Says Elephants Can't Dance? Inside IBM's Historic Turnaround* (HarperBusiness, 2002. ISBN: 0-060-52379-4)

3.1.1 Competition

There are certain facts of life that your professors in school didn't tell you (or perhaps they just didn't want to acknowledge them). For instance, there may be times when your coworkers actually pose a threat to your career. Although corporate rhetoric may laud the benefits of teamwork, the truth is that life in the cube farm can boil down to a dirty game of "survival of the fittest." Not only do companies compete among themselves, but the employees within companies also compete. They compete for better assignments, better equipment, a nicer office, and a bigger salary. In volatile situations, like during market downturns, employees may compete just to keep their jobs. In a competitive environment, people will take all sorts of measures to gain an advantage over other employees. This can lead to behavior like hoarding information.

Hoarding Information

Scarcity is a fundamental concept in economics. Scarcity offers leverage. By being the sole source of a scarce commodity, you make yourself valuable. Everyone is expendable, but the truly salient question, then, is how much it would cost your employer to replace you. The more valuable you are, the more expensive it is for someone to replace you, and the more secure your position is.

Knowledge can be lost because people actively sabotage its dissemination. In an effort to become the sole proprietor of valuable information, someone may decide to hide what they know. For example, there may be only one guy in a database group who understands how a crucial part of the transaction manager functions. To make himself more difficult to replace, he can let the existing documentation intentionally become outdated, and then stockpile his own private stash of current information. If he were to be laid off, the company would have to regrow all of the relevant knowledge. The cost of doing so might be great enough that it would be cheaper to keep him on board even in dire circumstances.

> **NOTE** *As a maintenance engineer, I would dread the thought of touching this guy's transaction code. In fact, I'm pretty sure his name would quickly become a curse word. However, can I blame him for looking out for his own interests? If a corporation can replace a high-paid senior engineer with a college student, or an H1-B candidate, it will. It may seem alienating, but most CEOs view engineers like a commodity. The truth is that corporations exist to make money; everything else is secondary (and I mean* everything). *It's a game of leverage, and one that can get very ugly. So try to hate the sin instead of hating the sinner.*

During an economic recession, the daily routine at the average software company resembles a game of musical chairs, as people jockey for position and resources. The efficiency experts enter the scene, with their chainsaws, and start cutting up chairs.[2] When they are done, only so many free chairs are left, and eventually someone will have to go home empty-handed. Can you imagine how someone who has a wife and three kids feels in this situation? Can you blame them for wanting a little protection from the chainsaw man?

Stonewalling

A person who is the "expert" cannot plead ignorance when faced with a technical question in their area of expertise. This would undermine their reputation as an expert and decrease their market value. For this reason, stonewalling is the preferred tactic of a person who hoards information. People who stonewall will actively evade you in the hallway, refuse to answer their e-mails, and tell you that they are "very busy" when you make a pilgrimage to their office.

As a last resort, they will attempt to use intellectual violence to fend you off. Which is to say that they will blind you with so many technical terms and concepts that you won't get anything useful out of the conversation. Their

---

2. *Office Space.* Directed by Mike Judge. 90 min. Twentieth Century Fox, 1999.

goal is to give you as little concrete information as possible, while at the same time wasting enough of your time that you are forced to move on afterwards.

For instance, I once asked an information hoarder how he defined a transaction, and he said:

> *A transaction, in my optimized implementation, is a self-formatting Unicode data stream, of arbitrary size, between a set of orthogonal subsystems, on a geo-distributed LAN, using an application-level network protocol.*

Does this sound just a tad bit ambiguous? Yes, it does, and this was intentional. Never mind that the whole idea of a transaction has already been clearly defined by a number of computer scientists.[3] Never mind that he couched his explanation with a bunch of irrelevant information. He didn't think that I knew what a transaction was, so he thought he could take advantage of my ignorance and baffle me into submission.

Countertactics

If civility and patience are of little help, one way to foil stonewalling is to flush the guilty party out into the open. Form a posse. Talk to your supervisor and have them request a meeting, and make sure to invite a lot of high-ranking managers. This will minimize antics on the part of the stonewaller and make it very difficult for them to hold out. They will not want to look dim-witted or inhospitable in front of the very people who have influence over their career. If they do, then at least you have witnesses.

Make sure that you maintain a paper trail. If someone is stonewalling you, then you will want proof that they are doing it. Route copies of your e-mails to your supervisor, so that the person hoarding information knows that they are under observation and that failure to respond will be noted by others with more authority.

To avoid returning your e-mail and to provide as little hard evidence as possible, the person hoarding information may prefer to visit your cube and dish out a few vague abstractions. If this is the case, take careful notes of the conversation and then send the person (and your supervisor) a summary of the conversation "just to make sure" that you understood what they told you. This will prevent them from backpeddling later on. Make copies of your e-mails and store them in a safe place (remember what I said in Chapter 1).

Finally, always have the humility to admit when you don't understand something. Using intellectual violence effectively depends upon the victim being too embarrassed to ask what the offender is talking about. If you are

---

3. Jim Gray, *Transaction Processing: Concepts and Techniques* (Morgan Kaufmann, 1993. ISBN: 1-558-60190-2)

willing to ask what might seem like stupid questions, then you can force
knowledge hoarders to spell out their precious code in terms that normal
people can understand. Force them to define their terms and explain ambiguous points. Don't be intimidated if they seem to get flustered by your ignorance,
they're just venting because they're scared that someone has finally caught on
to them.

3.1.2 Attrition

Change is inevitable. You can embrace it or despise it, but either way it will
occur. To see what I mean, go back and visit your old high school sometime.
It might not even be there any more. The world rushes forward like some sort
of high-speed locomotive, and corporate America is no exception. Departments
rarely keep their exact composition for more than six months. People quit,
get fired, retire, have midlife crises, or move on to other positions during
a reorganization.

During my first real job in the software industry, I went through six managers in a two-year period. This rapid turnover, however, was just a symptom
of a larger problem. Disorder at the top of the food chain inevitably gains the
requisite inertia to come crashing down on those in the lower levels of the
hierarchy. Eventually, you begin to feel like you're part of a traveling circus that
goes from town to town, never staying in one place for more than a few days.
When you hit middle age, you become an old codger like me, wishing for the
return of your salad days and decrying the fact that the world is going to hell.

The very fact that a steady flow of people normally enters and leaves
a corporation contributes to a loss of knowledge. When people leave, the
scavengers pick through whatever doesn't get shredded or thrown out. The
new guy is left with the remaining skeleton. It's not a malicious phenomenon,
like information hoarding; rather it is an unintended consequence of the natural order. It's like some morbid reenactment of something you might see on
the Discovery Channel.

Countertactics

Turnover is *not* something you can fight directly. Not even Bill Gates, with his
billions, can oppose the passage of time. However, there are ways that you
can perform forensic investigation and track down live sources of useful
information.

Any revision control system worth its salt will track the history of individual files. Even if most of the original authors are gone, a few knowledgeable
engineers may still be left who are currently on other projects. See who
worked on the original files via revision control history, and then try to find
out whom they worked with and who their managers were. Someone might
even have an old organization chart lying around that specifies who worked

on what, five years ago. If you can't talk to the original author, see if you can talk to one of their old coworkers.

The key to this tactic is being persistent, like a journalist tracking down a big story. Don't stop until you've hit all the dead ends and exhausted every lead. Hell, it works for the FBI. The only reason that they caught John Allen Muhammad and Lee Boyd Malvo was because they followed this type of brute force approach.

There may be unusual instances in which everyone is gone, even the groundskeepers, and all that is left is an empty building. CEOs like Al Dunlap have been known to amputate entire divisions in order to boost shareholder value, and create ghost towns literally overnight.[4] If your predecessors got chainsawed, there is nothing you can do . . . other than work with what you have: moldy legacy source code. Later in the chapter, I will present strategies to use when you have nothing but old code.

3.1.3 Promotion

The *Peter Principle* is an observation made by Dr. Laurence Peter that states that employees within a corporation tend to be promoted to the level at which they are incompetent.[5] In some companies, all you have to do is survive long enough and you will find yourself in upper management. Ah, yes, greener pa$ture$.

For the original author, promotion can offer a means of escape. The person who wrote the first cut may have spent the past five years babysitting their creation. The application stopped being a job and morphed into a ball and chain that they had to drag around wherever they went. The fact that they had to constantly fix and update the unwieldy dinosaur prevented them from taking on bigger and better projects.

Promotion solves this problem. Not only does the promoted employee get to hire someone else to do their dirty work, but they also receive an informal license to forget everything that they knew. In extreme cases, the promotion may move the engineer into another division, where they can pretend that they never even worked on their old code. It's like the witness protection program. A bunch of federal marshals move you to Arizona, and you get to start a whole new life. Henry Hill never had it so good.

I knew a vice president who spent almost ten years on a CASE tool before he maneuvered himself into a promotion. Once he got his new office, in a building several miles away, he was given to bouts of amnesia. When asked about a specific subsystem of the CASE tool, he would look wistfully into the

---

4.   John A. Byrne, *Chainsaw: The Notorious Career of Al Dunlap in the Era of Profit-at-Any-Price* (HarperBusiness, 1999. ISBN: 0-066-61980-7)

5.   Laurence J. Peter and Raymond Hull (Contributor), *The Peter Principle* (Buccaneer Books, 1996. ISBN: 1-568-49161-1)

distance and say something like, "Oh, geez, it's been so long since I touched that code. Ah, uh, I don't remember how it works. I think your best bet is just to read the source code."

Countertactics

The problem with engineers who get promoted is that they now possess authority and are not as easy to cajole as low-level engineering grunts. By assuming the title of "manager," they no longer have to be an expert. They don't have to answer your questions because they supposedly have more important fish to fry. Their new position allows them to focus on higher-level administrative issues, and this gives them a credible excuse for conveniently forgetting vital technical minutiae. Like I said, promotion can be a really effective escape hatch.

If you need information from a person who has been promoted, you should treat them like someone who is hoarding information. Namely, you should use meetings and e-mail to establish a paper trail. The difference lies in how you encourage them to cooperate. Because your manager and the amnesiac may be peers in the hierarchy, it won't be as easy to pressure the amnesiac into a dialogue. Instead, your manager will need to go up a level in the chain of command to see if they can have their boss exert some influence. The key is to involve other people, publicize the results of meetings, and put a spotlight on people who might otherwise be unlikely to help if they could find some way to hide. Damn roaches.

3.2 Poorly Written Code

Another barrier that impedes software maintenance is sloppy implementation. Which is to say that the source code is hard to read and decipher. Sloppy implementation can be the product of bad design, obfuscation, blatantly misleading statements, or a combination of all three. When sloppy code pops up, either the original author was inexperienced, or the original author was intentionally trying to make things complicated (recall what I said about internal competition earlier in the chapter?).

Forewarned is forearmed. If you recognize the symptoms of the disease early, you are less likely to be victimized by them. In this section, I will expose you to the various ways in which a program can be rendered illegible.

It would be unfair of me to present you with problems without offering a few solutions. Thus, in section 3.3, I will discuss countermeasures that you can use to gain insight into a poorly written program.

3.2.1 Design Problems

Sometimes it's difficult to put the blame on any one thing. This is because the very foundations of a program may be rotten. The whole notion of structured design or object orientation may have been completely ignored in favor of quickly whipping out a working prototype. The implementing engineers may not have invested the time or energy to construct a sane blueprint. Instead, they hacked together an incoherent mess that somehow satisfied the requirements. Damn the torpedoes!

Cut-and-Paste Programming

In the first chapter, I discussed the need to implement routines and classes that have strong cohesion. Code that has been implemented through cut-and-paste programming lies at the other end of the spectrum; it has very weak cohesion, which is to say that nearly identical snippets of program logic exist in dozens of different locations throughout a program. This makes maintenance a nightmare because changing a single feature can require the source code to be modified in dozens of places. Even worse, the original developer might have slightly modified each occurrence of program logic so that changes cannot simply be repasted.

The mantra for cut-and-paste programming is

Cut, paste, modify,

Cut, paste, modify,

Cut, paste, modify

For example, take the following code. It prints out the mean and sample variance of an array of floating-point values.

```
/* CutAndPaste1.c ----------------------------------------------*/
#include<stdio.h>
#include<stdlib.h>
float computeSum(float data[], int size)
{
    float ret = 0;
    int i;
    for(i=0;i<size;i++){ ret = ret + data[i]; }
    return(ret);
}/*end computeSum----------------------------------------------*/
float computeMean(float data[], int size)
```

```
{
    return(computeSum(data,size)/((float)size));
}/*end computeMean-------------------------------------------------*/
float computeSampleVariance(float data[], int size)
{
    float mean;
    float *ptr;
    float meanSquares;
    int i;
    mean = computeMean(data,size);
    ptr = (float*)malloc(sizeof(float)*size);
    for(i=0;i<size;i++){ptr[i]=data[i]*data[i];}
    meanSquares = computeMean(ptr,size);
    free(ptr);
    return(meanSquares-(mean*mean));
}/*end computeSampleVariance------------------------------------*/
void printStats(float data[], int size)
{
    if(size<=0)
    {
        fprintf(stderr,"size must be positive\n");
        return;
    }
    printf("mean = %f\n",computeMean(data,size));
    printf("var = %f\n",computeSampleVariance(data,size));
    return;
}/*end printStats-----------------------------------------------*/
```

A cut-and-paste programmer would literally write this as follows:

```
/* CutAndPaste2.c --------------------------------------------*/
#include<stdio.h>
#include<stdlib.h>
void printStats(float data[], int size)
{
    float sum;
    float variance;
    int i;
    sum = 0;
    for(i=0;i<size;i++){ sum = sum + data[i]; }
    printf("mean = %f\n",sum/((float)size));
    sum = 0;
    for(i=0;i<size;i++){ sum = sum + (data[i]*data[i]); }
    variance = sum/((float)size);
    sum = 0;
    for(i=0;i<size;i++){ sum = sum + data[i]; }
    variance -= (sum/((float)size))*(sum/((float)size));
    printf("var = %f\n",variance);
    return;
}
```

Compared to the first version, the cut-and-paste version would be more difficult to maintain. Every single operation has been repeated in as many places as possible. You can imagine what would happen if you had 200,000 lines of code like this.

Spaghetti Code

In the first chapter, I discussed the need to implement routines and classes that have *loose coupling*. Spaghetti code is characterized by very strong coupling. Spaghetti code can defy even the most relentless attempt to decompose source code into separate modules. Everything is global. Everything can access everything else. Not only that, but standard program control structures are eschewed in favor of goto statements. Like a mound of spaghetti, when you try to pick up a few strands of pasta with your fork, you end up having to lift everything.

To get a taste for how truly awful spaghetti code can get, take a look at the following code. This short program reads in a set of integers, sorts them, and then prints them out. Nothing so simple ever looked so hard.

```
/*SpaghettiCode.c-------------------------------------------------*/
#include<stdio.h>
#define MAX_SIZE   10
long array[MAX_SIZE];
long temp;
int  nValues=0;
int  current;
int  outerIndex;
int  innerIndex;
void main(int argc, char* argv[])
{
    enterValues:
    printf("enter value [enter -1 to quit]:\n");
    scanf("%ld",&array[nValues]);
    fflush(stdin);
    if(array[nValues]==-1)
    {
        nValues--;
        goto sortValues;
    }
    if(nValues==MAX_SIZE-1){ goto sortValues; }
    nValues++;
    goto enterValues;

    sortValues:
    printf("entered %d integers\n",nValues+1);
```

```
outerIndex=0;
outerLoop:
if(outerIndex==nValues+1){ goto endOuterLoop; }

innerIndex=outerIndex;
innerLoop:
    if
    (
        (innerIndex>0)&&
        (array[innerIndex]<array[innerIndex-1])
    )
    {
        int temp = array[innerIndex];
        array[innerIndex]=array[innerIndex-1];
        array[innerIndex-1]=temp;
    }
    else{ goto endInnerLoop; }
    innerIndex--;
    goto innerLoop;
    endInnerLoop:

outerIndex++;
goto outerLoop;
endOuterLoop:

printf("\nsorted values are:\n");
if(nValues==0){ goto end; }
current=0;
displayValues:
printf("array[%d]=%ld\n",current,array[current]);
current++;
if(current==nValues+1){ goto end; }
goto displayValues;

end:
printf("program is ending\n");
return;
}
```

From the perspective of the original author, using global constructs may seem to make life easier because it saves them from having to worry about constantly changing the signatures of their routines. When they need something, they just access it.

However, the original developer also knows exactly what they are doing, and why. A maintenance engineer does not have this benefit. Furthermore, in the interest of saving time, the maintenance engineer needs to be able to isolate a certain region of functionality in the source code and treat it like a little black box. The only alternative is to read, and digest, the entire application. Not many maintenance engineers have this kind of time on their hands.

Excessive Abstraction

The road to hell is paved with good intentions. Encapsulating atomic types and using wrappers can make it easier for source code to accommodate change. However, any tactic taken to an extreme is unhealthy. You can end up wrapping things so heavily that you lose sight of what you are dealing with, to the extent that someone has to descend through 50 levels of hierarchy to see what is actually being modified.

Here is an example of what I'm talking about:

```
struct TextValue
{
    char *string;
};
struct TextField
{
    struct TextValue textValue;
};
struct SimpleKeyField
{
    struct TextField textField;
};
struct RelationalKeyField
{
    struct SimpleKeyField simpleKeyField;
};
struct KeyField
{
    struct RelationalKeyField relationalKeyField;
};
```

All you're really working with is a string. However, this string has been wrapped, and rewrapped, so many times that it's hard to see this. In practice, this type of nesting would be spread out over several files (to make it less obvious, naturally). Traversing these different layers during a debugging session is very tedious unless you know exactly what you are looking for.

3.2.2 Obfuscation

Obfuscate   *To make unclear or indistinct*

In this section, I will present some of the more popular ways to obfuscate code in C. To obfuscate source code is to deliberately make it hard to read. Obfuscation tools exist that automate the process, but obfuscation can also be done by hand. To see the masters at work, visit the International Obfuscated C Coding Content (IOCCC) Web site.[6] Some anonymous programmer submitted the following source code to the IOCCC in 1984:

```
#include <stdio.h>
int i;main(){for(;i["]<i;++i){--i;}"];read('-'-'-',i+++"hell\
o, world!\n",'/'/'/'));}read(j,i,p){write(j/p+p,i---j,i/i);}
```

Just in case you're curious: this program does compile and run. It is a cruel version of the canonical "hello world" program. This program puts the "hell" in "hello."

Preprocessor Pyrotechnics

Using preprocessor directives maliciously carries the same stigma as using chemical weapons on the battlefield. Unfortunately, once they have been used, the damage has already been done, and the best that you can hope for is speedy justice for the guilty party.

The #define directive has been the subject of abuse more than any other. I suppose that it was probably introduced in an attempt to save memory. Given that directives are digested by the preprocessor at compile time, they do not take up any space in the resulting binary. If you were to declare global constants using variables, the size of the executable in memory would be increased to accommodate them.

For example, you could define the constants TRUE and FALSE in two ways:

```
#define TRUE        1==1
#define FALSE       !TRUE
/* --OR-- */
unsigned short int TRUE = 1;
unsigned short int FALSE = 0;
```

If you defined the constants by declaring variables, as I did in the second case, then you would end up making the executable's memory image at least 32 bits larger. If your application uses a couple hundred constants, then you can save memory by switching to macros.

The #define directive can be used to create a pseudo language. For example, using #define you can replace normal C code with your own homespun syntax:

```
#include<stdio.h>
#define LOOP(n) for(i=0;i<n;i++){
#define NEXT    }
```

---

6.   http://www.ioccc.org/

```
void main(int argc, char *argv[])
{
    int i;
    LOOP(4)
    scanf("%d",&i);printf("%d",i);
    NEXT
}
```

Someone perusing this sort of source code might think that they have accidentally stumbled onto a legacy BASIC or Fortran program (hint, hint).

The #define directive can also be used to alias variables. The confusion that results, when you expect to see one thing, and see another, can be augmented when items are assigned an alias multiple times. For example, the following structures can be used to represent compound conditions:

```
/*alias.c ------------------------------------------------------*/
enum LogicalOperator{AND,OR,XOR,NOT,NULL_OP};
enum RelationalOperator{LESS,GREATER,EQUAL};
struct Field
{
    char *fieldName;    //stores the name of a field
};

//forms a single condition element (i.e. (A>B) )
struct ConditionElement
{
    enum RelationalOperator op;
    struct Field leftField;
    struct Field rightField;
};

#define MAX_CONDITIONS  8
//a series of condition elements (i.e. (A>B)OR(B<C) )
struct Condition
{
    int nElements;
    int opArray[MAX_CONDITIONS-1];
    struct ConditionElement elementArray[MAX_CONDITIONS];
};
```

The following function appends a condition element onto the end of a condition:

```
void addConditionElement
(
    struct Condition *condition,
    struct ConditionElement *leftElement,
```

```
    enum LogicalOperator op,
    struct ConditionElement *rightElement
)
{
    int currentIndex;
    currentIndex = (*condition).nElements;

    if(currentIndex>=MAX_CONDITIONS-1){ return; }

     (*condition).elementArray[currentIndex]=*leftElement;
     (*condition).opArray[currentIndex]=op;
     (*condition).elementArray[currentIndex+1]=*rightElement;

    if(op==NULL_OP){ (*condition).nElements++; }
    else{ (*condition).nElements+=2; }
}
```

You can use macros to redraft this function into something that is harder to read:

```
#define CND          struct Condition
#define CNDELM       struct ConditionElement
#define OP           enum LogicalOperator
#define cnd          *condition
#define cnd_EA       (cnd).elementArray
#define cnd_OA       (cnd).opArray
#define cnd_SZ       (cnd).nElements

void addConditionElement2
(
    CND cnd,
    CNDELM *leftElement,
    OP op,
    CNDELM *rightElement
)
{

    int currentIndex;
    currentIndex = cnd_SZ;
    if(currentIndex>=MAX_CONDITIONS-1){ return; }
    cnd_EA[currentIndex]=*leftElement;
    cnd_OA[currentIndex]=op;
    cnd_EA[currentIndex+1]=*rightElement;
    if(op==NULL_OP){ cnd_SZ++; }
    else{ cnd_SZ+=2; }
}
```

Note how the macros replace the otherwise obvious expressions with a terse shorthand notation. If you didn't have the header files containing the macro definitions in front of you, you probably wouldn't recognize what you were looking at. In fact, you can imagine what would happen if the macros were buried somewhere in a little-used header file. You might quickly glance at the code and mistakenly think that it has nothing to do with the Condition structure.

The #ifdef directive and related conditional directives are often used to help port C to different platforms. At compile time, a specific macro can be defined on the compiler's command line such that a certain snippet of code is included in the final program.

For example, the following code defines the size of an integer, in bytes, on different platforms:

```
#ifdef   INTEL_8088
    #define INT_SIZE    2
#endif
#ifdef   IBM_RS6000
    #define INT_SIZE    8
#endif
```

These directives, however, can be abused just like all the others. One truly odious tactic involves making the inserted source code different each time that a header file is included. The following header file varies the value that the macro VALUE assumes each time that the header file is included. If the header file is processed only once, VALUE will correspond to the integer value 1. If the header is processed three times, VALUE will correspond to the value 3. The impact of this type of code can be devious.

```
#ifdef PASS
    #undef     VALUE
    #define    VALUE    2
    #undef     PASS
    #define    PASS2
#elif defined PASS2
    #undef     VALUE
    #define    VALUE    3
    #undef     PASS2
#else
    #undef     VALUE
    #define    VALUE    1
    #define    PASS
#endif
```

Nesting

Heavily nesting blocks of code is another way to undermine the readability of a program. The switch statement is particularly vulnerable to excessive nesting.

> **NOTE** *The* switch *statement's original intent was to sidestep the overhead of the* if-else *loop by sticking to integer comparison. If you take a look at an assembly code listing, you'll see that* switch *is* usually *more efficient than* if-else *statements.*

On January 15, 1990, an error in a switch statement, written in C, brought down AT&T's long distance system.[7] During the nine-hour crash, millions of calls were unable to get through. The problem originated in the System 7 software that ran AT&T's 4ESS call switching hardware. This software contained a switch statement that executed an unintended break.

Take the following source code as an example:

```
void switchExample()
{
    switch(1)
    {
        case 1:
        {
            if(TRUE)
            {
                if(TRUE)
                {
                    break;
                }
                printf("expected break to activate this code\n");
            }
        }
        break;
    }
    printf("break skipped intended code\n");
}
```

When this code is executed, the following output will be printed to the screen:

```
break skipped the intended code
```

Look at the first clause in the case statement: it contains an if block with a break statement. The intent of the programmer was to use the break statement to escape out of the innermost if loop. However, according to the ANSI

---

7.   Bruce Sterling, *The Hacker Crackdown* (Bantam Books, 1993. ISBN: 0-553-56370-X)

guidelines for C, the break statement terminates the immediately enclosing while, do, for, or switch statement. The ANSI standard says nothing about impacting an if-else statement.

Merged Statements

Back in the late 1950s, Ken Iverson invented a mathematical notation that evolved into a language called APL (A Programming Language). It gained enough of a following that in 1966 APL was implemented on IBM's System 360 mainframe. APL is infamous for its ability to create undecipherable programs that fit on a single line.

For instance, the following APL program takes a list of strings, stored in a vector X, and sorts them according to length:

```
X[X+.¬' ';]
```

This is one reason why APL has been called a "write-only" language (you can write it, just don't try to read it). The same general effect can be duplicated in C by merging separate statements into a single line. To this end, the op= class of operators and the ternary selection operator are very handy.

```
var <<=(var>mask^mask)?var/(&var)[mask/(mask+1)]:var&&mask;
```

Obscure Language Features

Some programmers feel the need to demonstrate that they have mastered every aspect of a language by using as many of syntactic eccentricities as possible. Some of the more esoteric features may be unnecessary, annoying, or just plain obsolete.

The following example demonstrates some of C's advanced, obsolete, and unusual constructs:

- A function pointer

- A function with a variable number of arguments

- A long jump

- Use of the ternary operator on the left-hand side

- The offsetof() macro

- The auto keyword

131

```
/* UseEveryFeature.c --------------------------------------------*/
#include <stdio.h>
#include <stdarg.h>
#include <stddef.h>
#include <setjmp.h>
typedef struct ElementStruct
{
    long field1;
    long field2;
    long field3;
}Element;
#define FIELD1  offsetof(Element,field1)
#define FIELD2  offsetof(Element,field2)
#define FIELD3  offsetof(Element,field3)
jmp_buf environment;
void printElements(Element *ptr,...)
{
    va_list marker;

    va_start(marker,ptr);

    while(ptr!=NULL)
    {
        printf("%ld\n",*((long*)((char*)ptr + FIELD1)));
        printf("%ld\n",*((long*)((char*)ptr + FIELD2)));
        printf("%ld\n",*((long*)((char*)ptr + FIELD3)));
        ptr = va_arg(marker,Element*);
    }

    va_end(marker);

    longjmp(environment,1);
    printf("should skip this\n");
    return;
}/*end printElements----------------------------------------------*/
void main()
{
    auto Element element;
    auto returnVal;
    void (*fp)(Element *ptr,...);

    element.field1=11;
    element.field2=22;
    element.field3=33;
    fp = printElements;

    (*((1==1)?&element:NULL)).field1 = 13;
```

```
    if(returnVal = setjmp(environment))
    {
        printf("returned from long jump\n");
        goto destination;
    }

    (*fp)(&element,NULL);
    destination:
    return;
}/*end main--------------------------------------------------------*/
```

When this somewhat odd program is run, the following output is produced:

```
13
22
33
returned from long jump
```

In the previous code, the printElements() function prints out the field values of a NULL-terminated list of Element variables. The printElements() routine is invoked via a function pointer. Once inside printElements(), the offsetof() macro is used to access the individual fields of each Element variable. A long jump then sends program control to the end of main(), and the program exits normally. Note the use of the auto keyword is unnecessary but legal (local variables are auto by default).

In general, well-written code should be easy for the average engineer to follow. Forcing the reader to sit with a copy of the ANSI standard[8] in their lap is not an indicator of superior code; it's a sign that someone, with a lot of time on their hands, is showing off. For Pete's sake, stop it!

Bad Identifiers

Descriptive variable names are a necessity for maintaining code. The readability of a program depends very heavily on the accuracy of its naming scheme. Most compilers support identifiers in excess of 128 characters. Microsoft's Visual Studio C compiler, by default, supports identifiers up to 247 characters in size (although this can be configured to be larger or smaller). The bad news is that the compiler will accept any identifier that obeys the minimal ANSI requirements. This means that there is nothing to stop some nimrod from naming a variable after his ex-girlfriend or pet dog.

---

8. American National Standards Institute (ANSI) C Standard, Document Number ISO/IEC 9899:1999

```
int SuzyQ;
char *snoopy;
```

One way to drive a maintenance programmer insane is to use similarly spelled identifiers that differ by only one character:

```
for(x_l1=0;x_1l<x_ll;x_11++)
{
    x_1l = x_11+x_ll;
    x_l1++;
}
```

The previous snippet of code relies on the fact that lowercase *L* and the digit *1* look very similar. Mixing and matching the digit *0* and uppercase *O* can create similar confusion.

Some software texts recommend, for the sake of brevity, to use abbreviated or truncated variable names. In my opinion, although this does cut down on line size, I think that this approach can lead to problems:

```
void PrcBInNdNbr(Nd *nd);
```

In case you were wondering, this prototype declares a routine that Processes Binary Instruction Node Numbers. It took me a few days to figure this out. Don't even ask me what `RmLtDBOdEtr` means.

> **NOTE** *In the old days, back when 16 kilobytes was a lot of memory, some of the compilers placed length restrictions on variable names to save space and boost performance. This may explain strange naming schemes in legacy code.*

Power Tools

The easiest way to obfuscate code is to use a tool. An obfuscator is a member of the compiler species. However, instead of generating low-level machine code as an output, it generates a less-readable version of the same high-level source code that was supplied as input.

Let's take the following simple program:

```
#include<stdio.h>
void sortList(int *array,int size)
{
    int temp;
    int i;
```

```
    int j;
    for(i=1;i<size;i++)
    {
        for(j=i;(j>0)&&(array[j]<array[j-1]);j--)
        {
            temp = array[j];
            array[j]=array[j-1];
            array[j-1]=temp;
        }
    }
}
void printList(int *array,int size)
{
    int i;
    for(i=0;i<size;i++)
    {
        printf("[%d]=%d\n",i,array[i]);
    }
}
void main()
{
    int array[]={2,7,3,8,1,9,4,6,5};
    sortList(array,9);
    printList(array,9);
}
```

I ran this program through CFog,[9] a shareware obfuscator:

```
C:\>fog source.c > output.c
```

This command will generate a file named output.c that contains the obfuscated version:

```
#include<stdio.h>
 void  i_d6 ( int  *  i_d7 , int  i_d8 ){ int  i_d9 ;
 int  i_d10 ;
 int  i_d11 ;
 for ( i_d10  = 1;
 i_d10  <  i_d8 ;
 i_d10  ++ ){ for ( i_d11  =  i_d10 ;
( i_d11  > 0) && ( i_d7 [ i_d11 ] <  i_d7 [ i_d11  - 1]);
 i_d11  -- ){ i_d9  =  i_d7 [ i_d11 ];
 i_d7 [ i_d11 ] =  i_d7 [ i_d11  - 1];
 i_d7 [ i_d11  - 1] =  i_d9 ;
}}} void  i_d12 ( int  *  i_d7 , int  i_d8 ){ int  i_d10 ;
```

---

9. http://www.bookcase.com/library/software/msdos.devel.lang.c.html

```
for ( i_d10  = 0;
i_d10  <  i_d8 ;
i_d10  ++ ){ printf ("\133\45\144\135\75\45\144\n"
, i_d10 , i_d7 [ i_d10 ]);
}} void  main (){ int  i_d7 [] = {2,7,3,8,1,9,4,6,5};
i_d6 ( i_d7 ,9);
i_d12 ( i_d7 ,9);
}
```

Obfuscators for C are fairly rare these days, seeing how easy it is to compile without including debug symbols. Java, on the other hand, is a much more active area of research because Java class files contain mandatory symbolic information. The nature of Java class files has resulted in a number of high-quality obfuscation tools. One of my favorites is an open source product named RetroGuard.[10]

3.2.3 Misleading Code

Misleading code is subtler than blatant obfuscation. This is because it looks readable. In this sense, it is more dangerous because it gives you a false sense of security. You may *think* you understand the code. However, when push comes to shove and a bug appears, your superficial understanding will disintegrate as you realize that you don't really know what's going on.

More Bad Identifiers

One way to confuse a maintenance engineer is to use nothing but abstract names. Some less-scrupulous engineers justify this tactic by claiming that it keeps things flexible and facilitates modification later on. In certain situations, this excuse has merit. In other situations, the names are so nebulous that they could mean anything. For example, examine the following routine prototype:

```
DataElement *process(DataElement *dataElement);
```

The previous prototype creates more questions than it answers. The identifiers don't really tell you anything. For instance, what is a DataElement? It implies that perhaps it is one member (i.e., an element) of a group of data items; but that's all. What is the data used for? How does it fit into the domain model? What exactly does process() do to the data? Does it modify the argument somehow?

---

10. http://www.retrologic.com

Another way to toy with a maintenance engineer is to use names that are synonymous. Consider the following set of prototypes:

```
void run(char *command);
void perform(char *command);
void system(char *command);
void execute(char *command);
void invoke(char *command);
```

From the perspective of a person looking at this code for the first time, these functions all appear to do the same thing. They all seem to run a native command. Imagine how confusing it would be if all of these functions took actions that were dramatically different.

Side Effects

This technique is one of the most sinister of them all. If you want to prevent someone from using the divide-and-conquer approach to understanding your program, make sure that all you routines have side effects that are not implied by the name, or type signature. In practice, side effects usually occur when a routine manipulates a global variable.

For example, the following code appears to check a list of arguments to see if they are sane. However, it also sorts them, invokes the garbage collector, and toggles a global variable.

```
int checkArguments(int *array, int size)
{
    int temp;
    int i;
    int j;
    if(size<0)
    {
        return(SIZE_ERROR);
    }
    for(i=0;i<size;i++)
    {
        if(isOutOfRange(array[i]))
        {
            badArgument(array[i]);
            return(RANGE_ERROR);
        }
    }
    for(i=1;i<size;i++)
    {
        for(j=i;(j>0)&&(array[j]<array[j-1]);j--)
        {
```

```
        temp = array[j];
        array[j]=array[j-1];
        array[j-1]=temp;
    }
}
collectFreeMemory(*environment);
programState = DATA_STATE;
}
```

Side effects work in opposition to cohesion. Remember, a strongly cohesive function is focused on doing one thing. When a function has side effects, it does many things (some of which may be completely unrelated).

3.3 Reverse Engineering

Never attribute to malice that which can be adequately explained by stupidity.

—Hanlon's Razor

In section 3.2, I presented a collection of bad habits that can transform a program into a big ball of mud. Surprisingly, this phenomenon is typically a product of history rather than malice. More code gets haphazardly slapped on top of more code until almost no one understands much of anything. In this section, I am going to offer you a collection of strategies and tactics that you can use to deal with this type of source code. If you are determined, and you judiciously use the tools that I provide, you will be able to (eventually) decipher even highly obfuscated code.

3.3.1 General Strategies

Later in the chapter, I will offer specific techniques that you can use to reverse engineer software. Before you can use these techniques, however, you must have an underlying game plan to direct their use. That is what this section is about.

Top Down vs. Bottom Up

There are two ways to tackle a large program. You can either start at the high-level interfaces (and work your way down), or you can search out the low-level routines and follow them up to the top. The common goal of both of these techniques is to come up with an *invocation tree* (see Figure 3-1).

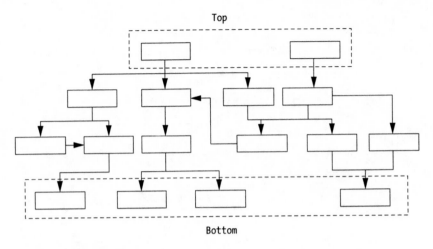

Figure 3-1. Invocation tree

I prefer to work from the bottom up, which is to say that I begin by isolating all the functions that do not invoke any functions (other than standard library calls). This gives me a set of atomic building blocks. Next, I isolate the layer of functions that invoke these atomic functions. This process continues until all the layers are delineated.

> **NOTE** *If you can get your hands on the requisite cash, I would suggest using a UML modeling tool like Rational Rose. This will allow you to generate a graphical synopsis of your code base that most engineers can easily interpret. Be warned, products like Rational Rose are not cheap. If you do not have several thousand dollars on hand, you may have to stick to the least-common-denominator solution and use an invocation tree.*

If your application is a morass of spaghetti code, it may not resolve to a neatly layered tree, like the one in Figure 3-1. Furthermore, you may not be able to isolate atomic routines. Every routine may end up calling at least one other routine in the system (see Figure 3-2), which has been known to happen in legacy COBOL programs. This doesn't mean that the invocation tree doesn't have merit; it just means that creating the tree will be more frustrating because it will be more difficult to trace.

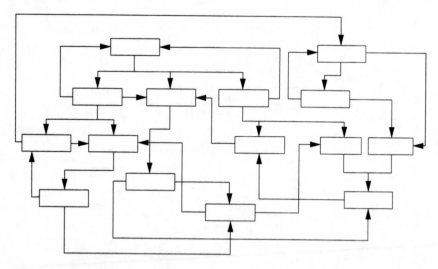

Figure 3-2. Spaghetti code invocation tree

Search Out Atomic Types

Regardless of how abstract a program is, everything inevitably boils down to atomic data types (memory addresses, integers, characters, and floating-point values). If you think about it, object instances are just the blobs of memory that store field values. These fields can, if you're persistent enough, be resolved to atomic data types.

For example, take the following class declarations:

```
class Address
{
    private:
    char *street;
    char *state;
    char *zip;

    public:
    Address(char* street, char *state, char *zip);
    char *getStreet();
    char *getState();
    char *getZip();
};
class Employee
```

```
{
    private:
    Address *address;
    char *name;
    int age;

    public:
    Employee(Address* address, char *name, int age);
    char *getName();
    int getAge();
};
```

If the following snippet of code were to be executed on an Intel Pentium:

```
Employee employee(&address,"Jim Hill",43);
printf("%d\n",sizeof(employee));
```

the output shown here would be streamed to the screen:

```
12
```

An instance of the Employee class will be realized as a 12-byte blob of memory (see Table 3-1). The Employee class has three member variables and three member functions. All instances of the Employee class share the same three member functions, which exist at a fixed location in the program's code segment. The size of the member functions doesn't count towards the size of the instance because it's the same for each instance. Only the member fields contribute to the size of the instance because they are the only parts that will be unique to each instance. In essence, an object in memory is nothing more than a fancy type of a structure variable.

Table 3-1. Employee *Object Constituents*

Field	Data Type	Size (80586)
address	Pointer	4
name	Pointer	4
age	Integer	4

The moral of the story is this: even high-level constructs like objects resolve to clumps of data. If you can't seem to understand what's going on in a program, sometimes it's a good idea to track down a set of atomic values and follow them as the program executes. This will give you the ability to see what the program is doing at the most fundamental level.

Start with the Database Tables

A program that consists of 50,000 lines of code may only use three or four database tables. If this is the case, then one way to reverse engineer the program is to start with the database tables. This will provide you with insight because most applications that use a database are tightly coupled, architecturally, to the storage schema that they use. By understanding the tables, you have an implicit understanding of the program that uses them.

For example, I once worked with a legacy CASE tool that generated business logic conditions. The tool was a winding maze of undecipherable K&R C. However, I knew that the tool only used a small set of four database tables (see Table 3-2).

Table 3-2. CASE Tool Tables

Table	Use
Cnd	Represents a condition; this is the top of the hierarchy.
CndElm	Breaks conditions down into condition elements and logical operators.
CndExp	Represents a condition expression, which consists of two fields and a relational operator.
Fld	Stores information about a specific field.

Rather than diving headfirst into the code, I started by decomposing the four tables (see Tables 3-3, 3-4, 3-5, and 3-6). Figuring out what each field, in each table, represented took a lot of digging. I spent several days making phone calls, tracking down contributing engineers, and fiddling with the CASE tool itself.

Table 3-3. The Condition Table (Cnd)

Column	Meaning	Example
id	The integer identifier of the condition	7
name	The ASCII name of the condition	"AC-200-CND1"
elm	The integer identifier of the first element	24

Table 3-4. The Condition Element Table (CndElm)

Column	Meaning	Example
id	The integer identifier of the element	24
expr1	The integer identifier of the left-hand expression	11
op	The logical operator	0
expr2	The integer identifier of the right-hand expression	13
next	The integer identifier of the next element	-1

Table 3-5. The Condition Expression Table (CndExp)

Column	Meaning	Example
id	The integer identifier of the expression	11
field1	The integer identifier of the left-hand field	32
op	The relational operator	2
field2	The integer identifier of the right-hand field	33

Table 3-6. The Field Table (Fld)

Column	Meaning	Example
id	The integer identifier of the field	32
name	The ASCII name of the field	"fieldA"
tbl	The integer identifier of the table owning the field	114

In this case, I started out knowing only the table names and the column names. I uncovered everything else through detective work. For example, to better understand what got placed in the tables, I played around with the tool and recorded what got inserted when I created a new condition. As I forged ahead, I discovered that the integers used to represent operators corresponded to macro definitions in the source code:

```
#define AND    0   //logical AND
#define OR     1   //logical OR
#define GT     2   //relational ">"
#define GTE    3   //relational ">="
#define EQ     4   //relational "=="
```

Rather than use strings to identify things in the database, the original author had decided to use numeric values for speed. For example, if you dumped the CndElm table's contents (I used an in-house tool named dbdump) you would get something like this:

```
$ dbdump -database dictionaryDB  -table CndElm

Table CndElm[id,expr1,op,expr2,next]
24    11    0    13    -1
25    3     1    15    26
26    11    1    15    27
27    8     0    12    -1
33    43    1    15    34
34    7     0    9     -1
6 records in file
```

Performing this sort of detective work actually told me a lot about how conditions were formed and manipulated. For example, assume you have the following condition:

```
(fieldA > fieldB) AND (fieldB==fieldC)
```

This condition consists of a single condition element. Because of this, the next field in the CndElm table for this element would have a value of –1. The condition element's two expressions are concatenated by a logical AND operator. If a condition element consists of only a single expression, the logical operator and second expression field would both be –1 in the CndElm table.

By understanding how expressions were concatenated to form conditions, and how they were persisted, I could bootstrap an initial traversal of the tool's source code. Furthermore, I discovered that the naming scheme in the source code was very similar to the naming scheme used in the database. So once I had decrypted the database tables, I automatically knew what many of the program's variables represented. Success breeds success.

Time Investment

Climbing a learning curve takes time. It's like getting physically fit; there are no miracle pills or secret diets. If you try to implement a fix before you have climbed the curve, you are more likely to introduce more bugs than you resolve. *People who think otherwise are either trying to sell you snake oil or are hopelessly naive.*

The problem is that people don't want to face the reality of the learning curve. It does not sound sweet to the ears. Most managers don't want to hear about how much time it's going to take to really understand a program. They want to hear, "Yes sir, tomorrow." This reminds me of people who want to lose weight by trying the Hollywood 48-Hour Miracle Diet. The worst lies are the ones that we tell ourselves (which is why salespeople always try to make us think that it's our idea).

If your supervisor is pushing you into the deep end too fast, send your supervisor an e-mail voicing your concern and make sure to save a hard copy of the e-mail (remember what I said about creating a paper trail). This way, if your quick-and-dirty fix crashes the system, you will be able to defend yourself. If placed in the spotlight, your boss may decide to redirect the blame to you in order to save their own skin: "Oh, it's that new guy. I had a feeling he wasn't going to work out."[11]

A program that has been well designed and cleanly implemented will have only a moderately steep learning curve. You will probably be able to climb the curve, isolate the offending snippet of code, and make a clean getaway without losing any sleep. If a program is a legacy monster that has been hacked to death over the years by a random stream of engineers, then you had better bring a sleeping bag with you into work. In extreme cases, you might want to break out your resume. Managers have been known to give Sisyphean tasks to people whom they don't like[12] (with the intention that the person will get fed up and leave).

Rewriting

There may be rare instances in which the source code of an application has become so brittle, old, and intertwined with outmoded hardware that the cost associated with maintaining the application is greater than the cost of rewriting. Why spend eight months reverse engineering a 12-year-old legacy application when it would take you four months to implement a more stable version from scratch?

Consider the Chicago Stock Exchange. During the 1980s, the exchange ran its Midwest Automated Execution (MAX) operations using a trading system that was based on Digital Equipment Corporation's VMS Operating System. This system was mired in a centralized architecture that used a proprietary VMS network protocol to talk to clients. The source base that implemented MAX services consisted of tens of thousands of lines of clunky

---

11. Scott Adams, *Dilbert and the Way of the Weasel* (HarperBusiness, 2002. ISBN: 0-060-51805-7)

12. In the software industry, this is known as a *Corrective Action Procedure*.

structured code, which was irrevocably tied to VMS. For all intents and purposes, VMS died when Compaq bought DEC back in 1998. The IT people at the exchange knew they would have to construct a new system from scratch, or face the dangers associated with becoming outdated. In 1997, a complete rewrite is what Steve Randich, the CIO at the time, managed to pull off. The acting team of engineers replaced the old system with an ORB-based engine that used C++ objects to execute business rules. In addition, they implemented a distributed architecture that used an object database.

> **NOTE** *Because the Chicago Stock Exchange chose to go with Windows NT 4.0 as the deployment platform, Microsoft used this as a marketing opportunity. Microsoft even launched a Web site named* howstevedidit.com. *I find it interesting that they failed to mention that the Chicago Stock Exchange decided against using DCOM, SQL Server, and MTS (which were in fashion at the time). Microsoft also failed to mention that the Chicago Stock Exchange reboots their NT machines every day. There have been mainframes that have had uptimes on the order of years . . .*

Rewriting is not an option that old-timers will take lightly. You should expect significant resistance. Such is the nature of humans when they form groups. I think that Nicolo Machiavelli put it best, in his book *The Prince*:

> *And it ought to be remembered that there is nothing more difficult to take in hand, more perilous to conduct, or more uncertain in its success, than to take the lead in the introduction of a new order of things. Because the innovator has for enemies all those who have done well under the old conditions, and lukewarm defenders in those who may do well under the new. This coolness arises partly from fear of the opponents, who have the laws on their side, and partly from the incredulity of men, who do not readily believe in new things until they have had a long experience of them.*

3.3.2 Countermeasures

In the previous section, I outlined a few basic strategies that can be used to help understand what's going on in a legacy application. In this section, I will examine the tactics that can be used to implement those strategies.

Verify Behavior with a Debugger

As we saw earlier in the chapter, misleading identifiers and routines with side effects can make it damn near impossible to believe anything that you see. If you decide to take a program at face value, you may end up falling into a booby trap. Initially, you should not put any faith in a program's naming scheme. If you want to know what a variable is used for, or what a routine does, crank up a debugger and trace through the related execution paths. Rather than put all your faith in the previous author, place your trust in a debugger. Verify everything that you read. *Names can lie; debuggers do not.* Trust no one. The truth is out there.

Refactor

The only long-term approach to dealing with spaghetti code or cut-and-paste programming is to refactor it. You may be able to fix a bug over the short-term by simply plodding headlong through the code, but the gains you make will be temporal. Most production environments are large enough, and complicated enough, that you will have to relearn everything again the next time that you need to implement a fix. By refactoring the code, you are effectively lowering the learning curve when you revisit the code six months later.

The preventative medicine that I discussed in the first chapter of this book provides a tentative list of *proactive* techniques. Refactoring is *reactive*, and is performed postmortem. For an exhaustive treatment of refactoring, I would recommend Martin Fowler's book on the subject.[13]

Use the Profiler's Call Graph

During my discussion of the GNU Profiler (i.e., gprof), I demonstrated how the profiler generates a call graph. The profiler's call graph is really nothing more than a text-based version of the invocation tree you saw earlier. A call graph is indispensable when it comes to building an invocation tree because it saves you from having to read the code manually. For large programs, tracing through code for function calls can be tedious. Tedium for humans translates into careless errors. Rather than suffer from your own inevitable mistakes, let the profiler perform some of the work for you. This way, all you have to do is make a pass over the profiler's call graph and chart out the tree.

For example, given the following call graph:

```
index % time    self    children    called              name
                1.28    1.11        1/1                 main [2]
[1]     100.0   1.28    1.11        1                   longLoop [1]
                0.72    0.00        50000000/50000000   doMoreWork [4]
                0.39    0.00        50000000/50000000   doWork [5]
-----------------------------------------------------------
```

---

13. Martin Fowler et al., *Refactoring: Improving the Design of Existing Code* (Addison-Wesley, 1999. ISBN: 0-201-48567-2)

		0.00	2.39	1/1	__crt1_startup [3]
[2]	100.0	0.00	2.39	1	main [2]
		1.28	1.11	1/1	longLoop [1]

					<spontaneous>
[3]	100.0	0.00	2.39		__crt1_startup [3]
		0.00	2.39	1/1	main [2]

		0.72	0.00	50000000/50000000	longLoop [1]
[4]	30.2	0.72	0.00	50000000	doMoreWork [4]

		0.39	0.00	50000000/50000000	longLoop [1]
[5]	16.3	0.39	0.00	50000000	doWork [5]

The corresponding invocation tree is pretty easy to construct (see Figure 3-3).

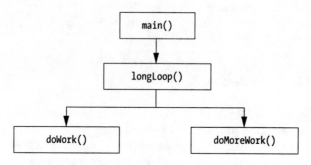

Figure 3-3. Sample invocation tree

Use a Beautifier

If you have stumbled onto code that is highly obfuscated, or which suffers from heavy nesting, you may want to consider using a beautifier. If an obfuscator is the Wicked Witch of the West, then the beautifier is the Good Witch of the North. A beautifier is a type of compiler that takes source code as an input, and generates an equivalent version that is easier to read. Most beautifiers do their job by adding blank lines, tabs, and spaces to force the code to adhere to a sane format.

Let's take a look at the source code obfuscated earlier in this chapter:

```
#include<stdio.h>
 void  i_d6 ( int  *  i_d7 , int  i_d8 ){ int  i_d9 ;
 int  i_d10 ;
 int  i_d11 ;
 for ( i_d10 = 1;
 i_d10 < i_d8 ;
 i_d10 ++ ){ for ( i_d11 = i_d10 ;
( i_d11 > 0) && ( i_d7 [ i_d11 ] < i_d7 [ i_d11 - 1]);
 i_d11 -- ){ i_d9 = i_d7 [ i_d11 ];
 i_d7 [ i_d11 ] = i_d7 [ i_d11 - 1];
 i_d7 [ i_d11 - 1] = i_d9 ;
}}} void i_d12 ( int * i_d7 , int i_d8 ){ int i_d10 ;
 for ( i_d10 = 0;
 i_d10 < i_d8 ;
 i_d10 ++ ){ printf ("\133\45\144\135\75\45\144\n"
, i_d10 , i_d7 [ i_d10 ]);
}} void  main (){ int  i_d7 [] = {2,7,3,8,1,9,4,6,5};
 i_d6 ( i_d7 ,9);
 i_d12 ( i_d7 ,9);
}
```

I will run this code through a beautifier, written by Christophe Beaudet, named GC (as in "Great Code"):

```
C:\_DOCS\code\docs\bookIdea\ch3\gc>gc -file-"src2.c"
GC GreatCode 1.138 by Christophe Beaudet
*****************************************
email: cbeaudet@club-internet.fr
url:   perso.club-internet.fr/cbeaudet
*****************************************
Type GC -help for options
Processing src2.c   (56 lines, 1417 characters)
```

I used GC to process a single file. If you want to use GC on an entire source tree, you will want to read the documentation that comes with GC. The beautified source code generated by GC looks like the following:

```
/*$T src2.c GC 1.138 04/21/03 12:44:59 */

#include <stdio.h>

void i_d6 (int *i_d7, int i_d8)
{
    int i_d9;
    int i_d10;
```

```
    int i_d11;
    for(i_d10 = 1; i_d10 < i_d8; i_d10++)
    {
        for(i_d11 = i_d10;
            (i_d11>0)&&(i_d7[i_d11]<i_d7[i_d11-1]);
             i_d11--)
        {
            i_d9 = i_d7[i_d11];
            i_d7[i_d11] = i_d7[i_d11 - 1];
            i_d7[i_d11 - 1] = i_d9;
        }
    }
}

void i_d12(int *i_d7, int i_d8)
{
    /*~~~~~~~*/
    int i_d10;
    /*~~~~~~~*/

    for(i_d10 = 0; i_d10 < i_d8; i_d10++)
    {
        printf("\133\45\144\135\75\45\144\n", i_d10, i_d7[i_d10]);
    }
}

void main(void)
{
    /*~~~~~~~~~~~~~~~~~~~~~~~~~~~~~~~~~~~~~*/
    int i_d7[] = { 2, 7, 3, 8, 1, 9, 4, 6, 5 };
    /*~~~~~~~~~~~~~~~~~~~~~~~~~~~~~~~~~~~~~*/

    i_d6(i_d7, 9);
    i_d12(i_d7, 9);
}
```

As you can see, the beautifier couldn't help us with the obscure variable names. It did, however, make the source code much easier to read. So, in a sense, using a beautifier is a good first step.

Run the Code Through a Preprocessor

The unwarranted use of preprocessor directives has been known to lead to "write-only" C code. If you are dealing with a program that has been overrun by preprocessor directives, one way to make the source code a little clearer is to run it through a preprocessor. The gcc compiler has an option that allows you to do just that.

For example, assume you are working with the following declarations:

```
struct Group
{
    char *manager;
    char *name;
};
#define MAX_GROUPS      15
#define MAX_OFFICES     10
#define MAX_DEPTS       5
struct Office
{
    char *address;
    struct Group groups[MAX_GROUPS];
};
struct Department
{
    char *name;
    struct Office offices[MAX_OFFICES];
};
struct Division
{
    char *name;
    struct Department departments[MAX_DEPTS];
};
#define DIV        division
#define DEPT       (DIV).departments[i]
#define OFFICE     (DEPT).offices[j]
#define GROUP      (OFFICE).groups[k]
#define TEAM       (GROUP).name
```

A statement like

```
TEAM = "NT Development";
```

can be misleading because it's easy to forget that you're actually dealing with a heavily nested structure. In fact, a new hire may glance at this code and then spend the next hour hopelessly looking for a TIME variable declaration.

```
char *TEAM;     //hey, where is it...damn, why did I take this job?
```

To expand out macros, and see what you are actually working with, you can use the -E option if you are compiling with gcc. The pr-processed source code will be streamed to standard output and must be piped to a file.

```
C:\>gcc -E source.c > processed.c
```

Using this feature, the previous line of source code expands out to

```
((((division).departments[i]).offices[j]).groups[k]).name ="NT Development";
```

Ah ha! Now you know what is really getting modified.

Use Class Browsers

Excessive generalization can lead to code that is like an onion. You peel off one layer, and there's a whole new layer underneath. Classes get wrapped until they are buried under a mountain of inheritance. If you feel like the original author was trying to blind you with abstraction, one way to achieve clarity is by using a GUI IDE that has class browsing facilities. Specifically, you'll need a tool that allows you to view the subclasses and parent classes of a given class. This is the quickest, and easiest, way to deal with unwieldy class hierarchies. A long-term solution to this problem would also include refactoring, as discussed earlier.

In older companies, you may come across grizzled veterans who are literally stuck in the 1970s. These Unix diehards refuse to cave in, and doggedly use the vi editor for everything. The problem with this character-based fascism is that it ignores the visual tools that can make environments like JBuilder so powerful.

For example, take a look at the 20+ classes in Figure 3-4. Imagine trying to track the relationships between these classes in your head. You would probably break out a pencil and paper and draw a diagram. If you were using a clunky old editor like vi, this is exactly what you would have to do. The problem with this approach is that you would be forced to constantly redraw the diagram in an effort to accommodate changes. With a contemporary IDE like Visual Studio, you can right-click a class and immediately see its children and parents.

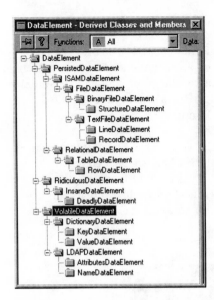

Figure 3-4. A derived class viewer

3.3.3 Creating a Knowledge Base

If you've successfully reverse engineered an application, you should make sure that you persist your newfound understanding so that the next guy can use it. Not only will this make you into something of a corporate hero, but it will also thwart all those pesky little information hoarders who made your job difficult to begin with. Remember, you cannot snag that high-paying architectural position unless you can find a person who can take over your current maintenance duties. By documenting your discoveries, you are making it easier (i.e., less expensive) for your bosses to promote you.

NOTE *To be fair, documentation is a double-edged sword. By documenting your findings, you are also making it easier for your employer to replace you. It depends, very heavily, on the corporate culture in which you work. I suppose, then, that it's up to you to take a look around you and decide upon a wise course of action. From a maintenance programmer's perspective, absent documentation is a capital offense; but from the perspective of the original author, absent documentation can translate into job security. I had an English professor who called this ethical relativism.*

Use the Least Common Denominator

The most effective way to disseminate information is via a Web server. The motivation behind this statement is one of pure economics. The Apache Web server can be downloaded for free and run on cheap commodity hardware.[14] Everyone, even your pointy-haired manager, has a Web browser installed; Microsoft has seen to that. Using the HTTP approach makes your material available to the broadest possible audience.

Once you have a server up and running, you will need to either translate your documentation to HTML or provide HTML links so that people can download your documentation (see Figure 3-5). If you opt for the latter option, it would be a good idea to stick with universal file formats, like Adobe's Portable Document Format (PDF). Adobe offers a PDF viewer that is free and has been ported to most desktop operating systems.[15]

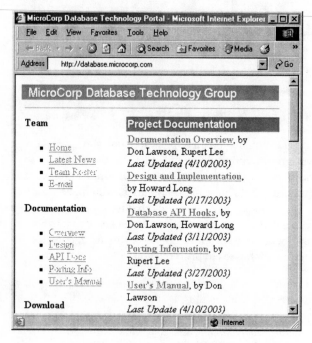

Figure 3-5. Web-enabled knowledge base

Building a Web-enabled knowledge base is easier than you might think. I've seen some development teams get them up and running in less than

---

14. http://www.apache.org

15. http://www.adobe.com/products/acrobat/

a day. In the long run, this kind of setup will pay itself off. People who want information about a project no longer have to locate team members and pester them for information. In addition, those same team members no longer have to stockpile Xeroxed copies of documentation to pass out to people. To get the most current information on a project, all someone has to do is point a Web browser at the team's Web server.

Place a Link in a Well-Known Spot

Once you have a Web-enabled knowledge base set up, the next challenge you will have will be publicizing it. In large corporate environments, it's easy for even the best sources of information to be lost. You could send e-mail to everyone, but people tend to ignore, or forget, this type of correspondence. Furthermore, most people are so busy that they don't have the extra bandwidth necessary to memorize half a dozen specific URLs.

People like to stick to simple retrieval cues. You're best bet is to make your knowledge base easy for everyone to find by placing a link to your Web server on the main corporate intranet. Every company has at least one well-known internal Web site that provides the corporate directory and human resources information. Make an announcement and then wait for the hits to begin (see Figure 3-6).

Figure 3-6. Link on a corporate intranet

3.4 Summary

The only way to reliably fix a malfunctioning program is to have a fundamental understanding of the program's requirements and how it implements those requirements. This is easier said than done, seeing as how most production programs are complicated behemoths. Simply reading through the source code does not always yield understanding.

In light of this, a number of strategies can be used to help decipher a large program:

- Create an invocation tree (use top-down or bottom-up approach)

- Search out and trace atomic data types

- Decipher the database schema, if data is persisted

- Be prepared to climb a learning curve

- If all else fails, the final option is to perform a rewrite

In applying these strategies, you will encounter obstacles. Table 3-7 provides a list of such obstacles and potential countermeasures.

Table 3-7. Countermeasure Summary

Obstacle	Countermeasure
Stonewalling	Maintain a paper trail, intellectual humility.
Attrition, the passage of time	Revision control file history, detective work.
Promotion, greener pa$ture$	Maintain a paper trail, have management make appeals.
Cut-and-paste programming	Refactor and revisit.
Spaghetti code	Use a debugger to identify dead code, refactor, and revisit.
Excessive class hierarchies	Use a class browser, refactor, and revisit.
Preprocessor abuse	Use compiler options, rewrite or delete directives.
Obfuscated code	Use a beautifier, refactor, and revisit.
Obscure, unnecessary, language features	Restate using more common language constructs.
Poorly chosen names	Verify purpose with a debugger, rename.
Routines with side effects	Decompose behavior with a debugger, refactor.

CHAPTER 4

Debugger Internals

In Chapter 2, I presented a short tutorial on using the GNU debugger. This chapter is dedicated to those curious souls who yearn to look under the hood and see how debuggers actually work. I will begin by discussing the different types of debuggers and then showing you how they perform basic debugging tasks (e.g., breakpoints and single stepping). Later on in the chapter, we will look more closely at symbolic debuggers and I will offer suggestions with regard to how they can be implemented. For those engineers interested in protecting intellectual property, I will end the chapter with a collection of techniques that can be used to thwart reverse-engineering tools.

157

4.1 Types of Debuggers

A debugger is a tool that allows you to examine the state of a running program from a neutral frame of reference. In other words, you can observe a process without having to worry about unintentionally influencing its execution path. You are not a part of the experiment; you can watch things objectively as they occur. As far as most scientific disciplines go, computer scientists have a unique and enviable advantage.

4.1.1 Machine Debuggers vs. Symbolic Debuggers

Recall how I defined a debugger in Chapter 2: it's a tool that allows the execution path of a process to be temporarily suspended such that the state of the process may be inspected and modified.

This definition is just a little ambiguous. The truth is you can view a machine's state from a couple of different levels. Specifically, you can view the state of a process at the machine level or at the abstract level of the program's source code. As a result, there are two basic types of debuggers: one gives you a view from ground zero and the other gives you a view from 10,000 feet.

Machine Debuggers

A *machine-level debugger* views a program in terms of very low-level hardware constructs. A machine debugger does not know anything about a program's variables or routines. It sees a program as a sequence of raw binary instructions and memory segments; the level of granularity is as discrete as it can get. From the perspective of a machine-level debugger, an executing program's state is defined by

- The contents of the processor's registers

- The values of the bytes in memory that the program occupies

The debug program that originally shipped with Microsoft's 16-bit DOS operating system in the 1980s is an excellent example of a machine-level debugger. On more recent versions of Windows, the debug command runs on top of a virtual DOS machine (VDM), which is basically a Windows program that acts like a DOS machine. The commands available to debug can be displayed by entering the help command at the debug prompt (?).

```
C:\>debug
-?
assemble      A [address]
compare       C range address
dump          D [range]
enter         E address [list]
fill          F range list
go            G [=address] [addresses]
hex           H value1 value2
input         I port
load          L [address] [drive] [firstsector] [number]
move          M range address
name          N [pathname] [arglist]
output        O port byte
proceed       P [=address] [number]
quit          Q
register      R [register]
search        S range list
trace         T [=address] [value]
unassemble    U [range]
write         W [address] [drive] [firstsector] [number]
```

NOTE   *The* debug *utility still ships with Windows, although now it runs inside of a virtual DOS machine (VDM), which is a 32-bit Win32 program that is used to simulate the 16-bit 8088 environment for legacy applications. You can still compile and run 16-bit DOS programs on Windows; you just have to be aware that what you're dealing with is a simulated 16-bit runtime.*

As you can see from the list of commands, debug is limited to working with bare-bones hardware information. For example, take the following simple program:

```
/* simple.c ----------------------------*/
int i;
int j;
void main()
{
    for(i=0;i<10;i++)
    {
        j=i;
    }
    return;
}
```

If this program is compiled using the "tiny" 16-bit memory model (i.e., everything fits in one 64-kilobyte memory segment), the following assembly language equivalent will be generated:

```
;-segment begins--------------------------
CSEG SEGMENT BYTE USE16 PUBLIC 'CODE'
ASSUME CS:CSEG, DS:CSEG, SS:CSEG
ORG 100H
here:
JMP _main
PUBLIC _main
_main:
        mov     word ptr CSEG:_i,0
        jmp     short @5
@4:     mov     ax,word ptr CSEG:_i
        mov     word ptr CSEG:_j,ax
@3:     inc     word ptr CSEG:_i
@5:     cmp     word ptr CSEG:_i,10
        jl      @4
@2:     jmp     short @1
@1:     RET
PUBLIC _i
_i DW 1 DUP(?)
PUBLIC _j
_j DW 1 DUP(?)
;-segment ends----------------------------
CSEG ENDS
END here
```

This assembler program can be built with Microsoft's MASM assembler and link tools:

```
C:\>ML /Zm -c simple.asm
C:\>LINK /TINY simple.obj
```

The .COM file, simple.com, generated by the linker can be loaded by debug for analysis. It is only 34 bytes in size. The debugger will copy the executable into memory and await further instruction.

```
C:\>debug simple.com
-
```

The unassemble command (u) can be used to display an assembly code version of simple.com.

```
-u
1488:0100 EB00         JMP      0102
1488:0102 C7061E010000 MOV      WORD PTR [011E],0000
1488:0108 EB0A         JMP      0114
1488:010A A11E01       MOV      AX,[011E]
1488:010D A32001       MOV      [0120],AX
1488:0110 FF061E01     INC      WORD PTR [011E]
1488:0114 833E1E010A   CMP      WORD PTR [011E],+0A
1488:0119 7CEF         JL       010A
1488:011B EB00         JMP      011D
1488:011D C3           RET
1488:011E 0000         ADD      [BX+SI],AL
```

This looks very similar to the previous assembly code listing. The difference is that labels have been replaced by integer addresses.

The registers command (r) displays the contents of the processor's registers and the next machine instruction in line to be executed.

```
-r
AX=0000  BX=0000  CX=0022  DX=0000  SP=FFFE  BP=0000  SI=0000  DI=0000
DS=1488  ES=1488  SS=1488  CS=1488  IP=0100   NV UP EI PL NZ NA PO NC
1488:0100 EB00         JMP      0102
```

Notice how the instruction pointer (IP) has the value 0x100. This is the offset address of the first instruction of the program's segment (there is only a single segment; the segment registers DS, ES, SS, and CS all contain the same value).

If you want to look at a particular region of memory, you can use the debug dump command (d).

```
-d 1488:0100
1488:0100  EB 00 C7 06 1E 01 00 00-EB 0A A1 1E 01 A3 20 01   .............. .
1488:0110  FF 06 1E 01 83 3E 1E 01-0A 7C EF EB 00 C3 00 00   .....>...|......
1488:0120  00 00 00 00 00 00 00 00-00 00 00 00 00 00 00 00   ................
```

```
1488:0130  00 00 00 00 00 00 00 00-00 00 00 00 00 00 00 00    ................
1488:0140  00 00 00 00 00 00 00 00-00 00 00 00 00 00 00 00    ................
1488:0150  00 00 00 00 00 00 00 00-00 00 00 00 00 00 00 00    ................
1488:0160  00 00 00 00 00 00 00 00-00 00 00 00 00 00 00 00    ................
1488:0170  00 00 00 00 00 00 00 00-00 00 00 00 00 00 00 00    ................
```

The previous command displays 128 bytes of memory starting at address 1488:0100, where 0x1488 is the address of the program's segment and 0x0100 is the offset into that segment.

As I mentioned earlier, in the eyes of a machine-level debugger, the registers and the contents of memory specify machine state. A machine-level debugger knows nothing about routines or specific variables. All its sees is a raw sequence of binary values. This is why most engineers prefer not to use a machine debugger unless they're really desperate. The granularity of machine instructions is so fine that it's easy to get lost among the trees and lose sight of the forest. It may be fun the first couple of times, but after a while using a machine-level debugger can get very tedious.

Symbolic Debuggers

A *symbolic debugger* (also known as a *source-level debugger*) views a program at the source code level, such that individual routines and variables can be examined at runtime. To a symbolic debugger, the state of a program is defined by its variables. Given that source code is much easier to read than machine code, most software engineers opt for a symbolic debugger if they have the chance.

The magic that facilitates source-level debugging is a program's *debug symbol table*. A program's symbol table is basically a small, self-contained database that consists of a collection of variable-length records. These records are generated and persisted by the compiler when it translates the program's source code into object code (see Figure 4-1). The records in each object code file get merged together into the final executable by the linker.

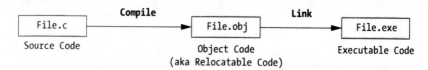

Figure 4-1. The standard build cycle

Depending on the format of the object code, debug symbol table records are typically placed in one of two locations:

- In the body of the object code itself

- In a separate file

For example, Microsoft's current proprietary solution is to place a program's debug information in a separate file. This special file is named with the .PDB extension (which stands for Program Database). The PDB debug format was introduced with Visual C++ 2.0. The motivation behind the PDB approach was to save the linker from performing extraneous disk I/O by placing everything in one spot.

Years ago, Microsoft's tools used to be able to place debug information directly into the object code, using a format known as CodeView (or STI). Up until Visual C++ 4.1, the linker and another Visual Studio tool named CVPACK could consolidate CodeView debug information and append it to the end of the executable. Naturally, executables with CodeView debug information could get pretty large and consume a lot of memory.

NOTE *The fine details of the PDB and STI debug record formats are complicated enough to fill up an entire book. If you have the urge to find out more, I would recommend visiting Microsoft's MSDN site.[1] My goal is to give you the general idea so that your understanding is flexible enough to accommodate different implementations.*

Debug symbol information maps functions and variables to locations in memory. This is what gives a symbolic debugger the fundamental advantage over a machine debugger. For instance, the source code-to-memory mapping allows a symbolic debugger to display the value of a variable, because the variable's identifier is matched to a specific location in the program's data segment (or stack, or heap). Not only that, but there will also be data-type information in the symbol table that will tell the debugger what type of data is being manipulated so that its value can be properly displayed (see Figure 4-2).

---

1.   http://msdn.microsoft.com

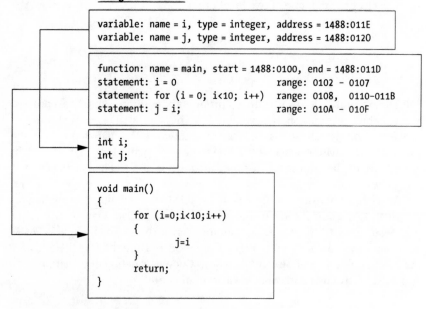

Figure 4-2. Debug information

This mapping also matches source code statements to ranges of bytes in memory. When you step into a source code statement, the symbolic debugger will look up the address range of the given statement in the program's debug records. Then it will simply execute the machine instructions in that range.

If you compile the previous C program using GNU's gcc compiler on a Pentium, you will get a 32-bit executable that you can debug with gdb. Unlike the DOS debug machine-level debugger, a symbolic debugger like gdb can be used to observe execution at the source-code level of granularity:

```
C:\>gdb simple.exe
(gdb) break simple.c:7
Breakpoint 1 at 0x16f5: file simple.c, line 7.
(gdb) run
Starting program: c:/simple.exe

Breakpoint 1, main () at simple.c:7
7                       j=i;
(gdb) s
5               for(i=0;i<10;i++)
(gdb) s

Breakpoint 1, main () at simple.c:7
7                       j=i;
```

```
(gdb) s
5                  for(i=0;i<10;i++)
(gdb) print i
$1 = 1
(gdb) print j
$2 = 1
(gdb)
```

In the previous debugging session, you stepped through code one high-level statement at a time and printed the values of specific variables. This beats the heck out of having to deduce program state information by deciphering the registers and dumping memory.

4.1.2 Debugging Infrastructures: Custom Built

All of the commercial operating systems provide hooks for debugging. These hooks are usually implemented as system calls to debugging facilities inside of the kernel. This is a necessity because debugging an application requires access to system data structures that exist in a protected region of memory (i.e., the kernel). The only way to manipulate these special data structures is to politely ask the operating system to do so on your behalf.

One exception to this rule occurs in the case of DOS. With DOS, a real-mode operating system, you can do damn near everything by yourself because memory protection does not exist.

DOS Debugging Interrupts

To implement a minimal DOS debugger, all you have to do is implement interrupt service routines for the following two Intel machine instructions:

- INT 0x3: Signals a breakpoint

- INT 0x1: Supports single stepping

The INT 0x3 instruction represents a breakpoint. When a program encounters an INT 0x3 instruction, the processor automatically locates the fourth entry in a special system data structure called the *interrupt vector table* (see Figure 4-3), or IVT for short (the table index begins at zero, so 0x3 is the fourth element). The IVT exists at the bottom of memory; it starts at address 0x00000. The processor uses the IVT entry to locate the corresponding *interrupt service routine* (ISR) in memory. Each interrupt table entry, known as a *vector*, has its own dedicated ISR. Each vector stores the real-mode segment:offset address of its ISR.

Interrupt Vector Table (IVT)

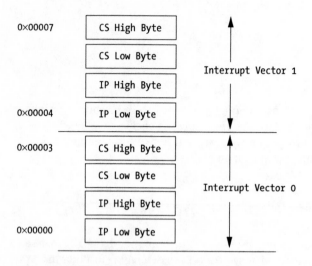

Figure 4-3. The interrupt vector table

Normally, the ISR for INT 0x3 does nothing; it's a dummy placeholder routine. In order to actually do something when an INT 0x3 instruction is encountered, you'll need to register your own ISR routine with the IVT so that your code is activated when an INT 0x3 instruction is processed. You can do this by placing the address of your ISR in the IVT.

The Intel processor has a register named FLAGS. This is actually the older, 16-bit version of the Pentium's 32-bit EFLAGS register. The ninth bit in the FLAGS register is called the *Trap Flag* (TF). When the TF flag is set (i.e., equal to 1), the processor will execute a single instruction and then automatically execute an INT 0x1 instruction. As with INT 0x3, this causes the ISR designated by the second entry in the IVT to be executed. As before, this ISR is a dummy placeholder that you will need to replace.

For example, if you compiled and ran the following program in DOS, nothing would happen:

```
void main()
{
    _asm{ int 0x3 }
    _asm{ int 0x1 }
    return;
}
```

In order to make INT 0x3 and INT 0x1 useful, you need to implement and register the necessary interrupt service routines.

However, there are a few tricky points you should be aware of:

- You cannot manipulate TF explicitly.

- The processor automatically disables TF when it invokes an ISR.

Fortunately, the nature of Intel interrupts offers you a way to indirectly alter TF. Specifically, when the processor encounters an interrupt and jumps to the corresponding ISR, it performs the following steps:

- Pushes FLAGS onto the stack

- Pushes the CS register onto the stack

- Pushes the IP register onto the stack (offset following interrupt)

- Clears TF

- Loads CS and IP with the values from the IVT vector

The processor automatically clears TF so that the debugger itself does not operate in single-step mode. If the debugger wants to single-step the program being debugged, it will have to manipulate the FLAGS value that was pushed onto the stack, so that when it is popped off TF will be updated.

A DOS Machine-Level Debugger

The following code implements a simple DOS debugging API. You can insert it into a 16-bit DOS application to include machine-level debugging services. Normally, a debugger examines a program by running it as a child process. In this case, however, you are going to tack debugging functionality onto the application itself using the enableDebug() and disableDebug() routines.

```
/* dosdebug.c---------------------------------------------------*/
#include<stdio.h>

//data types (addresses in DOS are 16 bits)
#define U2 unsigned short
#define U1 unsigned char

#define BOOLEAN     U2
#define TRUE        1==1
#define FALSE       !TRUE

//context of process (i.e., all the 8088 registers)
struct Context
{
    U2 rCS;
    U2 rDS;
```

```
    U2 rSS;
    U2 rES;

    U2 rIP;
    U2 rSP;
    U2 rBP;
    U2 rSI;
    U2 rDI;

    U2 rAX;
    U2 rBX;
    U2 rCX;
    U2 rDX;

    U2 flags;
};


//logical IVT vector, segment:offset address of ISR in memory
struct ISRVector
{
    U2 segment;
    U2 address;
};


//debugger's environment (save so you can restore it later)
//a single new vector replaces both INT 0x1 and INT 0x3 ISRs
struct Environment
{
    struct ISRVector oldBreakPointVector;
    struct ISRVector oldSingleStepVector;
    struct ISRVector newVector;
    U1 breakPointIndex;              //index into the IVT
    U1 singleStepIndex;              //index into the IVT
};


//high-level interface to code (i.e., what you see in main())
struct Environment *enableDebug();
void disableDebug(struct Environment *env);

//IVT entry manipulation
void swapISRVectors(struct ISRVector *, struct ISRVector *,U1 index);
void getISR(struct ISRVector *vector,U1 index);
void setISR(struct ISRVector *vector,U1 index);

//interrupt handler and debug services
void handleInterrupts(struct ISRVector *vector, int function);
```

```
//debugger implementation
BOOLEAN command(U2 *trace, struct Context *context);
void displayRegisters(struct Context *context);
void dumpMemory();
void help();

//very crude driver
void main()
{
    struct Environment *env;
    env = enableDebug();      //register new ISRs

    //do stuff (and provide a binary signature)

    _asm{ nop }     //0x90
    _asm{ int 3 }   //0xCC
    _asm{ nop }     //0x90
    _asm{ inc bx}   //0x43

    disableDebug(env);        //restore old "dummy" ISRs
    return;
}


#define GET_ADDRESS         1
#define BREAK_POINT_ISR     3
#define SINGLE_STEP_ISR     1

struct Environment *enableDebug()
{
    struct Environment *env;
    U2 size;

    size = sizeof(struct Environment);
    env = (struct Environment*)malloc(size);

    //special, 1-time call to get address of new ISR

    handleInterrupts(&((*env).newVector),GET_ADDRESS);
    (*env).breakPointIndex = BREAK_POINT_ISR;
    (*env).singleStepIndex = SINGLE_STEP_ISR;

    //replace old ISRs with new ISR entry in IVT

    swapISRVectors
    (
        &((*env).oldBreakPointVector),
        &((*env).newVector),
        (*env).breakPointIndex
    );
```

```
        swapISRVectors
        (
            &((*env).oldSingleStepVector),
            &((*env).newVector),
            (*env).singleStepIndex
        );
        return(env);
}/*end enableDebug----------------------------------------------*/
void disableDebug(struct Environment *env)
{
        setISR(&((*env).oldBreakPointVector),(*env).breakPointIndex);
        setISR(&((*env).oldSingleStepVector),(*env).singleStepIndex);
        free(env);
}/*end disableDebug---------------------------------------------*/
void swapISRVectors
(
        struct ISRVector *oldVector,
        struct ISRVector *newVector,
        U1 index
)
{
        getISR(oldVector,index);
        setISR(newVector,index);
        return;
}/*end swapISRVectors-------------------------------------------*/
void printISR(struct ISRVector *vector)
{
        printf("ISR[");
        printf("CS=%04X:",(*vector).segment);
        printf("IP=%04X]\n",(*vector).address);
        return;
}/*end printISR-------------------------------------------------*/

//get CS:IP values for ISR at specified index in IVT
void getISR(struct ISRVector *vector,U1 index)
{
        U2 segment;
        U2 address;
        _asm{ mov ah,0x35 }
        _asm{ mov al,index }
        _asm{ int 0x21 }
        _asm{ mov segment,ES }
        _asm{ mov address,BX }
        (*vector).segment = segment;
        (*vector).address = address;
        return;
}/*end getISR---------------------------------------------------*/
```

```
//set CS:IP values for ISR at specified index in IVT
void setISR(struct ISRVector *vector,U1 index)
{
     U2 segment;
     U2 address;
     segment = (*vector).segment;
     address = (*vector).address;

     //code uses DS, so you must save it and restore it (via PUSH/POP)

     _asm{ push ds }
     _asm{ mov ah,0x25 }
     _asm{ mov al,index }
     _asm{ mov ds,segment }
     _asm{ mov dx,address }
     _asm{ int 0x21 }
     _asm{ pop ds }
     return;
}/*end setISR--------------------------------------------------------*/

//I embedded the new ISR within the handleInterrupts() function.
//The problem is that an ISR does not utilize a stack frame, so
//variables that might otherwise be local have to be global
//(for encapsulation, don't access outside of handleInterrupts()).

struct Context context;
U2 trace;

U2 rCS;
U2 rDS;
U2 rSS;
U2 rES;

U2 rIP;
U2 rSP;
U2 rBP;
U2 rSI;
U2 rDI;

U2 rAX;
U2 rBX;
U2 rCX;
U2 rDX;
U2 flags;

void handleInterrupts
(
     struct ISRVector *vector,
     int function
)
```

```
{
    //special case, asking for address of ISR

    if(function==GET_ADDRESS)
    {
        U2 segment;
        U2 address;

        _asm{ mov AX,CS }
        _asm{ mov segment,AX }
        _asm{ mov AX,OFFSET start }
        _asm{ mov address,AX }

        (*vector).segment = segment;
        (*vector).address = address;
        return;
    }

    //ISR actually begins here...

    start:

    saveState:
    _asm{ sti }
    _asm{ mov rDS,DS }
    _asm{ mov rSS,SS }
    _asm{ mov rES,ES }

    _asm{ mov rSP,SP }
    _asm{ mov rBP,BP }
    _asm{ mov rDI,DI }
    _asm{ mov rSI,SI }

    _asm{ mov rAX,AX }
    _asm{ mov rBX,BX }
    _asm{ mov rCX,CX }
    _asm{ mov rDX,DX }

    /*
    interrupt stack    [IP]     = instruction following interrupt
                       [CS]     = code segment
                       [FLAGS]  = contents of flags register
    */
    clearTfFlag:
    _asm{ pop cx }
    _asm{ mov rIP,cx }
    _asm{ pop dx }
    _asm{ mov rCS,dx }
    _asm{ pop ax }
```

```
_asm{ mov flags,ax }
_asm{ and ax,0xFEFF } /* AX && 1111 1110 1111 1111*/
_asm{ push ax }
_asm{ push dx }
_asm{ push cx }

context.rCS = rCS;
context.rDS = rDS;
context.rSS = rSS;
context.rES = rES;
context.rIP = rIP;
context.rSP = rSP;
context.rBP = rBP;
context.rDI = rDI;
context.rSI = rSI;
context.rAX = rAX;
context.rBX = rBX;
context.rCX = rCX;
context.rDX = rDX;
context.flags = flags;


invokedDebuggerLoop:
trace = FALSE;
while(command(&trace,&context)){}
printf("leaving debug API\n");

if(!trace){ goto restoreState; }

setTfFlag:
_asm{ pop cx }
_asm{ pop dx }
_asm{ pop ax }
_asm{ or ax,0x0100 } /* AX || 0000 0001 0000 0000*/
_asm{ push ax }
_asm{ push dx }
_asm{ push cx }

restoreState:
_asm{ mov SP,rSP }
_asm{ mov BP,rBP }
_asm{ mov DI,rDI }
_asm{ mov SI,rSI }

_asm{ mov AX,rAX }
_asm{ mov BX,rBX }
_asm{ mov CX,rCX }
_asm{ mov DX,rDX }
```

```
        endISR:
        _asm{ iret }

        return;
}/*end handleInterrupts--------------------------------------------*/
BOOLEAN command(U2 *trace, struct Context *context)
{
        U1 ch;

        printf("-");
        scanf("%c",&ch);
        fflush(stdin);

        switch(ch)
        {
            case 'r':
            {
                displayRegisters(context);
            }break;
            case 'd':
            {
                dumpMemory();
            }break;
            case 'T':
            {
                *trace=FALSE;
                printf("tracing disabled\n");
            }break;
            case 't':
            {
                *trace=TRUE;
                printf("tracing enabled\n");
            }break;
            case 'q':
            {
                return(FALSE);
            }break;
            default:
            {
                help();
            }
        }
        return(TRUE);
}/*end command---------------------------------------------------*/
void displayRegisters(struct Context *context)
{
        printf("CS=%04X ",(*context).rCS);
        printf("DS=%04X ",(*context).rDS);
        printf("SS=%04X ",(*context).rSS);
        printf("ES=%04X\n",(*context).rES);
```

```
    printf("IP=%04X ",(*context).rIP);
    printf("SP=%04X ",(*context).rSP);
    printf("BP=%04X\n",(*context).rBP);

    printf("SI=%04X ",(*context).rSI);
    printf("DI=%04X\n",(*context).rDI);

    printf("AX=%04X ",(*context).rAX);
    printf("BX=%04X ",(*context).rBX);
    printf("CX=%04X ",(*context).rCX);
    printf("DX=%04X\n",(*context).rDX);

    printf("FLAGS=%04X\n",(*context).flags);
}/*end displayRegisters---------------------------------------------*/
U1 getByteValue(U2 segment,U2 currentOffset)
{
    U1 value;
    _asm{ mov ES,segment }
    _asm{ mov BX,currentOffset }
    _asm{ mov al,ES:[BX] }
    _asm{ mov value,al }
    return(value);
}/*end getByteValue-------------------------------------------------*/

//display bytes as lines of 16 (in groups of 4)

#define FOUR_BYTES      4
#define LINE_BREAK      16

int isEndOfDisplayGroup(index)
{
    if((index>0)&&((index%FOUR_BYTES)==0)){ return(TRUE); }
    return(FALSE);
}/*end isEndOfDisplayGroup-----------------------------------------*/
int isEndOfDisplayLine(index)
{
    if((index>0)&&((index%LINE_BREAK)==0)){ return(TRUE); }
    return(FALSE);
}/*end isEndOfDisplayLine------------------------------------------*/
void displayByte(U2 index,U2 segment,U2 currentOffset)
{
    if((index==0)||isEndOfDisplayLine(index))
    {
        printf("\n");
        printf("[%04X][%04X] ",segment,currentOffset);
    }
    else if(isEndOfDisplayGroup(index))
    {
        printf("-");
    }
```

```
        printf(" %02X",getByteValue(segment,currentOffset));
        return;
}/*end displayByte-----------------------------------------------*/


#define DUMP_LIMIT      128


void dumpMemory()
{
        U2 segmentAddress;
        U2 offsetAddress;
        U2 i;

        printf("enter segment: ");
        scanf("%X",&segmentAddress);
        fflush(stdin);

        printf("enter offset: ");
        scanf("%X",&offsetAddress);
        fflush(stdin);

        for(i=0;i<DUMP_LIMIT;i++)
        {
                displayByte(i,segmentAddress,offsetAddress+i);
        }
        printf("\n");
}/*end dumpMemory------------------------------------------------*/
void help()
{
        printf("--commands--\n");
        printf("r     display registers\n");
        printf("d     dump memory starting at addr\n");
        printf("t     step into next instruction\n");
        printf("T     turn off single-stepping\n");
        printf("q     quit\n");
        return;
}/*end help-----------------------------------------------------*/
```

Using the DOS Debugger

When this debugging API has been grafted onto a program, the program will
run until it hits its first breakpoint. Once the first breakpoint has been
reached, you can take a look at the registers with the r command.

```
C:\>debuggedApp.exe
-r
CS=0F25 DS=1187 SS=1187 ES=0070
IP=068B SP=0E26 BP=0E34
```

```
SI=055E DI=055E
AX=0F98 BX=0FA0 CX=050D DX=03D5
FLAGS=3206
```

Then, you can peruse the memory image of the process being debugged using the d command. Notice, you should be able to spot the byte pattern that you placed in main() (i.e., 0x90 0xCC 0x90 0x43). The IP register is pointing to the address of the byte directly after the interrupt instruction (i.e., 0xCC).

```
-d
enter segment: f25
enter offset: 0680
[0F25][0680]  02 56 57 E8-  24 FF 89 46-  FC 90 CC 90-  43 FF 76 FC
[0F25][0690]  E8 9F FF 83-  C4 02 E9 00-  00 5F 5E 8B-  E5 5D C3 00
[0F25][06A0]  B4 30 CD 21-  3C 02 73 05-  33 C0 06 50-  CB BF 87 11
[0F25][06B0]  8B 36 02 00-  2B F7 81 FE-  00 10 72 03-  BE 00 10 FA
[0F25][06C0]  8E D7 81 C4-  7E 06 FB 73-  10 16 1F E8-  6A 02 33 C0
[0F25][06D0]  50 E8 F7 04-  B8 FF 4C CD-  21 36 A3 20-  02 86 E0 36
[0F25][06E0]  A3 1E 02 8B-  C6 B1 04 D3-  E0 48 36 A3-  DE 01 BB E0
[0F25][06F0]  01 36 8C 17-  83 E4 FE 36-  89 67 04 B8-  FE FF 50 36
```

You can also toggle the single-stepping flag so that the application executes a single instruction and then returns control to the debugger.

```
-t
tracing enabled
-q
```

You've quit the debugger, via the q command, but it will automatically return control to the debugger once the single step has occurred. You can verify that an instruction has been executed by looking at the incremented value of the IP register.

```
leaving debug API
-r
CS=0F25 DS=1187 SS=1187 ES=1187
IP=068C SP=0E26 BP=0E34
SI=055E DI=055E
AX=0F98 BX=0FA0 CX=050D DX=03D5
FLAGS=3306
-T
tracing disabled
-q
leaving debug API
```

Sure enough, IP has incremented from 0x068B to 0x068C.

Whew. As you can see, there are a lot of little details to take care of when you build your debugging services from the ground up. Interrupt service routines are touchy creatures to work with. One wrong move, and your machine can come crashing down. I implemented this code on Windows 2000 using Visual C++ version 1.52, and even in a protected environment like Windows 2000, I was able to blue screen my machine by corrupting the VDM that ran my code. Which, interestingly enough, demonstrates how you can still crash a protected-mode operating system with a real-mode application.

4.1.3 Debugging Infrastructures: System Calls

At the other end of the spectrum, opposite DOS, is Windows. Windows has a fairly sophisticated memory protection scheme. This means that if you want to write a debugger, you'll need to rely on the Win32 system calls.

The Windows Debugging API

The Win32 API has roughly 15 system calls dedicated to debugging. For instance, a Win32 debugger can either load a new process or attach itself to a running process. The CreateProcess() routine loads a new process into memory such that the debugger is the parent process and the program being debugged is a child process. The DebugActiveProcess() system call allows the debugger to latch on to a program that is already executing.

In Windows, debugging interrupts are buried deep within the kernel. There are probably only a handful of engineers at Microsoft who can view the source code that implements the corresponding interrupt service routines. Several layers of abstraction have wrapped the hardware-specific details. Ordinary programmers like you and me see these interrupts as events that the operating system generates.

```
ok = WaitForDebugEvent(&event,INFINITE);
if(!ok){ displayError(); }

while(event.dwDebugEventCode!=EXIT_PROCESS_DEBUG_EVENT)
{
    ok = processDebugEvent(&event,&processInfo);
    if(!ok){ break;}

    ok = ContinueDebugEvent
    (
        processInfo.dwProcessId,
        processInfo.dwThreadId,
        DBG_CONTINUE
    );
    if(!ok){ displayError(); break; }
```

```
ok = WaitForDebugEvent(&event,INFINITE);
if(!ok){ displayError(); break; }
}
```

Most debuggers use some sort of loop to process debug events and take the appropriate actions. To this end, there are two important system calls. The WaitForDebugEvent() system call causes the debugger to pause until it receives a debugging event from the program that it is debugging. Once a program has sent a debugging event, it will remain in a state of suspended animation until the ContinueDebugEvent() system call is invoked by the debugger.

Tables 4-1 through 4-4 list the various calls by function.

Table 4-1. Starting a Process

Call	Description
CreateProcess	Loads a process to be debugged
DebugActiveProcess	Attaches the debugger to a running process

Table 4-2. Debugging Loops

Call	Description
WaitForDebugEvent	Blocks until it receives a debugging event
ContinueDebugEvent	Resumes execution
SetDebugErrorLevel	Sets an error-level threshold

Table 4-3. Calls for Manipulation

Call	Description
GetThreadContext	Retrieves the context of a thread
ReadProcessMemory	Reads the memory of a process
SetThreadContext	Sets the context of a thread
WriteProcessMemory	Modifies the memory of a process

Table 4-4. Calling the Debugger

Call	Description
DebugBreak	Manually produces a breakpoint exception
FatalExit	Transfers execution control to the debugger
IsDebuggerPresent	Indicates if a process is being debugged
OutputDebugString	Sends a message to the debugger

A number of calls allow the debugger to manipulate the program that it is debugging. For example, the ReadProcessMemory() system call allows the debugger to access the address space of the program being debugged. The GetThreadContext() system call returns the context of the thread currently being debugged. A thread's context is represented programmatically by a CONTEXT structure. The makeup of CONTEXT varies from one hardware platform to the next. Anyone familiar with the Intel assembler will recognize a number of well-known registers in the Pentium version that have been included.

```
 typedef struct _CONTEXT
{
    DWORD ContextFlags;
    DWORD   Dr0;
    DWORD   Dr1;
    DWORD   Dr2;
    DWORD   Dr3;
    DWORD   Dr6;
    DWORD   Dr7;
    FLOATING_SAVE_AREA FloatSave;

    DWORD   SegGs;
    DWORD   SegFs;
    DWORD   SegEs;
    DWORD   SegDs;

    DWORD   Edi;
    DWORD   Esi;
    DWORD   Ebx;
    DWORD   Edx;
    DWORD   Ecx;
    DWORD   Eax;
```

```
DWORD    Ebp;
DWORD    Eip;
DWORD    SegCs;
DWORD    EFlags;
DWORD    Esp;
DWORD    SegSs;

} CONTEXT;
```

There are also system calls that the program being debugged can invoke to interact with the debugger. For instance, the OutputDebugString() system call causes the debugger to print a string to standard output. This allows a program to log relevant messages during a debugging session. The IsDebuggerPresent() routine can be invoked by a program to check and see if it is being debugged. The DebugBreak() call can be used to manually produce a breakpoint event, and the FatalExit() routine causes the program being debugged to transfer program control to the debugger.

A Windows Machine-Level Debugger

The following code implements a subset of these system calls to build a simple Win32 machine-level debugger:

```
/* windebug.c -------------------------------------------------------*/
#include<stdio.h>
#include<windows.h>

#define RETURN_OK          0
#define RETURN_ERROR       1

//data types (addresses in Windows 2000 are 32-bits)

#define BOOLEAN        int
#define U4             unsigned long

/*++++++++++++++++++++++++++++++++++++++++++++++++++++++++++++++++++++
+ Declaration                                                        +
++++++++++++++++++++++++++++++++++++++++++++++++++++++++++++++++++++*/

//this class handles the command line

#define MAX_ARGUMENTS      3
```

```
class CommandLine
{
    private:
    int argc;
    char *argv[MAX_ARGUMENTS];

    BOOLEAN fileExists(char *fname);
    void printHelp();

    public:
    CommandLine(int argc, char *argv[]);
    BOOLEAN validArguments();
    char* getFileName();
    char* getArgument();
};


/*++++++++++++++++++++++++++++++++++++++++++++++++++++++++++++++++++++++++
+ Definitions                                                            +
++++++++++++++++++++++++++++++++++++++++++++++++++++++++++++++++++++++++*/

CommandLine::CommandLine(int argc, char *argv[])
{
    int i;
    (*this).argc = argc;
    for(i=0;i<MAX_ARGUMENTS;i++)
    {
        (*this).argv[i]=NULL;
        if(argv[i]!=NULL)
        {
            (*this).argv[i]=argv[i];
        }
    }
    return;
}/*end constructor-------------------------------------------------*/

#define FILE_INDEX              1
#define NO_ARGUMENT          2
#define HAS_ARGUMENT         3

BOOLEAN CommandLine::validArguments()
{
    switch(argc)
    {
        case NO_ARGUMENT:
        case HAS_ARGUMENT:
        {
            if(!fileExists(argv[FILE_INDEX]))
```

```
                {
                        printf("%s does not exist\n",argv[FILE_INDEX]);
                        return(FALSE);
                }
        }break;
        default:
        {
                printHelp();
                return(FALSE);
        }
    }
    return(TRUE);
}/*end validArguments------------------------------------------------*/

BOOLEAN CommandLine::fileExists(char *fname)
{
    FILE* file;
    file = fopen(fname,"r");
    if(file==NULL)
    {
            return(FALSE);
    }
    fclose(file);
    return(TRUE);
}/*end fileExists--------------------------------------------------*/

void CommandLine::printHelp()
{
    printf("usage:dbg program.exe [argument]\n");
    return;
}/*end printHelp--------------------------------------------------*/

char* CommandLine::getFileName()
{
    return(argv[FILE_INDEX]);
}/*end getFileName------------------------------------------------*/

char* CommandLine::getArgument()
{
    switch(argc)
    {
        case HAS_ARGUMENT:
        {
                return(argv[FILE_INDEX+1]);
        }break;
    }
    return(NULL);
}/*end getArgument------------------------------------------------*/
```

```
/*++++++++++++++++++++++++++++++++++++++++++++++++++++++++++++++++++++
+ Declaration                                                       +
++++++++++++++++++++++++++++++++++++++++++++++++++++++++++++++++++++*/


//represents the process being debugged

class Debugee
{
     private:
     char *fileName;
     char *argument;
     void getSecurity(SECURITY_ATTRIBUTES *, SECURITY_DESCRIPTOR *);

     public:
     Debugee(char *fileName, char *argument);
     PROCESS_INFORMATION getProcessHandle();
};


/*++++++++++++++++++++++++++++++++++++++++++++++++++++++++++++++++++++
+ Definitions                                                       +
++++++++++++++++++++++++++++++++++++++++++++++++++++++++++++++++++++*/

Debugee::Debugee(char *fileName, char *argument)
{
     (*this).fileName = fileName;
     (*this).argument = argument;
}/*end constructor--------------------------------------------------*/

PROCESS_INFORMATION Debugee::getProcessHandle()
{
     PROCESS_INFORMATION processInfo;
     STARTUPINFO startUpInfo;
     SECURITY_ATTRIBUTES attributes;
     SECURITY_DESCRIPTOR descriptor;

     BOOLEAN ok;
     getSecurity(&attributes,&descriptor);
     GetStartupInfo(&startUpInfo);

     ok = CreateProcess
     (
         fileName,           //executable
         argument,           //command line
         &attributes,        //process security descriptor
         &attributes,        //thread security descriptor
         FALSE,              //inherits handles of debugger
         DEBUG_ONLY_THIS_PROCESS,
```

```
        NULL,            //use environment of calling process
        NULL,            //current directory of calling process
        &startUpInfo,
        &processInfo     //handles for debugee
    );
    if(!ok)
    {
        printf("could not load %s\n",fileName);
        exit(RETURN_ERROR);
    }
    return(processInfo);
}/*end getProcessHandle----------------------------------------*/

void Debugee::getSecurity
(
    SECURITY_ATTRIBUTES *attributes,
    SECURITY_DESCRIPTOR *descriptor
)
{

    InitializeSecurityDescriptor
    (
        descriptor,
        SECURITY_DESCRIPTOR_REVISION
    );

    (*attributes).nLength =sizeof(SECURITY_ATTRIBUTES);
    (*attributes).lpSecurityDescriptor=descriptor;
    (*attributes).bInheritHandle =TRUE;
    return;
}/*end getSecurity-------------------------------------------*/

/*+++++++++++++++++++++++++++++++++++++++++++++++++++++++++++++++++++
+ Declaration                                                       +
++++++++++++++++++++++++++++++++++++++++++++++++++++++++++++++++++++*/

//Command-line debugger

class Debugger
{
    private:
    PROCESS_INFORMATION *processInfo;

    void displayRegisters();
    void displayMemory();
    void displayByte(U4 index,U4 address,char byte);
    BOOLEAN isEndOfDisplayGroup(U4 index);
    BOOLEAN isEndOfDisplayLine(U4 index);
```

```
      public:
      Debugger(PROCESS_INFORMATION *processInfo);
      void processDebugCommand();
};


/*+++++++++++++++++++++++++++++++++++++++++++++++++++++++++++++++++++++++
+ Definitions                                                          +
+++++++++++++++++++++++++++++++++++++++++++++++++++++++++++++++++++++++*/

Debugger::Debugger(PROCESS_INFORMATION *processInfo)
{
      (*this).processInfo = processInfo;
}/*end constructor-------------------------------------------------*/


void Debugger::processDebugCommand()
{
      BOOLEAN exitLoop;
      char ch;

      exitLoop=FALSE;
      while(!exitLoop)
      {
          printf("-");
          scanf("%c",&ch);
          fflush(stdin);
          switch(ch)
          {
              case 'r':{ displayRegisters(); }break;
              case 'd':{ displayMemory(); }break;
              case 'q':{ exitLoop = TRUE; }break;
          }
      }
      printf("exiting command loop\n");
      return;
}/*end processDebugCommand----------------------------------------*/


void Debugger::displayRegisters()
{
      BOOLEAN ok;
      CONTEXT context;
      ok = GetThreadContext
      (
          (*processInfo).hThread,
          &context
      );
      if(!ok)
      {
          printf("could not get context\n");
          return;
      }
```

```
      printf(" CS=%081X",context.SegCs);
      printf(" DS=%081X",context.SegDs);
      printf(" SS=%081X",context.SegSs);
      printf(" ES=%081X",context.SegEs);
      printf(" FS=%081X",context.SegFs);
      printf(" GS=%081X\n",context.SegGs);

      printf(" EIP=%081X",context.Eip);
      printf(" ESP=%081X",context.Esp);
      printf(" EBP=%081X\n",context.Ebp);

      printf(" EAX=%081X",context.Eax);
      printf(" EBX=%081X",context.Ebx);
      printf(" ECX=%081X",context.Ecx);
      printf(" EDX=%081X\n",context.Edx);
      printf(" EDI=%081X",context.Edi);
      printf(" ESI=%081X\n",context.Esi);
      printf(" EFLAGS=%081X\n",context.EFlags);
      return;
}/*end displayRegisters----------------------------------------------*/


void Debugger::displayMemory()
{
      BOOLEAN ok;
      char *buffer;
      unsigned long address;
      unsigned long nbytes;
      unsigned long i;

      printf("[base address]:");
      scanf("%1X",&address);
      fflush(stdin);

      printf("[# bytes]:");
      scanf("%1X",&nbytes);
      fflush(stdin);

      buffer = (char*)malloc(nbytes);

      ok = ReadProcessMemory
      (
          (*processInfo).hProcess,
          (LPCVOID)address,
          buffer,
          nbytes,
          &nbytes
      );
      if(!ok)
```

```
        {
            printf("could not read memory\n");
            free(buffer);
            return;
        }

        for(i=0;i<nbytes;i++)
        {
            displayByte(i,address+i,buffer[i]);
        }
        printf("\n");
        free(buffer);
        return;
}/*end displayMemory----------------------------------------------*/

void Debugger::displayByte
(
        U4 index,
        U4 address,
        char byte
)
{

        if((index==0)||isEndOfDisplayLine(index))
        {
            printf("\n");
            printf("[%08X] ",address);
        }
        else if(isEndOfDisplayGroup(index))
        {
            printf("-");
        }

        printf(" %02X",(unsigned char)byte);
        return;
}/*end displayByte-------------------------------------------------*/

#define FOUR_BYTES      4
#define LINE_BREAK     16

BOOLEAN Debugger::isEndOfDisplayGroup(U4 index)
{
        if((index>0)&&((index%FOUR_BYTES)==0)){ return(TRUE); }
        return(FALSE);
}/*end isEndOfDisplayGroup-----------------------------------------*/

BOOLEAN Debugger::isEndOfDisplayLine(U4 index)
{
        if((index>0)&&((index%LINE_BREAK)==0)){ return(TRUE); }
        return(FALSE);
}/*end isEndOfDisplayLine------------------------------------------*/
```

```
/*++++++++++++++++++++++++++++++++++++++++++++++++++++++++++++++++++++++
+ Declaration                                                          +
++++++++++++++++++++++++++++++++++++++++++++++++++++++++++++++++++++++++*/

//Handles debug events

class DebugEventHandler
{
     private:
     DEBUG_EVENT *event;
     PROCESS_INFORMATION *processInfo;

     void displayError();

     BOOLEAN processDebugEvent();
     void printDebugEvent(DEBUG_EVENT *event);

     BOOLEAN processExceptionEvent();
     void printExceptionEvent(DEBUG_EVENT *event);

     public:
     void startDebugLoop(PROCESS_INFORMATION);
};

/*++++++++++++++++++++++++++++++++++++++++++++++++++++++++++++++++++++++
+ Definitions                                                          +
++++++++++++++++++++++++++++++++++++++++++++++++++++++++++++++++++++++++*/

void DebugEventHandler::startDebugLoop(PROCESS_INFORMATION processInfo)
{
     BOOLEAN ok;

     (*this).processInfo = &processInfo;
     (*this).event = (DEBUG_EVENT*)malloc(sizeof(DEBUG_EVENT));

     ok = WaitForDebugEvent(event,INFINITE);
     if(!ok){ displayError(); }

     while((*event).dwDebugEventCode!=EXIT_PROCESS_DEBUG_EVENT)
     {
         ok = processDebugEvent();
         if(!ok){ break;}

         ok = ContinueDebugEvent
         (
             processInfo.dwProcessId,
             processInfo.dwThreadId,
             DBG_CONTINUE
         );
         if(!ok){ displayError(); break; }
```

```
            ok = WaitForDebugEvent(event,INFINITE);
            if(!ok){ displayError(); break; }
      }

      if((*event).dwDebugEventCode==EXIT_PROCESS_DEBUG_EVENT)
      {
            printf("debugged process has exited, ");
      }
      printf("exiting debugger\n");

      free(event);
      return;
}/*end startDebugLoop-------------------------------------------*/


void DebugEventHandler::displayError()
{
      LPVOID lpMsgBuf;
      FormatMessage
      (
            FORMAT_MESSAGE_ALLOCATE_BUFFER|
            FORMAT_MESSAGE_FROM_SYSTEM,
            NULL,
            GetLastError(),
            MAKELANGID(LANG_NEUTRAL, SUBLANG_DEFAULT),
            (LPTSTR) &lpMsgBuf,
            0,
            NULL
      );
      printf("error: %s\n",lpMsgBuf);
      LocalFree(lpMsgBuf);
      return;
}/*end displayError--------------------------------------------*/


BOOLEAN DebugEventHandler::processDebugEvent()
{
      printDebugEvent(event);

      switch((*event).dwDebugEventCode)
      {
            case EXCEPTION_DEBUG_EVENT:
            {
                  printExceptionEvent(event);
                  return(processExceptionEvent());
            }break;
      }
      return(TRUE);
}/*end processDebugEven----------------------------------------*/
```

```
void DebugEventHandler::printDebugEvent(DEBUG_EVENT *event)
{
    switch((*event).dwDebugEventCode)
    {
        case EXCEPTION_DEBUG_EVENT:
        {
            printf("EXCEPTION_DEBUG_EVENT\n");
        }break;
        case CREATE_THREAD_DEBUG_EVENT:
        {
            printf("CREATE_THREAD_DEBUG_EVENT\n");
        }break;
        case CREATE_PROCESS_DEBUG_EVENT:
        {
            printf("CREATE_PROCESS_DEBUG_EVENT \n");
        }break;
        case EXIT_THREAD_DEBUG_EVENT :
        {
            printf("EXIT_THREAD_DEBUG_EVENT \n");
        }break;
        case EXIT_PROCESS_DEBUG_EVENT:
        {
            printf("EXIT_PROCESS_DEBUG_EVENT\n");
        }break;
        case LOAD_DLL_DEBUG_EVENT:
        {
            printf("LOAD_DLL_DEBUG_EVENT\n");
        }break;
        case UNLOAD_DLL_DEBUG_EVENT:
        {
            printf("UNLOAD_DLL_DEBUG_EVENT\n");
        }break;
        case OUTPUT_DEBUG_STRING_EVENT:
        {
            printf("OUTPUT_DEBUG_STRING_EVENT\n");
        }break;
        case RIP_EVENT :
        {
            printf("RIP_EVENT \n");
        }break;
        default:{ printf("bad event code\n"); }
    }
    return;
}/*end printDebugEvent-----------------------------------------------*/

BOOLEAN DebugEventHandler::processExceptionEvent()
{
    EXCEPTION_DEBUG_INFO debugInfo;
    EXCEPTION_RECORD record;
    Debugger debugger(processInfo);
```

```
        debugInfo = ((*event).u).Exception;
        record = (debugInfo).ExceptionRecord;

        switch(record.ExceptionCode)
        {
            case EXCEPTION_BREAKPOINT:
            {
                debugger.processDebugCommand();
            }break;
            default:
            {
                printf("debug exception not handled");
                return(FALSE);
            }break;
        }
        return(TRUE);
}/*end processExceptionEvent----------------------------------------*/

void DebugEventHandler::printExceptionEvent(DEBUG_EVENT *event)
{
        EXCEPTION_DEBUG_INFO exceptionInfo;
        EXCEPTION_RECORD record;

        exceptionInfo = ((*event).u).Exception;
        record = (exceptionInfo).ExceptionRecord;

        switch(record.ExceptionCode)
        {
            case EXCEPTION_BREAKPOINT:
            {
                printf("EXCEPTION_BREAKPOINT\n");
            }break;
            default:{ printf("record code not handled\n"); }
        }
        return;
}/*end printExceptionEvent------------------------------------------*/

/*++++++++++++++++++++++++++++++++++++++++++++++++++++++++++++++++++++
+ Driver                                                            +
++++++++++++++++++++++++++++++++++++++++++++++++++++++++++++++++++++*/

//program entry point

int main(int argc, char *argv[])
{
        CommandLine commandLine(argc,argv);
```

```
if(!commandLine.validArguments())
{
    return(RETURN_ERROR);
}

Debugee debugee
(
    commandLine.getFileName(),
    commandLine.getArgument()
);

DebugEventHandler handler;
handler.startDebugLoop(debugee.getProcessHandle());
return(RETURN_OK);
}
```

This program is basically the Win32 equivalent of the 16-bit debugging API I presented earlier in the chapter. The primary difference between the two is that the Win32 version loads the program to be debugged as a child process.

Using the Windows Debugger

The 32-bit Windows console program that I constructed, to illustrate how a debugger operates, looks like the following:

```
/* simple2.c ---------------------------------------------------*/
#include<stdio.h>
int i;
int j;

void main()
{
    //do stuff (create signature)

    _asm{ nop }              //0x90
    _asm{ int 3 }            //0xCC
    _asm{ nop }              //0x90
    _asm{ inc bx}            //0x66 0x43

    for(i=0;i<10;i++)
    {
        j=i;
    }
    fprintf(stdout,"j=%d\n",j);
    fflush(stdout);
    return;
}
```

Note how I used in-line assembly code syntax to embed a binary signature in the final executable (i.e., 0x90 0xCC 0x90 0x66 0x43). This will allow me to test the debugger's memory dumping facilities later on. I also placed an INT 0x3 instruction in the program. In 32-bit code, as well as in 16-bit code, this interrupt represents a breakpoint. The INT 0x3 instruction will cause my debugger to pause and display a command prompt.

```
C:\>windebug simple2.exe
exiting command loop
EXCEPTION_DEBUG_EVENT
EXCEPTION_BREAKPOINT
-
```

As with the DOS version, the Win32 debugger has an r command to display the registers:

```
-r
 CS=00000197 DS=0000019F SS=0000019F ES=0000019F FS=0000495F GS=00000000
 EIP=00401018 ESP=0064FDEC EBP=0064FDF8
 EAX=00770380 EBX=00540000 ECX=00000001 EDX=007703F0
 EDI=00000000 ESI=816A0C64
 EFLAGS=00000212
```

Now that I know where the EIP register is pointing, I can dump the region of memory nearby using the d command and look for the binary signature that I mentioned earlier.

```
-d
[base address]:00401010
[# bytes]:20

[00401010]   55 8B EC 53- 56 57 90 CC- 90 66 43 C7- 05 74 3F 41
[00401030]   00 00 00 00- 00 EB 0D A1- 74 3F 41 00- 83 C0 01 A3
```

The signature I'm looking for starts at address 0x00401016.

By issuing the q command, I can exit the debugging loop and allow the child process to complete its execution path.

```
-q
exiting command loop
j=9
debugged process has exited, exiting debugger
```

In the previous source code, I constructed a machine-level debugger. If you wanted to build a symbolic debugger, you would have to read the executable's symbol table. It's there, in the debug build; I merely took the easy way out and ignored it. Constructing a symbolic debugger would entail explaining the organization and use of Microsoft's Portable Executable (PE) and PDB file formats (which could easily take up an entire book). Windows has a DLL named IMAGEHLP.DLL that provides an API for accessing PE debug information so that you don't have to do it yourself. The API assumes that the reader is familiar with the PE file format. Interested readers are directed to Microsoft's online description of the IMAGEHLP API.[2]

4.1.4 Debugging Infrastructures: Interpreters

Debugging an interpreted language is much more direct than the system call approach because all of the debugging facilities can be built directly into the interpreter. With an interpreter, you have unrestricted access to the execution engine; the entire thing runs in user space instead of kernel space. Nothing is hidden. All you need to do is add extensions to process breakpoint instructions and support single stepping.

A Simple Interpreter

To demonstrate what I'm talking about, I am going to implement a crude interpreter named vm. This interpreter executes low-level instructions, so you could probably call my implementation a virtual machine (hence the name). My implementation reads a bytecode file into memory and sequentially executes its instructions.

In terms of execution environment, there are five general-purpose integer registers (R0, R1, R2, R3, R4) and an instruction pointer (IP) that stores the address of the next instruction to be executed.

The vm virtual machine obeys the instruction set specified in Table 4-5. The nuts and bolts are pretty straightforward. The virtual machine starts by validating command-line arguments and determining the size of the bytecode executable. Next, the virtual machine sets up its context by loading the bytecode into memory and initializing its registers. The virtual machine will execute instructions until it hits a breakpoint.

---

2. http://msdn.microsoft.com/library/default.asp?url=/library/en-us/
    debug/base/image_help_library.asp

Table 4-5. vm *Instruction Set*

Opcode	Encoding	Format	Meaning
PUT	0x0	PUT constant, R	Put constant value into register R.
STORE	0x1	STORE R, address	Place the contents of register R into memory.
LOAD	0x2	LOAD address, R	Place the integer at address into register R.
MOV	0x3	MOV R1, R2	Copy contents of R1 into R2.
ADD	0x4	ADD R1, R2, R3	R3 = R1 + R2
SUB	0x5	SUB R1, R2, R3	R3 = R2 – R1
STOP	0x6	STOP	Halt execution.
PRINT	0x7	PRINT R	Print the contents of register R.
BREAK	0x8	BREAK	Execute a breakpoint.

The source code that implements vm is slightly long-winded but easy to understand. It can be downloaded from the Apress Web site (http://www.apress.com).

As I mentioned before, adding debugger functionality to an interpreter is trivial. In this case, it was as easy as plugging in two new functions (i.e., handleBreakPoint() and handleSingleStep()) to the interpreter's execute() routine and defining a new breakpoint instruction.

To take the interpreter for a spin, I manually built a bytecode file named program.run:

```
/* bytecode ------------------------------------------------------*/
#include<stdio.h>

#define R0           0
#define R1           1
#define R2           2
#define R3           3
#define R4           4

#define PUT          0    //PUT      constant,R*
#define STORE        1    //STORE    R*,address
#define LOAD         2    //LOAD     address,R*
#define MOV          3    //MOV      R*,R*
#define ADD          4    //ADD      R*,R*,R*
#define SUB          5    //SUB      R*,R*,R*
#define STOP         6    //STOP
#define PRINT        7    //PRINT    R*
#define BREAK        8    //BREAK
```

```
#define write(arg)              fputc(arg,filePointer)

void main()
{
      FILE *filePointer;
      filePointer = fopen("program.run","wb");

      //address 0          encoding:(0x8)
      write(BREAK);

      //address 1          encoding:(0x0 0xAA 0xBB 0xCC 0xDD 0x0)
      write(PUT);
      write(0xAA); write(0xBB); write(0xCC); write(0xDD);
      write(R0);

      //address 7          encoding:(0x3 0x0 0x2)
      write(MOV);
      write(R0);
      write(R2);

      //address 10         encoding:(0x1 0x2 0x25 0x00 0x00 0x00)
      //(store at 0x25 = 37 )
      write(STORE);
      write(R2);
      write(0x25); write(0x00); write(0x00); write(0x00);

      //address 16         encoding:(0x2 0x25 0x00 0x00 0x00 0x4)
      write(LOAD);
      write(0x25); write(0x00); write(0x00); write(0x00);
      write(R4);

      //address 22         encoding:(0x4 0x2 0x4 0x1 )
      write(ADD); write(R2); write(R4); write(R1);

      //address 26         encoding:(0x5 0x2 0x4 0x1)
      write(SUB); write(R2); write(R4); write(R1);

      //address 30         encoding:(0x7 0x1)
      write(PRINT); write(R1);

      //address 32         encoding:(0x6)
      write(STOP);

      //address 33, static data storage at end of file
      //use for load and store instructions
```

```
write(0x00);write(0x00);write(0x00);write(0x00);
write(0x00);write(0x00);write(0x00);write(0x00);
write(0x00);write(0x00);write(0x00);write(0x00);
write(0x00);write(0x00);write(0x00);write(0x00);

fclose(filePointer);
return;
}
```

After feeding the name of this bytecode file to the interpreter, on the command line, the first instruction (which is a breakpoint) will invoke the debugger. Breakpoints automatically place the interpreter into single-step mode, so even if you quit the debugger, the interpreter will execute the next instruction and then immediately return to the debugger command prompt.

```
C:\>vm program.run
BREAK POINT HIT
-q
PUT DDCCBBAA,R0
-r
IP=00000007
R0=DDCCBBAA
R1=00000000
R2=00000000
R3=00000000
R4=00000000
single-stepping on
-q
MOV R0,R2
-
```

As with all of the other debuggers in this chapter, there is a command to display the state of the registers and a command to dump memory.

```
-r
IP=0000000A
R0=DDCCBBAA
R1=00000000
R2=DDCCBBAA
R3=00000000
R4=00000000
single-stepping on
-q
STORE R2,00000025
-d
[address]:0
nbytes:48
```

```
[00000000]   08 00 AA BB-  CC DD 00 03-  00 02 01 02-  25 00 00 00
[00000010]   02 25 00 00-  00 04 04 02-  04 01 05 02-  04 01 07 01
[00000020]   06 00 00 00-  00 AA BB CC-  DD 00 00 00-  00 00 00 00
-
```

If you want to turn single stepping off, you can invoke the T command and the interpreter will go back to its natural state. In the case of program.run, the interpreter will execute a few additional instructions, print out the value of the R1 register, and then hit the STOP instruction.

```
-T
single-step off
-q
R1=00000000
C:\>
```

To add symbolic debugging features, I would have to define a symbol table format, encode this information as a stream of bytes, and persist these bytes inside of the bytecode file itself, or in a separate file. Naturally, the Context structure would need an additional field to point to this symbolic metadata after the interpreter loads the information into memory. I would also have to construct an API that could read and query this symbolic information and then integrate this API into the getCommand() routine. Adding symbolic debugging features to the vm interpreter could easily double or triple the lines of code (and that's a conservative guess).

4.1.5 Kernel Debuggers

In the previous three sections, we looked at several different types of debuggers:

- A 16-bit debugger implemented as a user library

- A 32-bit debugger that manipulates a child process

- A debugger embedded inside an interpreter

In the case of the 16-bit debugger, the debugging code was implemented as a user library. DOS has no memory protection scheme, such that everything (including the kernel) runs in the same address space. In other words, everything runs in user mode (or, equivalently, everything runs in kernel mode). The underlying services supporting debugging are completely transparent. The 16-bit debugger code does not use the operating system as an agent; it does everything by itself.

In the case of the interpreter, you are in a situation similar to that of the 16-bit debugger. Everything runs in the same address space. There are no barriers between the debugging code and the main execution engine. In addition, all of the gory details of the runtime environment are spelled out completely via the interpreter's source code. The debugger can access anything that it needs to, and does not need to go through a third party.

In the case of the 32-bit debugger, the debugging code was implemented as a user application. The debugger runs in a designated region of memory outside of the kernel (i.e., in user mode). The program being debugged also runs in user mode, as a child process of the debugger. As such, the mechanics of debugging are both hidden and abstracted by the operating system. All that you know is that breakpoint instructions are somehow translated into system events that *magically* get funneled back to the debugger.

The Need for Kernel Debuggers

When an operating system institutes strict memory protection, a special type of debugger is needed to debug the kernel. You cannot use a conventional user-mode debugger because memory protection facilities (like segmentation and paging) prevent it from manipulating the kernel's image. Instead, what you need is a *kernel debugger.*

A kernel debugger is an odd creature that commandeers control of the processor so that the kernel can be examined via single stepping and breakpoints (see Figure 4-4). This means that the kernel debugger must somehow sidestep the native memory protection scheme by merging itself into the operating system's memory image. Some vendors perform this feat by designing their debuggers as device drivers, or loadable kernel modules.

Commercial operating systems like Windows often embed code to support kernel debugging within the kernel itself. For example, a special version of the Windows kernel known as the *checked build* (or *debug build*) contains extra validation code and a full complement of debug symbol information. This allows a checked kernel to be examined by a source-level debugger.

The code embedded in the operating system, which supports kernel debugging, typically allows the kernel debugger to exist on a separate machine. By placing the kernel debugger on a remote machine, it is insulated from whatever goes on inside of the kernel. If the kernel being observed crashes, then the kernel debugger can watch it happen from a safe distance.

The kernel being debugged runs on what is known as the *target machine.* The remote kernel debugger runs on what is known as the *host machine.* The two systems typically communicate via a bare-bones hardware-level protocol (i.e., a null modem connection). Anyone walking through the halls of a Microsoft campus would likely see several of these dual-computer setups (see Figure 4-5).

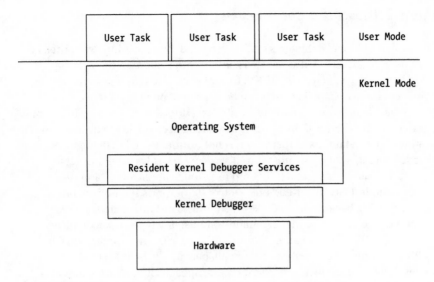

Figure 4-4. Kernel debugger subverts control of the processor

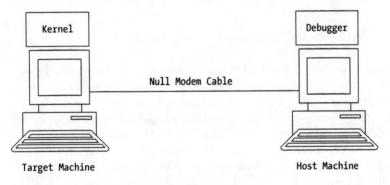

Figure 4-5. Remote debugging setup

NOTE *The RS-232 is a standard hardware-level protocol for serial data communication between Data Terminal Equipment (DTE) and Data Communication Equipment (DCE). In days of yore, the DTE was usually a dummy terminal and the DCE was a modem. In the case of kernel debugging, you're dealing with two DTE devices and so you need a special type of serial cable called a* null modem *that will fool each DTE into thinking that it is talking to a DCE.*

Kernel Debuggers for Windows

A number of kernel debuggers can be used to debug the Windows kernel. For instance, KD and WINDBG.EXE are two kernel debuggers that ship with the Windows Device Driver Kit (DDK).[3] Compuware also sells a powerful debugging tool named SoftICE, which can be used to debug the Windows kernel.[4]

KD is a command-line debugger (i.e., I386KD.EXE on Intel hardware) that is geared towards kernel debugging. It can debug user-mode applications, but it cannot set breakpoints in them, so it is not normally used to debug user-mode programs. KD is the most primitive of the three kernel debuggers. WINDBG.EXE can be used to debug both user-mode applications and the kernel. It has a modest GUI front-end and, unlike KD, supports symbolic debugging.

SoftICE is basically WINDBG.EXE on steroids. The SoftICE debugger is a source-level debugger that can handle almost any type of executable, including 16-bit DOS binaries, VxDs, and 32-bit Windows applications. In addition to supporting remote debugging over a TCP/IP link, SoftICE does a better job of tracking machine execution. Specifically, SoftICE can seamlessly follow the transition from user mode to kernel mode (and vice versa). This way, you can place a breakpoint in a Win32 program and monitor the path of execution as it makes its way in and out of the kernel.

4.1.6 Interface: Command Line vs. GUI

In case you haven't noticed, it's all about program state. Different debuggers offer different ways for a user to view the state of a running program. Some debuggers, like gdb, provide only a simple, but consistent, command-line interface. Other debuggers are integrated into slick GUI environments. To be honest, I lean towards the GUI debuggers because they are capable of presenting and accessing more machine state information at any given point in time. With a GUI debugger, you can easily monitor dozens of program elements simultaneously.

On the other hand, if you are developing an application that will be deployed on multiple platforms, it may be difficult to find a GUI IDE that runs on all of them. This is the great equalizer for command-line debuggers. The GNU debugger may not have a fancy interface, but it looks (and behaves) the same everywhere. Once you jump the initial learning curve, you can debug executables on any platform that gdb has been ported to.

---

3. http://www.microsoft.com/ddk/

4. http://www.compuware.com/products/driverstudio/ds/

4.2 Symbolic Debugger Extensions

My emphasis in the last section was on machine-level debuggers. Symbolic debuggers have a few extra twists and turns when it comes to using breakpoints and performing single-step execution. In this section, I will discuss both of these topics in more detail.

4.2.1 Dynamic Breakpoints

In the previous section, I used static breakpoint instructions that were manually inserted at compile time. An alternative to this approach is to dynamically insert breakpoints into a program's memory image at runtime. As you will see later on, this allows symbolic debuggers to single-step through a program at the source code level.

Unlike static breakpoints, which exist for the duration of a program's life cycle, symbolic debuggers usually work with dynamic breakpoints. The insertion, and removal, of dynamic breakpoints obeys the following scheme:

- The debugger identifies the first opcode of a statement.

- The debugger saves the opcode and replaces it with a breakpoint.

- The debugger digests the breakpoint and halts execution.

- The debugger restores the original opcode.

- The debugger leaves the opcode or swaps in another breakpoint.

For example, take the following statement in C:

```
total = total + value;
```

On the Intel hardware platform, this statement would translate into a series of three machine instructions.

```
00006   8b 45 f8    mov     eax, DWORD PTR _total$[ebp]
00009   03 45 fc    add     eax, DWORD PTR _value$[ebp]
0000c   89 45 f8    mov     DWORD PTR _total$[ebp], eax
```

To place a dynamic breakpoint on this statement, the debugger would take the first opcode (0x8B) and replace it with a breakpoint instruction (0xCC. When the debugger encounters this breakpoint, it will replace the breakpoint with the opcode and then execute the entire statement.

Once the statement has been executed, the debugger then has the option to swap back in the breakpoint or to leave the instruction alone. If the breakpoint was originally inserted via an explicit request by the user (i.e., break source.c:17), it will be reinserted. However, if the breakpoint was initially inserted to support single stepping, the breakpoint will *not* be reinserted.

4.2.2 Single Stepping

Single stepping in a machine-level debugger is simple: the processor simply executes the next machine instruction and returns program control to the debugger. For a symbolic debugger, this process is not as simple because a single statement in a high-level programming language typically translates into several machine-level instructions. You can't simply have the debugger execute a fixed number of machine instructions because high-level source code statements vary in terms of how many machine-level instructions they resolve to.

To single-step, a symbolic debugger has to use dynamic breakpoints. The nature of how dynamic breakpoints are inserted will depend upon the type of single stepping being performed. There are three different types of single stepping:

- Single stepping into (the next statement)

- Single stepping out of (a routine)

- Single stepping over (the next statement)

Stepping into Code

When a symbolic debugger *steps into* a source code statement, it scans the first few machine instructions to see if the statement is a function invocation. If the first opcode of the next instruction is not part of a function invocation, the debugger will simply save the opcode and replace it with a breakpoint. Otherwise, the debugger will determine where the function invocation jumps to, in memory, and replace the first opcode of the function's body with a breakpoint such that execution pauses after the function has been invoked (see Figure 4-6).

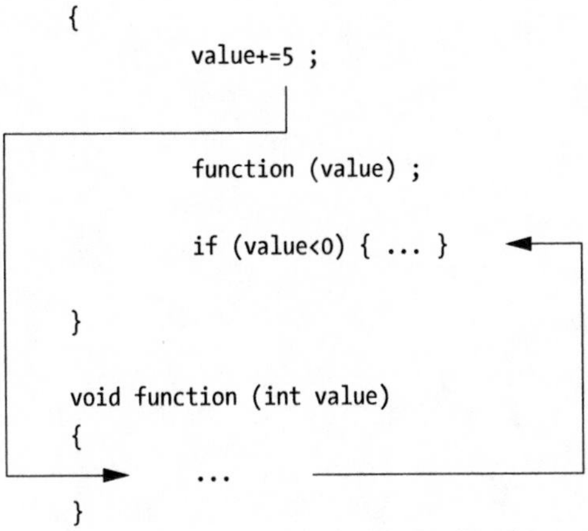

```
{
        value+=5 ;

        function (value) ;

        if (value<0) { ... }

}

void function (int value)
{
        ...
}
```

Figure 4-6. Stepping into and out of a function

Stepping out of Code

When a source-level debugger steps out of a routine, it looks through the routine's activation record for a return address. It then saves the opcode of the machine instruction at this return address and replaces it with a breakpoint. When program execution resumes, the routine will complete the rest of its statements and jump to its return address. The execution path will then hit the breakpoint, and program control will be given back to the debugger. The net effect is that you are able to force the debugger's attention out of a function and back to the code that invoked it.

Stepping over Code

When a source-level debugger steps over a statement, it queries the program's symbol table to determine the address range of the statement in memory (this is one scenario in which the symbol table *really* comes in handy). Once the debugger has determined where the statement ends, it saves the opcode of the first machine instruction following the statement and replaces it with a breakpoint. When execution resumes, the debugger will regain program control only after the path of execution has traversed the statement (see Figure 4-7).

```
{
        value+=5 ;

        function (value) ;

        if (value<0) { ... }
}
```

Figure 4-7. Stepping over a statement

4.3 Countertactics

Given enough time and effort, any program can be reverse engineered. The goal, then, is to make it as painful as possible for a malicious engineer to figure out how things work. In light of this, there are steps that you can take that will make it difficult for someone to peek at your program with a debugger. In this section, I will examine a few of these steps.

4.3.1 System Calls

Some operating systems provide a special call that will indicate if the current process is being executed under the auspices of a debugger. For example, the KERNEL32.DLL in Windows exports a function named IsDebuggerPresent(). You can wrap this call in an innocuous little routine like chk().

```c
#include<windows.h>
BOOL chk()
{
    typedef BOOL (*FunctionPointer)();
    BOOL returnValue;

    HINSTANCE handle;
    FunctionPointer functionPointer;

    handle = LoadLibrary("KERNEL32.DLL");
    if(handle==NULL){ return; }

    functionPointer =
    (FunctionPointer)GetProcAddress
    (
    handle,
    "IsDebuggerPresent"
    );
```

```
if(functionPointer==NULL){ return; }
returnValue = functionPointer();
FreeLibrary(handle);
return(returnValue);
}
```

The trick to this technique is to call chk() immediately. This will increase the likelihood that the code will get a chance to execute before the debugger encounters the first breakpoint.

```
void main(int argc, char *argv[])
{
    if(chk()){ useWierdConfiguration(); }     //call this before anything else
    ...
}
```

If a debugger is present, you can force the program to behave strangely, and send the person debugging your application on a wild-goose chase. Recall that I mentioned in Chapter 2 that debuggers are unique tools because they allow the user to observe a program from a neutral frame of reference. By inserted code like chk(), you are forcing the user into a warped quantum universe where the very act of observation influences the output of the program.

4.3.2 Remove Debug Information

One simple way to make debugging more expensive is to remove debugging information from your deliverable. This can be done by stripping debug information (with a tool like GNU's strip utility) or by setting your development tools to generate a release build.

Some business software companies prefer to strip debug information and accept the associated performance hit, because it allows sales engineers to perform an on-site diagnosis. When sales engineers make a house call, all that they need to do in order to take a look under the hood is insert the debug information and crank up a debugger.

The gcc compiler uses the -g option to insert debug information in the object code that it generates. If this option is not specified, then no symbol information will be included for debugging purposes.

```
gcc -o program  source.c
```

If you try and debug this with gdb, it will complain that it cannot find any debugging symbols. The absence of debugging symbols will make it very difficult to see what's going on in terms of anything but raw machine state.

```
C:\>gdb program.exe
 (no debugging symbols found)...
(gdb)
```

The Threat of Decompilers

The absence of debugging symbols will not stop everyone. Some decompilers out there can take machine code and recast it as high-level source code. The good news is that these tools tend to generate code that is difficult to read and use arbitrary naming conventions. In other words, the cure is almost as bad as the illness.

Take the following simple program:

```c
#include<stdio.h>
float average(float *array,int size)
{
    int i;
    float sum;
    for(i=0;i<size;i++){ sum+=array[i]; }
    return(sum/size);
}
void main()
{
    float array[]={ 1,2,3,4,5,6,7,8 };
    printf("average=%f\n",average(array,8));
    return;
}
```

I compiled this program with Visual Studio to create a PE binary named average.exe. Next, I fed average.exe to a decompiler named Rec[5] that was written by an Italian engineer named Giampiero Caprino. Rec took the raw binary and used it to produce reconstituted C code.

```
C:\> rec average.exe
Reading prototype files...
warning: addtype: complex int redefined
average.exe is an NT executable of 0x18800 (100352) bytes
Image base : 0x00400000,  Entry point : 0x00001210
0x00001000 - 0x00012400  ( 70656) .text
0x00013000 - 0x00014400  (  5120) .rdata
0x00015000 - 0x00019200  ( 16896) .data
0x0001b000 - 0x0001b800  (  2048) .idata
0x0001c000 - 0x0001ce00  (  3584) .reloc
```

---

5.   http://www.backerstreet.com/rec/rec.htm

```
Validating strings...
Finding references...
Finding procedures...
Done.
Decompiling 0041237e - 004123ff (1/323)
Left 1168 assembly statements, 7 assembly nodes
Translation complete - 8802 translated statements in 0 sec.
```

The source file that this decompiler produced, average.rec, was a 14,149-line monster C program that I wouldn't wish on my worst enemy. In fact, I might even venture to say that the C code is even less legible than pure assembly code.

Here's a snippet of the reverse-engineered C code so you can see what I'm talking about:

```
/*--using old K&R C function declaration--*/
L00401380(A8)
void  A8;
{
    if(*L00419028 != 2)
    {
        L00404E60();
    }
    L00404EB0(A8);
    return(*L00415a54(255));
}
```

4.3.3 Code Salting

If memory footprint is not a big issue, and you don't mind a slight perfor-mance hit, one way to foil a debugger is to periodically salt your code with unnecessary statements. This will make it easy for someone trying to reverse engineer your code to become lost among the trees and lose sight of the for-est, so to speak.

For example, take the simple program that I presented in the previous section. It would be possible to salt and obfuscate the average() routine to the extent that it would be almost unrecognizable:

```
 float l1(float *l2, int l3)
{
    int l4;
    float l5;
    float l8;
    int l7;
    goto l6;
    if(l3==0){ l5=l2[0]+5; }
```

```
16:
for(14=0,17=0;14<13;14++)
{
    15+=12[14];
    goto 111;
    112:
    goto 113;
    111:
    18=12[17];
    17++;
    goto 112;
    113:
    18++;
}
18 = (15+(17^17))/13;
return(18);
}
```

Even if you shipped this program with debug symbols intact, it would be difficult to figure out what was happening (particularly if you believed that each statement had a legitimate purpose).

4.3.4 Mixed Memory Models

There are robust debuggers, like SoftICE, that can gracefully make the jump between user mode and kernel mode. However, not many debuggers can make the jump between two different memory models. Windows in particular is guilty of allowing this kind of abomination to occur. On Windows, this phenomenon is generally known as *thunking,* and it allows 16-bit code and 32-bit code to fraternize.

The three types of thunking on Windows are described in Table 4-6.

Table 4-6. Thunking Techniques

Thunk	Platform	Use
Generic	Windows NT/2000/XP	A 16-bit program invokes code in a 32-bit DLL.
Flat	Windows 95/98/ME	16-bit and 32-bit DLLs call each other's functions.
Universal	Windows 3.1	A 16-bit program invokes code in a 32-bit Win32s DLL.

Universal thunking is of little use, seeing as how Windows 3.1 is, for all intents and purposes, an extinct operating system. In case you're wondering, in the early 1990s Win32s was a special extension package that allowed 32-bit applications to run on Windows 3.1 and Windows 3.11. It was often bundled with development tools. Back in 1995, the Borland 4.5 C++ compiler had an install option for Win32s.

With the advent of Windows XP, the Windows 95/98/ME bloodline met its end. Like universal thunking, planned obsolescence has relegated flat thunking to the garbage heap. This is probably a good thing, seeing as how flat thunking was such a complicated procedure. To give you an idea of what was involved, here are the basic steps involved in building a flat thunking bridge:

1. Write a thunk script.

2. Compile the script with thunk.exe to produce assembly code.

3. Assemble the generated code twice (i.e., 16-bit, 32-bit object code).

4. Create a 16-bit DLL and link it with the 16-bit .OBJ file.

5. Create a 32-bit DLL and link it with the 32-bit .OBJ file.

Generic thunking is facilitated entirely by an API. There are Win32 functions like the following:

- LoadLibraryEx32W()

- CallProc32W()

- FreeLibrary32W()

These functions are declared in WOWNT16.H. They allow 16-bit code to load and invoke a 32-bit Win32 DLL. Because this mechanism is API driven, most of the internal operation is hidden from view. Windows XP currently supports this approach.

4.4 Summary

A debugger is a tool for examining the state of a running program from a neutral frame of reference. There are two basic types of debuggers, which are distinguished based on how they describe the state of a program:

- Machine-level debugger

- Symbolic debugger

A machine debugger views a program in terms of its raw machine state. Raw machine state consists of

- The contents of the processor's registers

- The contents of program memory

A symbolic debugger views a program in terms of high-level constructs like routines and variables, such that the program's state is defined by the values stored in its variables.

A symbolic debugger relies heavily on the presence of a symbol table, which maps program constructs to locations in memory. Debug symbol information is inserted by the compiler and then arranged into its final form by the linker. Many different executable file formats exist (e.g., ELF, COFF, PE), and each one has its own way of storing debug symbol information.

A kernel debugger is a special type of debugger that can be used to examine the native operating system. Kernel debuggers are usually implemented as device drivers, or loadable kernel modules, so that they can access the kernel's memory image. There are both machine-level kernel debuggers and symbolic kernel debuggers.

You have a number of ways to implement a debugger. The approach used depends both upon the nature of the runtime environment and the type of program that you want to debug (see Table 4-7).

Table 4-7. Techniques for Building a Debugger

Implementation	Runtime	Type of Executable
System call API	Protected-mode memory	User application
Device driver interface	Protected-mode memory	Operating system kernel
Custom extensions	Interpreter	User application

Regardless of the type of debugger that you are working with, all debuggers rely on the same basic mechanisms to analyze the state of a running program:

- Breakpoints

- Single stepping

Breakpoints suspend the normal flow of execution and yield program control to the debugger. Breakpoints can be placed statically in a program, at compile time, or inserted (and removed) dynamically by the debugger.

Breakpoints are typically implemented as a special opcode. On the Intel Pentium, breakpoints are realized as an interrupt instruction. In the case of DOS, service routines that handle this interrupt can be explicitly registered in the interrupt vector table. In the case of Windows, the mechanism for handling breakpoints is a proprietary black box (although you might be able to find out the truth by doing some disassembly with a kernel debugger).

Single stepping allows a debugger to execute a program's statements one at a time. Machine-level debuggers single-step by executing a single machine instruction and then returning program control to the debugger. Single stepping for symbolic debuggers is a little more involved because a single high-level source code statement can translate into a varying number of machine instructions. Symbolic debuggers use debug symbol information, dynamic breakpoints, and limited code scanning to single-step through high-level source code.

CHAPTER 5

Optimization: Memory Footprint

Premature optimization is the root of all evil in programming.

—Donald Knuth, *Literate Programming*

Inside every fat person is a thin person screaming to get out.

—Richard Simmons

Too much is always better than not enough.

—J. R. "Bob" Dobbs, 1961 speech in San Francisco

In the beginning of the book, I stated that two prototypical tribulations beset the maintenance engineer:

- Repairing bugs

- Improving program performance

The previous four chapters have been devoted to the first problem. This chapter, and the next, will be devoted to the second problem.

A computer program has two basic resources at its disposal:

- Processor time (i.e., CPU cycles)

- Memory

This is how it has been since the beginning of time (i.e., 1941).[1] A high-performance program will use both of these resources sparingly. In other words, it will be as small, and as fast, as possible. The art of taking an application and making it more efficient is known as *optimization*. When it comes to optimizing a program, Donald Knuth is correct: the worst thing that you can do is blindly optimize your code as you implement it. *Premature optimization is akin to making a pact with Lucifer.* Sure, you'll get what you want . . . but only by paying a terrible price. This is because optimization introduces bugaboos like complexity and context-sensitive restrictions. These bugaboos can undermine the long-term integrity of a program by making it brittle and resistant to change.

Before you make a pass at optimization, you should

- Fully test and debug your code.

- Profile your code to identify bottlenecks.

- Use a better algorithm as an alternative to optimizing.

Before you start trying to ramp up execution speed, it's a good idea to verify that you have an operational version of your program. This way, if your attempts at optimizing are unsuccessful, you still have a properly functioning build that you can fall back on. Think of this practice as an insurance policy.

Once you have a stable build, you should take the time to design a barrage of stress tests. You can use these tests to profile your application and locate performance bottlenecks. The motivation behind this is to minimize the number of locations in the source code that you optimize. If you optimized everything, your source code would disintegrate into an unholy mess. By using a profiler, you narrow down the list of suspected offenders so that you have half a chance of keeping your code readable.

In the late 1800s, an Italian economist named Vilfredo Pareto originally stated the *Pareto Principle*, otherwise known as the *80:20 rule*.[2] Pareto discovered that roughly 80 percent of the wealth in Italy was owned by 20 percent of

---

1.   In 1941, Konrad Zuse built the Z3, the first program-controlled electromechanical digital computer.

2.   Luigino Bruni, *Vilfredo Pareto and the Birth of Modern Microeconomics* (Edward Elgar, 2002. ISBN: 1-840-64532-6)

the population. The 80:20 rule has since been adopted in computer science. In computer science, the 80:20 rule says that 80 percent of the CPU's time is consumed by 20 percent of a program's source code. This is why profiling is so important; you want to identify the 20 percent of your code that is eating up processor time and focus on that. Optimizing the other 80 percent is a waste of time.

Finally, if you have a bottleneck in your crosshairs, before you pull the trigger and do something that you might regret later, try using a better algorithm. It doesn't matter how much you optimize a bubble sort routine, it will always be slower than an implementation of quick sort. If your binary search trees are unbalanced, then use a 2-3 tree or a red-black tree. If your stack is being overrun, then pass arguments by reference instead of by value. Always look for an algorithmic solution before you break out the dangerous weaponry.

> **NOTE** *I suddenly know how my father felt when he bought me a pellet gun for my 13th birthday. He warned me to be careful with it and not to point it at anyone. However, I also think he knew that I would be sorely tempted to abuse my privileges. Nevertheless, he let me have a pellet gun because he probably thought that it would teach me (one way or another) about the trade-offs between freedom and responsibility. In the same spirit, I can strongly advise you to consider using a better algorithm; but in the end, it's your decision. Some of the optimization techniques that I discuss are a little extreme. So don't come crying to me if you can't read your own code two weeks later . . . I warned you.*

Now that I've issued this perfunctory warning, let's break out the pellets and start shooting.

5.1 Forgotten History

In the early days, memory was a precious commodity. For example, Control Data's model 6600 computer had roughly 476 kilobytes of core memory (i.e., 65,000 60-bit words). The CDC 6600 was released in 1964 and sold for around $7 million. When the CDC 7600 was released in 1971, it was five times as fast as the 6600. The engineers who wrote software for the 7600 were blown away. The emotional response of seeing this type of performance jump was much stronger than the logical response ("WOW" versus "I say, good show.").

The problem is that this emotional response obscures the logical one, and people forget to push as hard as they can in areas like performance. There were engineering teams at Control Data working on the 7600 that failed to meet their performance benchmarks. The team leads said, "Well, we thought that the processor would be so fast that we wouldn't have to optimize."

Back in 1983, I used to go to work with my father on Saturday so that I could sneak some time in on his IBM 8088 PC. Once you took all the BIOS code into account, the 8088 had 640 kilobytes of usable memory. It also had a clock speed of 5 megahertz. Fast forward to 2003. Anyone with a few hundred dollars can walk into a computer store and walk out with a gigabyte of memory. Processors now have a transistor design rule on the order of 0.10 microns and clock speeds up in the gigahertz range (see Table 5-1). With the advent of Intel physical address extensions, Pentium Pro processors (and later) can expand their address space to 64 gigabytes.

Table 5-1. The Evolution of the Intel Desktop Processor

Processor	Year	Design Rule	Clock Speed	Address Space
8088	1979	3 micron	5 MHz	1MB
80186	1982	3 micron	10 MHz	1MB
80286	1982	1.5 micron	6 MHz	16MB
80386	1985	1.5 micron	16 MHz	4GB
80486	1989	0.8 micron	25 MHz	4GB
Pentium (80586)	1993	0.8 micron	60 MHz	4GB
Pentium II	1997	0.35 micron	233 MHz	4GB\64GB
Pentium III	1999	0.25 micron	450 MHz	4GB\64GB
Pentium IV	2000	0.18 micron	1.4 GHz	4GB\64GB

These kinds of advances have lulled the current generation of software engineers into complacency. Back in the 1960s, your program may have had only 16 kilobytes of memory, and you had to work diligently in order to keep from running out of space. Three decades later, during the 1990s, none of the engineers that I worked with even gave it a second thought. In fact, if a program ran out of memory, the immediate solution was to go out and buy more. "Dude, 64 megabytes isn't going to do it, maybe we should see how it works with 128."

Planned Obsolescence

In 1996, I worked for an insurance company in Cleveland that was in the process of rolling out Windows 95. The CIO had a 166 MHz Pentium, which at the time was a sweet ride (particularly when everyone else had 33 MHz 80486 machines). One day I visited the CIO, George Mazelis, in his corner office and watched, with subdued amusement, as his machine buzzed under the strain of running Windows 95. He looked up at me and said, "Oh brother, this OS is a *dog*."

By 1996 standards, he was right. Windows 95 was as slow as tar. I suppose that the engineers at Microsoft were not that concerned. They knew that, in a year or two, hardware would be available (to normal mortals) that would be able to run Windows 95. If Reverend Bill and his 33 MHz clunker couldn't handle the load, then all the better because it meant that he would be forced to shell out his hard-earned cash for a new computer. From the perspective of Intel executives, the memory and processor requirements of Windows 95 was good for business!

The underlying assumption seems to be that you can pack as much as you want into memory and Gordon Moore's rule of thumb will take care of everything else. I hate this attitude. I hate it because if effectively lowers the bar. There are strategies and tactics that exist that can be used to make efficient use of memory. Programmers worth their salt will take enough pride in their work to use them.

5.2 Program Layout in Memory

Running programs are organized as blocks of memory called *segments*. Segmentation can be physical, in that the processor enforces it. Or segmentation can be logical, such that the processor will not forbid a program from performing unregulated manipulation of its own memory image. Every production operating system in existence today (i.e., Windows, Linux, Solaris, HP-UX, AIX, IRIX, and z/OS) implements physical segmentation.

Table 5-2 lists the four types of program segments.

Table 5-2. Memory Segment Types

Segment	Use	Life Span
Code segment	Instructions	Long term
Data segment	Global variables	Long term
Stack	Local variables, routine parameters	Short term
Heap	Dynamic storage	Varies

All programs can be decomposed into two fundamental ingredients:

- Instructions

- Storage

Instructions are always placed in the code segment. The data segment, stack, and heap are all used for different types of storage. The data segment, stack, and heap are distinguished by how their storage is allocated and their life span during execution.

The type of segments that a program uses and their arrangement in memory depends upon the tools used to develop the program, in addition to the requirements instituted by the native operating system (see Figure 5-1).

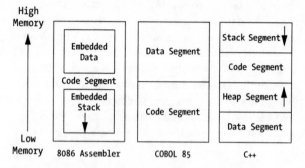

Figure 5-1. Different segmentation schemes

NOTE *The arrows in Figure 5-1 are meant to indicate that the stack allocates storage starting from a high address and then moves downwards, towards low memory. The heap, on the other hand, starts at a low address and allocates storage moving upwards towards higher memory. The arrangement of the segments in this figure is also somewhat arbitrary. Specifically, the exact location of the different segments, relative to each other, is typically determined by the host operating system. One operating system may place the data segment above the code segment, and another operating system may place the data segment below the code segment.*

5.2.1 Scenario: A Single Segment

You can use Microsoft's MASM assembler to create programs in DOS that consist of a single code segment. Such single-segment programs obey what is known as the *tiny memory model*.

In tiny memory model programs, static data must be embedded within the code segment. Tiny memory model programs also have a stack segment, but the stack segment uses the same region of memory as the code segment. In other words, the stack pointer is placed somewhere in the code segment with the guarded expectation that it will not run into any instructions.

Here is an example of a tiny memory model x86 program:

```
;single.asm-----------------------------------
.386
codeSegment SEGMENT USE16
ASSUME CS:codeSegment, DS:codeSegment, SS:codeSegment, ES:codeSegment
ORG 100H
;instructions--------------------------------
startHere:
PUSH DS
MOV AH,0H
PUSH AX

MOV [stackAddress],SP
MOV SP,OFFSET newStack

MOV AX,OFFSET message1
PUSH AX
CALL printMessage

MOV AX,OFFSET message2
PUSH AX
CALL printMessage

MOV SP,[stackAddress]
RETF

;embedded storage----------------------------
stackAddress      DW?
message1          DB "Hey Moe! Hey Larry! "
terminate1        DB '$'
message2          DB "woo-woo-woo"
terminate2        DB '$'

;embedded stack------------------------------
stackStorage      DB 31 dup ('01')
newStack          DB 01H

;more instructions---------------------------
printMessage:
PUSH BP
MOV  BP,SP
MOV  AH,09H
MOV  DX,[BP+4]
INT 21H
POP BP
RET
codeSegment ENDS
END startHere
```

In the previous assembly code, both global variables (message1 and message2) and a stack (newStack) exist. The stack was actually defined in two parts (stackStorage and newStack) so that the top of the stack could be referenced by name. Both the data and the stack have been placed smack in the middle of the code segment. Strictly speaking, they are both part of the code segment; it's just that the processor doesn't get the chance to execute them because it hits a RETF instruction.

Here is the build command:

```
C:\> ML /AT single.asm
```

When you run this application, the following message is printed to the screen:

```
C:\>single.com
Hey Moe! Hey Larry! woo-woo-woo
```

5.2.2 Scenario: Code and Data Segments Only

COBOL 85 programs are composed exclusively of global data and global routines, such that every operation can be performed within the confines of a code segment and data segment.

Take a look at the following classic COBOL application:

```
000010 @OPTIONS MAIN
000013 IDENTIFICATION DIVISION.
000020 PROGRAM-ID. COBOLPROGRAM.
000021*-------------------------------------------------------
000022 ENVIRONMENT DIVISION.
000023 CONFIGURATION SECTION.
000026 INPUT-OUTPUT SECTION.
000027*-------------------------------------------------------
000028 DATA DIVISION.
000029 WORKING-STORAGE SECTION.
000030 01 REVENUE   PIC 9(3)v99   VALUE 000.00.
000031 01 CHARGES   PIC 9(3)v99   VALUE 000.00.
000032 01 BALANCE   PIC S9(3)v99  VALUE 000.00.
000033 01 CRT-VAL   PIC ZZZ.ZZ.
000034*-------------------------------------------------------
000035 PROCEDURE DIVISION.
000036 MAIN-CODE SECTION.
000037 MAIN.
000038 MOVE 70.00 TO REVENUE.
000039 MOVE 40.50 TO CHARGES.
```

```
000040 PERFORM COMPUTE-BALANCE.
000050 STOP RUN.
000060 SUBROUTINE SECTION.
000070 COMPUTE-BALANCE.
000080 MOVE REVENUE TO BALANCE.
000090 SUBTRACT CHARGES FROM BALANCE.
000091 MOVE BALANCE TO CRT-VAL.
000100 DISPLAY  " BALANCE: " CRT-VAL.
```

The previous program prints out the following:

```
BALANCE:  29.50
```

The working storage section of the program defines four global variables (REVENUE, CHARGES, BALANCE, and CRT-VALUE). The procedure division consists of two global routines (MAIN and COMPUTE-BALANCE). There are no local variables and no dynamically allocated variables. Hence, there is no need for a stack segment or a heap segment.

5.2.3 Scenario: All Four Segment Types

C compilers, like the one that ships with Visual Studio, can construct programs that use all four types of segments. Consider the following program that prints out the binary equivalents of two integers:

```c
/* allSegments.c-------------------------------------------------*/
#include<stdio.h>
#include<stdlib.h>
unsigned long var;
void printBinary(unsigned long *pointerArg)
{
    unsigned long mask;
    int bitSize;
    int i;

    if(pointer==NULL){ pointerArg = &var; }

    mask = 1;
    bitSize = sizeof(var)*8;
    for(i=0;i<bitSize;i++)
    {
        if(mask&(*pointerArg)){ printf("1"); }
        else{ printf("0"); }
        mask*=2;
    }
}
```

```
    printf("\n");
    return;
}/*end printBinary---------------------------------------------*/
void main()
{
    unsigned long *pointer;
    pointer = (unsigned long*)malloc(sizeof(unsigned long));
    var = 0xFF00FF00;
    *pointer=0xFFFF0000;
    printBinary(NULL);
    printBinary(pointer);
    free(pointer);
    return;
}
```

This program can be broken down and its different parts classified according to the memory segment to which they belong (see Table 5-3).

Table 5-3. Segment Occupants in `allSegments.c`

Segment	Program Elements
Code segment	The instructions in the bodies of `main()` and `printBinary()`
Data segment	`var`
Stack	`pointer`, `pointerArg`, `mask`, `bitSize`, `i`

This program has all the colors of the memory segment rainbow. Unlike the previous two programs, the routines in `allSegments.c` define local variables, and the `printBinary()` routine has an input parameter. Local variables and routine parameters are both facilitated by using the stack (I will discuss how this is done in Section 5.5 later in the chapter). In addition, the heap is also used because you dynamically allocate an integer in `main()` via a call to `malloc()`.

5.3 Code Segment

One way to make efficient use of memory is to minimize the size of a program's code segment. A program's instructions are placed in its code segment. Hence, to minimize the size of a code segment, you must limit the number of instructions therein. This section examines a few techniques that can be used towards this end.

5.3.1 Cut-and-Paste Programming

To an engineer pressured by a deadline, cut-and-paste programming may seem like a good idea. It's a quick way to leverage the code you've already written to build something slightly different. I know analysts at an ERP company who, when they wanted to build a new display screen for a given program, would just gut the 4GL code of an existing screen and copy it over into a new source file. In the short term, perhaps this offers return on investment.

In the long term, however, not only does it hurt maintainability, but it also leads to bloated code. If an error crops up in a snippet of cut-and-paste code, that error will exist in multiple places instead of just one place. Consider the following source code, which edits the fields of an employee database record:

```
/* CutAndPaste.c---------------------------------------------------*/
#include<stdio.h>
#include<string.h>
#include<ctype.h>
#define BOOLEAN     int
#define TRUE        1==1
#define FALSE       !TRUE
#define CODE_SIZE   4
BOOLEAN editEmployeeRecord
(
    char *companyID,    //[letter][letter][letter][letter]
    char *employeeID,   //[digit][digit][digit][digit]
    char *division,     //[letter][letter][letter][letter]
    char *project       //[letter][letter][letter][letter]
)
{
    int i;

    if(companyID==NULL){ return(FALSE); }
    if(strlen(companyID)>CODE_SIZE){ return(FALSE); }
    for(i=0;i<CODE_SIZE;i++)
    {
        if(!isalpha(companyID[i])){ return(FALSE); }
    }

    if(employeeID==NULL){ return(FALSE); }
    if(strlen(employeeID)>CODE_SIZE){ return(FALSE); }
    for(i=0;i<CODE_SIZE;i++)
    {
        if(!isdigit(employeeID[i])){ return(FALSE); }
    }
```

```
    if(division==NULL){ return(FALSE); }
    if(strlen(division)>CODE_SIZE){ return(FALSE); }
    for(i=0;i<CODE_SIZE;i++)
    {
        if(!isalpha(division[i])){ return(FALSE); }
    }

    if(project==NULL){ return(FALSE); }
    if(strlen(project)>CODE_SIZE){ return(FALSE); }
    for(i=0;i<CODE_SIZE;i++)
    {
        if(!isalpha(project[i])){ return(FALSE); }
    }
    return(TRUE);
}
```

As you can see, many of the steps needed to edit these fields can be consolidated. The engineer who wrote this code might have been too lazy to take the mental effort to do so. Or, even worse, perhaps they thought that if they wrote more lines of code, they would look more productive (some pointy-haired managers use ridiculous metrics like this).

The best way to deal with cut-and-paste programming is to refactor your code so that each logical operation is performed in one place, and one place only. Let's take the previous source code and recast it so that things are less redundant:

```
/* CutAndPaste.c-------------------------------------------------*/
#include<stdio.h>
#include<string.h>
#include<ctype.h>
#define BOOLEAN         int
#define TRUE            1==1
#define FALSE           !TRUE
#define FIELD_ALPHA     1
#define FIELD_DIGIT     2
#define CODE_SIZE       4
BOOLEAN isFieldOK(char *field, int type)
{
    int i;

    if((field==NULL)||(strlen(field)>CODE_SIZE))
    {
        return(FALSE);
    }
```

```
    switch(type)
    {
        case FIELD_ALPHA:
        {
            for(i=0;i<CODE_SIZE;i++)
            {
                if(!isalpha(field[i])){ return(FALSE); }
            }
        }break;
        case FIELD_DIGIT:
        {
            for(i=0;i<CODE_SIZE;i++)
            {
                if(!isdigit(field[i])){ return(FALSE); }
            }
        }break;
        default:{ return(FALSE); }
    }
    return(TRUE);
}/*end isFieldOK -----------------------------------------------*/
BOOLEAN editEmployeeRecord
(
    char *companyID,   //[letter][letter][letter][letter]
    char *employeeID,  //[digit][digit][digit][digit]
    char *division,    //[letter][letter][letter][letter]
    char *project      //[letter][letter][letter][letter]
)
{
    if
    (
        isFieldOK(companyID,FIELD_ALPHA)&&
        isFieldOK(employeeID,FIELD_DIGIT)&&
        isFieldOK(division,FIELD_ALPHA)&&
        isFieldOK(project,FIELD_ALPHA)
    )
    {
        return(TRUE);
    }
    return(FALSE);
}/*end editEmployeeRecord-------------------------------------*/
```

Checking a field via a cut-and-paste statement uses up 140 bytes of code segment memory per check (on a Pentium IV).

```
//140 bytes per shot
if(employeeID==NULL){ return(FALSE); }
if(strlen(employeeID)>CODE_SIZE){ return(FALSE); }
for(i=0;i<CODE_SIZE;i++)
```

227

```
{
    if(!isdigit(employeeID[i])){ return(FALSE); }
}
```

A call to the consolidated isFieldOK() code uses only 11 bytes, which translates into a few lines of assembly code.

```
; isFieldOK(companyID,FIELD_ALPHA);
push    1
mov     eax, DWORD PTR _companyID$[ebp]
push    eax
call    isFieldOK
```

This might not seem like much, but when you consider that a typical business application suite may end up editing several hundred different fields, the memory savings can add up.

5.3.2 Macros

Traditionally, macro operations have been used to speed up an application, the motivation being that if you can prevent the execution path from jumping around, the processor can stay in its cache longer and avoid the overhead of making a jump. A processor can execute a stream of sequential instructions faster than code that makes frequent jumps.

If you're an engineer developing software that will be deployed on a mainframe with 64 gigabytes of primary memory, one way to speed up an application is to replace every function with a macro such that every operation is effectively expanded inline. I have spoken with engineers who worked at Cray Research who took this very approach.

> **NOTE** *Some compilers provide an option so that function invocations will be expanded inline. For example, the* gcc *compiler has the* -finline-functions *option that will expand all simple functions inline. The compiler uses a heuristic algorithm to decide which functions are "simple."*

Now let's look at the other end of the spectrum: embedded software. Embedded programs exist in a world that has a very limited amount of memory. If an embedded application runs out of storage, it has nowhere to go. Desktop and server operating systems have a disk drive, which the operating system can dip into if it wants to artificially expand its address space. Embedded systems do not have access to disk storage. An embedded system may have 512 kilobytes of memory, and that's it.

Engineers who develop embedded software will jump through all sorts of hoops to ensure that a program has no redundant instructions. Typically, this means favoring functions over macros such that size is minimized at the expense of speed. An embedded program may have a small footprint, but it will also spend much of its time jumping around memory.

Consider the following source code:

```c
#include<stdio.h>
#define BOOLEAN         int
#define TRUE            1==1
#define FALSE           !TRUE
#define R0              0
#define R1              1
#define R2              2
#define R3              3
#define R4              4
#define R5              5
#define isRegister(reg)         ((reg>-1)&&(reg<(R5+1)))?TRUE:FALSE
BOOLEAN isValidRegister(int reg)
{
    return(((reg>-1)&&(reg<(R5+1)))?TRUE:FALSE);
}
void main()
{
    isValidRegister(R0);
    isRegister(R0);
}
```

The previous code uses two different mechanisms to check register macros (i.e., R0, R1 . . . R5). Invoking the isValidRegister() function requires 10 bytes of memory on a Pentium processor.

```
; isValidRegister(R0);
push    0
call    isValidRegister
add     esp, 4
```

The problem with this approach is that the processor has to spend time managing a stack frame and then jumping to the body of the function. The macro, when referenced in code, translates into 28 bytes of serial code.

```
; isRegister(R0);
cmp     DWORD PTR _reg$[ebp], -1
jle     SHORT $L149
cmp     DWORD PTR _reg$[ebp], 6
jge     SHORT $L149
mov     DWORD PTR -8+[ebp], 1
```

```
jmp      SHORT $L150
$L149:
mov      DWORD PTR -8+[ebp], 0
$L150:
```

Using the macro costs over twice as much, in terms of memory, as invoking the function. The moral of the story is this: if you use macros to speed up your programs, you should be aware of the memory-related expenses that they incur.

5.3.3 Dead Code

Of all the techniques you can use to shrink a program's code segment, removing dead code from your source tree offers the quickest return on investment. Dead code consists of operations that are never executed by program control. Dead code usually creeps into a code base that is subject to frequent, and sometimes dramatic, changes by people who are not familiar with it. The mindset of such people is "Uh, I don't know what this does and I'm too scared to mess with it. My code doesn't depend on it, and things seem to work, so I'll just leave it alone."

This mindset can cause megabytes of memory to be wasted. I worked at an online bank were the build cycle included 4,000 different source code files. The problem was nobody knew which files were being used and which files were dead. It compiled, and it worked, so people just kept checking in new files without removing the old ones. Over ten years, no one worked up the requisite courage to prune the source tree. It has grown into an intertwined morass of ASCII text that has resisted three separate house-cleaning attempts.

Dead code is one consequence of the Lava Flow antipattern.[3] The Lava Flow antipattern occurs in code that has been frequently altered, without proper documentation, to provide extensions for fashionable technologies that come and go. (How many of you remember Microsoft's OLE2 framework, or Borland's Owl Windows API?) Lava Flow code tends to stick around, "just in case." By the time that the technology has been pushed onto the trash heap by the latest, greatest thing, the engineers who implemented it are gone, and the new engineers are too scared to touch it because nothing is documented and the existing program works properly.

---

3.   http://www.antipatterns.com/lavaflow.htm

5.4 Data Segment

Another way to make efficient use of memory is to minimize the size of a program's data segment. The data segment is used to provide storage space for global variables. Hence, to minimize the size of a data segment, you must limit the proliferation of global data. This section examines a few techniques that can be used towards this end.

5.4.1 Dual-Use Data Structures

In military parlance, a dual-use technology is one that can be used not only for normal manufacturing purposes, but also for military purposes. For example, in November 2002, a German inventor named Frank Behlke sold a batch of 44 high-voltage switches (valued at $70,000) to businessmen who had ties to Iran. The switches can be used to break up kidney stones, or to initiate a nuclear explosion.[4]

Even computers are considered to be a dual-use technology. In January 2003, Silicon Graphics pleaded guilty to selling a million dollars worth of supercomputer equipment to a Russian nuclear laboratory in 1996.

There are dual-use data structures in C. In other words, C has data structures that can be used for unrelated activities. By using dual-use data structures, you allow your code to do more with less.

Pointers

Take a look at the following global variable definitions:

```
char    *charPointer;
short   *shortPointer;
int     *intPointer;
long    *longPointer;
float   *floatPointer;
double  *doublePointer;
```

On Windows, these global variables consume 24 bytes of storage in the data segment (the compiler allocates a double word for each pointer variable). Depending on how these variables are used in the program, you might be able to get away with replacing these six variables with a single global variable.

---

4. David Crawford, "How Hunch May Have Hindered the Nuclear Ambitions of Iran," *The Wall Street Journal*, May 6, 2003

```
void        *voidPointer;
```

This could save up to 20 bytes of storage space. Regardless of the data type pointed to, the address used to point to an area of storage is always the same size. This allows you to write a statement like this one:

```
double pi = 3.14159265358979323846264433832795;
voidPointer = (void*)&pi;
printf("%e",*((double*)voidPointer));
```

If you don't mind using just-in-time casting, you can get away with using void pointers for a lot of different operations without having to worry about what you're pointing to.

Naturally, there is a downside. For example, the following code will cause most compilers to emit an error message:

```
if(voidPointer[0] == voidPointer[1])
{
        //do something
}
```

The void type does not have a data type size associated with it. This means array-like references to actual values are meaningless because there is no way to determine the actual offset address of a particular void array element.

Some engineers may be just a little dismayed by my recommendations. I admit, reusing a pointer variable to store the address of different data types is a potentially dangerous tactic. In light of this, recycling pointers should be used only in situations where you are absolutely desperate to conserve every single byte of memory.

Unions

A *union* is a type of data structure that has fallen into disuse since the days of 16-kilobyte memory cores. A union definition allocates a block of memory that can be treated like several different data structures. The compiler facilitates this by allocating just enough memory for the largest data structure. This saves space by allowing you to give a chunk of storage multiple personalities.

For example, consider the following declarations. You declare two structures, and then declare a union that can act like either of the two structures.

```
struct Employee
{
    char *name;   //4 bytes
    char *ID;     //4 bytes
};
```

```
struct Message
{
    int type;         //4 bytes
    int queueIndex;   //4 bytes
    char *payLoad;    //4 bytes
};
union DualUse
{
    struct Employee employee;
    struct Message message;
};
```

If you define a global variable of type DualUse as follows:

```
union DualUse dualUse;
```

the compiler will allocate 12 bytes of storage for the union because the larger of the two structures, Message, requires 12 bytes. For example, the Visual Studio compiler emits the following assembly code to represent this global variable:

```
DATA      SEGMENT
COMM      dualUse:BYTE:0cH
DATA      ENDS
```

These 12 bytes of storage can be used to store a Message structure variable or an Employee structure variable (see Figure 5-2).

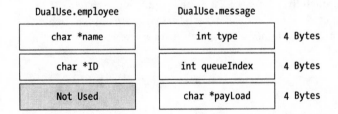

Figure 5-2. The dualUse *global variable has split personalities*

By including union variables, you have the option of using one block of memory for different purposes. This can save you storage space.

5.4.2 Bit Fields

One convention used in C is to define a BOOLEAN type and then use this new type to represent Boolean flags.

```
#define BOOLEAN unsigned char
BOOLEAN flag1;
BOOLEAN flag2;
BOOLEAN flag3;
BOOLEAN flag4;
BOOLEAN flag5;
BOOLEAN flag6;
BOOLEAN flag7;
BOOLEAN flag8;
```

These definitions take up 8 bytes of memory. By using bit fields, you could compress all 8 bytes into a single byte.

```
struct Flags
{
    BOOLEAN flag1:1; //1 bit
    BOOLEAN flag2:1;
    BOOLEAN flag3:1;
    BOOLEAN flag4:1;
    BOOLEAN flag5:1;
    BOOLEAN flag6:1;
    BOOLEAN flag7:1;
    BOOLEAN flag8:1;
};
struct Flags flags; //takes up 1 byte ( 8 bits == 8 flags )
```

A bit field is a type of structure field in which you can specify the number of bits used. In terms of memory consumption, this is a dramatic improvement over the approach that defines a separate variable for each flag.

In order to set or clear the value of a bit field, masks are applied behind the scenes to the structure variable. For example, the statement

```
flags.flag6 = TRUE;
```

gets translated to the following Intel assembly code:

```
mov     al, BYTE PTR _flags
or      al, 32   ; 32 = 00100000B
mov     BYTE PTR _flags, al
```

Using Masks Directly

An alternative to using bit fields is to explicitly use integer variables and masks. I have seen engineers use this on platforms where the C compiler that they were using did not support bit fields.

```
#define FLAG1    0x1;
#define FLAG2    0x2;
#define FLAG3    0x4;
#define FLAG4    0x8;
#define FLAG5    0x10;
#define FLAG6    0x20;
#define FLAG7    0x40;
#define FLAG8    0x80;
BOOLEAN storage;
```

To access a specific field, you perform a bit-wise AND.

```
if(storage&FLAG6)
{
    printf("flag6 is on\n");
}
else
{
    printf("flag6 is off\n");
}
```

To set a specific field, you perform a bit-wise OR.

```
storage = storage | FLAG6;
```

To clear a field, you perform a bit-wise AND in addition to a bit-wise complement.

```
storage = storage & (~FLAG6);
```

5.4.3 Compression Algorithms

If you have a large amount of global data that remains fairly static during the life cycle of the application, one way to save space is to compress the global data and then decompress when you need to access it. Naturally, there is a performance hit, because you are trading speed for space; but this is a viable alternative in some cases.

Some simple algorithms like Huffman coding can be used to compress ASCII text. But for the general case of binary or text data, the zlib compression library is an excellent choice.[5] The source code to zlib is highly portable, unencumbered by patents, and (best of all) free. Mark Adler and Jean-loup

---

5. http://www.gzip.org/zlib/

Gailly originally implemented the zlib code. The algorithm used by zlib is the same as that in the GNU Zip (gzip), a utility that can be found on every Linux installation. Considering that Jean-loup is the author/maintainer of gzip, this should not come as a surprise.

If you are working on Windows, zlib can be compiled as a DLL. There is a Web site from which this version of the source code can be downloaded.[6]

The following steps can be used to build the zlib DLL:

1. Run Visual Studio's VCVARS32.BAT batch file.

2. Move the Makefile.nt file to the zlib source code directory.

3. Move zlib.dnt to the zlib source code directory.

4. Run the command nmake -f makefile.nt.

This will generate a file named zlib.dll.

The two functions exported by this DLL that you will be interested in are compress() and uncompress(). The following short program illustrates their use:

```c
/* useZlibDLL.c ----------------------------------------------------*/
#include<stdio.h>
#include<windows.h>
#define BUFFER_SIZE      100
char text[BUFFER_SIZE];
char compress[BUFFER_SIZE];
char decompress[BUFFER_SIZE];
void main()
{
    typedef int (*FunctionPointer)
     (
        char *dest,
        unsigned long *destLen,
        const char *source,
        unsigned long sourceLen
    );
    FunctionPointer functionPointer;
    HINSTANCE handle;
    unsigned long length;
    unsigned long capacity;
    unsigned long i;

    for(i=0;i<=BUFFER_SIZE;i++){ text[i]='A';}
```

6.   http://www.winimage.com/zLibDll/

```
handle = LoadLibrary("ZLIB.DLL");
if(handle==NULL){ return; }

functionPointer =(FunctionPointer)GetProcAddress(handle,"compress");
if(functionPointer==NULL){ return; }

 (*functionPointer)(compress,&length,text,BUFFER_SIZE);

printf("output length=%u\n",length);
for(i=0;i<length;i++)
{
    printf("%c",compress[i]);
}
printf("\n");

functionPointer =(FunctionPointer)GetProcAddress(handle,"uncompress");
if(functionPointer==NULL){ return; }

capacity = BUFFER_SIZE;
 (*functionPointer)(decompress,&capacity,compress,length);

printf("output length=%u\n",capacity);
for(i=0;i<capacity;i++)
{
    printf("%c",decompress[i]);
}
printf("\n");

FreeLibrary(handle);
return;
}
```

When this program is executed, the following output should appear on the screen:

```
output length=12
x£stñ= _e
output length=100
AAAAAAAAAAAAAAAAAAAAAAAAAAAAAAAAAAAAAAAAAAAAAAAAAAAA
AAAAAAAAAAAAAAAAAAAAAAAAAAAAAAAAAAAAAAAAAAAAAAAAA
```

The previous program starts by compressing 100 "A" characters into an array of 12 bytes. The uncompress routine expands the data back to its original form.

5.5 Stack Segment

The stack segment is a block of bytes in memory that functions like a first in, last out (FILO) data structure. Computer stacks typically grow downwards, from high memory to low memory. In other words, when a new item is inserted on to the stack, the stack pointer (i.e., the ESP register on Intel) is decremented to point to that item's first byte (see Figure 5-3).

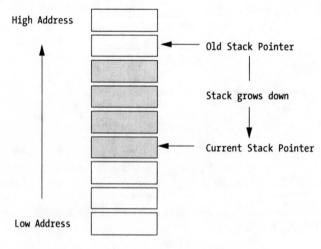

Figure 5-3. The stack segment grows down

There are two ways to manipulate the stack pointer:

- Indirectly, via the PUSH and POP instructions

- Directly, by manipulating the stack pointer

The PUSH instruction places new data on the stack. For example, the following places the contents of the 32-bit EAX register on the stack:

```
PUSH EAX
```

The stack pointer is decremented to point to the first byte of the most recent item pushed on (see Figure 5-4).

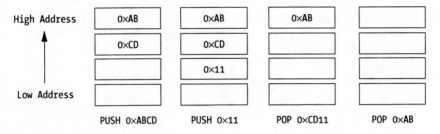

Figure 5-4. PUSH *and* POP *instructions*

The POP instruction removes data from the stack and places it in the location specified by the operand. For example, it takes the top 4 bytes from the stack and places them in the EAX register:

```
POP EAX
```

The stack pointer is incremented to point to the first byte of the next item on the stack (see Figure 5-4).

Manual manipulation of the stack pointer, via addition and subtraction, is a very fast way to allocate and free space on the stack. The one catch is that you'll have to populate the stack manually also.

5.5.1 Activation Records

The primary use of the stack is to serve as a temporary storage space for local variables, function parameters, and return addresses. Specifically, when a routine is invoked, the following items are pushed onto the stack (see Figure 5-5):

- The state of the variables in the invoking routine

- Storage space for the return value, if one is used

- The arguments fed to the routine, if arguments are passed

- The return address (of the instruction following the invocation)

- The current value of the stack frame pointer (i.e., EBP)

- Storage space for variables local to the routine being called

The exact order of the items in the activation record is not set in stone, and can vary from one compiler to the next. So the list that I just provided is one possible combination.

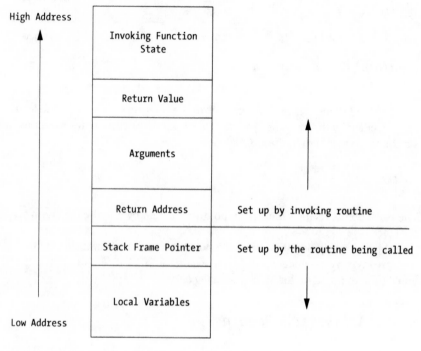

Figure 5-5. A generic activation record

The stack region displayed in Figure 5-5 is known as an *activation record* (or *stack frame*), because every time that a routine is invoked (i.e., activated) one of these constructs must be created on the stack. The invoking routine and the routine being called split up the work needed to build an activation record. The invoking routine typically sets up everything but the stack frame pointer and local variable storage. The routine being called sets up these last two items.

When the routine being called is ready to return, it uses the return address (pushed on by the invoking function) to jump back to the body of the invoking function. Typically, the invoking routine will then extract the return value from the stack and restore its state. Once this has occurred, the invoking function will manually increment the stack pointer and wipe out the activation record.

You may be wondering what a stack frame pointer is, and why you need to push it onto the stack. A stack frame pointer is usually a register (i.e., the EBP register on Intel) that is used to serve as a positional marker. The routine being invoked will push the current value of the stack frame pointer onto the stack (so that it can be restored later) and then set the stack frame pointer (EBP) to the current value of the stack pointer (ESP). For example, routines implemented on the Intel platform will execute the following steps in setting up their part of the stack frame:

1. PUSH EBP onto the stack.

2. Copy ESP into EBP.

3. Decrement ESP to make room for local storage.

The EBP register now holds the value of ESP after you pushed the old value of EBP. This allows elements in the stack frame to be referenced relative to the contents of the stack frame pointer (i.e., EBP) instead of having to specify a concrete address.

Elements above the stack frame pointer are addressed indirectly by adding an integer value to the stack frame pointer. Elements below the stack frame pointer are addressed indirectly by subtracting an integer value from the stack frame pointer. In this manner, the entire stack frame can be accessed via indirect addressing.

NOTE *There are two ways to specify the address of a variable.* Direct addressing *specifies an address in memory explicitly with a numeric value. For example, in assembly language programming, when you specify an address with a label (e.g.,* JMP myLabel*), you are using direct addressing because the assembler will replace the label with an address.* Indirect addressing *specifies an address in memory by indicating a register and an optional offset to add to the contents of the register (e.g.,* JMP [EBP-6]*).*

By now you may be thoroughly confused. Don't worry. The best way to understand all this is through an example. Consider the following program:

```
float average(float *array, int size)
{
    int i;
    float average;

    for(i=0;i<size;i++)
    {
        average +=array[i];
    }
    average = average/size;
    return(average);
}
```

```
void main()
{
    float array[] = {3.24,1.1,5.6,7.8};
    float sampleMean;

    sampleMean = average(array,4);
    printf("%e\n",sampleMean);
    return;
}
```

The Intel assembly code equivalent to this program looks like this:

```
TEXT      SEGMENT
_array$ = 8
_size$ = 12
_i$ = -8
_average$ = -4
_average PROC NEAR
    push    ebp
    mov     ebp, esp
    sub     esp, 8

    mov     DWORD PTR _i$[ebp], 0
    jmp     SHORT $L145
$L146:
    mov     eax, DWORD PTR _i$[ebp]
    add     eax, 1
    mov     DWORD PTR _i$[ebp], eax
$L145:
    mov     ecx, DWORD PTR _i$[ebp]
    cmp     ecx, DWORD PTR _size$[ebp]
    jge     SHORT $L147
    mov     edx, DWORD PTR _i$[ebp]
    mov     eax, DWORD PTR _array$[ebp]
    fld     DWORD PTR _average$[ebp]
    fadd    DWORD PTR [eax+edx*4]
    fstp    DWORD PTR _average$[ebp]
    jmp     SHORT $L146
$L147:
    fild    DWORD PTR _size$[ebp]
    fdivr   DWORD PTR _average$[ebp]
    fst     DWORD PTR _average$[ebp]

    mov     esp, ebp
    pop     ebp
    ret     0
_average ENDP
_TEXT ENDS
_TEXT SEGMENT
```

```
_array$ = -20
_sampleMean$ = -4
_main PROC NEAR
      push    ebp
      mov     ebp, esp
      sub     esp, 20     ; 00000014H

      mov     DWORD PTR _array$[ebp], 1078942761      ; 404f5c29H
      mov     DWORD PTR _array$[ebp+4], 1066192077    ; 3f8ccccdH
      mov     DWORD PTR _array$[ebp+8], 1085485875    ; 40b33333H
      mov     DWORD PTR _array$[ebp+12], 1090099610   ; 40f9999aH

      push    4
      lea     eax, DWORD PTR _array$[ebp]
      push    eax
      call    average
      add     esp, 8
      fst     DWORD PTR _sampleMean$[ebp]

      mov     esp, ebp
      pop     ebp
      ret     0
_main   ENDP
_TEXT   ENDS
END
```

Now let's step through the important parts. The main() function begins by pushing two 32-bit arguments onto the stack (the size of the array and then the address of the array). The call instruction, in addition to jumping to the average() function, pushes the 32-bit return address onto the stack.

```
push    4
lea     eax, DWORD PTR _array$[ebp]
push    eax
call    average
```

This puts a total of 12 bytes on the stack. Notice how *no storage* for the return value was placed on the stack. I will explain this a little later. Once program control has made it to the average() function, EBP is pushed onto the stack, assigned a new value, and then 8 bytes are allocated on the stack for local variable storage.

```
push    ebp
mov     ebp, esp
sub     esp, 8
```

This gives you the stack frame shown in Figure 5-6.

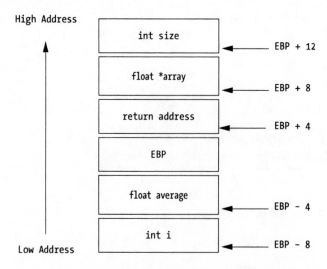

Figure 5-6. Illustrating use of the stack frame pointer

The average() function does its song and dance and then stores the final average value in the Intel ST floating-point register. This register will be used to ferry the return value back to main(), as opposed to using the stack. Now you know why storage for a return value was *not* allocated on the stack by main().

```
fild    DWORD PTR _size$[ebp]
fdivr   DWORD PTR _average$[ebp]
```

The average() function restores the ESP register, pops off the EBP value, and then returns program control to main(). This effectively wipes out everything that average() allocated on the stack.

```
mov    esp, ebp
pop    ebp
ret    0
```

When main() gets the ball back in its corner, it wipes out the rest of the stack and then accesses the return value that was temporarily stuck in ST.

```
add    esp, 8
fst    DWORD PTR _sampleMean$[ebp]
```

This ends the stack frame's life cycle.

Using a stack frame helps to implement useful features like recursion. If you merely used registers to store a routine's local variables, a function that called itself would end up destroying its existing set of local variables. Using the stack also is a neat way to implement function-based scope. When you enter a function, the corresponding stack frame gets created and the variables magically appear. When the function returns, the activation record gets wiped out, and this prevents the local storage from being accessed by other parts of the program.

5.5.2 Function Parameters

Looking at the makeup of the activation record in Figure 5-5, you should be able to see that the number of arguments that you pass to a function impacts the size of the activation record. Thus, one way to make efficient use of the stack segment is to limit the number of arguments that you pass to a routine.

What kind of limit should you put on the number of routine parameters? As a rule of thumb, I would suggest that you pass no more than six arguments to a routine. If you have to pass more than six arguments, then I would suggest that you wrap the arguments in a structure.

For example, if you are dealing with a function like the following:

```
void processOrder
(
    char *customerID,
    char *DoDCode,
    int isBulkBuyer,
    char *productID,
    int quantity,
    int tiaGovFlag
)
{
        //do stuff
}
```

you may want to rewrite it so that it uses a compound data type as an argument:

```
struct OrderInfo
{
    char *customerID,
    char *DoDCode,
    int isBulkBuyer,
    char *productID,
    int quantity,
    int tiaGovFlag
};
void processOrder(struct OrderInfo orderInfo)
{
        //do stuff
}
```

Not only does this cut down on stack frame size, but it also makes your code more flexible. The type signature of the routine is now based on a structure whose internals can change without requiring the function signature itself to change.

But wait! There is a catch to this approach.[7] Passing a structure by value can be a dangerous proposition because the entire thing has to be placed in the stack frame. For example, consider the following code:

```
struct StringStructure
{
    char array[64];
};
void routine(struct StringStructure string)
{
        //do stuff
}
void main()
{
    struct StringStructure string;
    routine(string);
}
```

When `main()` invokes `routine()` and passes it a copy of `string`, all 64 bytes will be passed. To see this, take a look at a snippet of this program's assembly code listing:

```
sub     esp, 64      ; 00000040H
mov     ecx, 16      ; 00000010H
lea     esi, DWORD PTR     string$[ebp]
mov     edi, esp
rep     movsd
call    routine
```

By wrapping a character array in a structure, you end up passing the whole array to the invoked function. Fortunately, there is an easy solution: instead of passing structures by value, *always pass them by reference.*

```
struct StringStructure
{
    char array[64];
};
void routine(struct StringStructure *string)
{
        //do stuff
}
```

---

7.   Always read the fine print.

```
void main()
{
    struct StringStructure string;
    routine(&string);
}
```

The preceding code uses only 4 bytes of space on the stack to pass the argument.

```
lea     eax, DWORD PTR    string$[ebp]
push    eax
call    routine
```

The punch line to all of this is, always minimize the number of arguments you pass to a routine. Wrap them in a structure if you must, but make sure to pass the structure by reference.

5.5.3 Local Variables

Aside from routine parameters and the return value, the other big-ticket item on the activation record is the local storage for the routine being invoked. To minimize local storage, you need to put a limit on the size of a routine's local variables. For example, the following is a bad idea:

```
void routine()
{
    char buffer[10240];    //allocates local 10KB buffer
    //do stuff
}
```

This function will have to allocate 10 kilobytes of space on the stack.

```
push      ebp
mov     ebp, esp
mov     eax, 10240
call      chkstk
sub     esp, 10240
```

A recursive function that behaves like this could cause a stack overflow. This explains why the compiler quietly inserted the __chkstk function.

The best way to prevent a stack overflow is to declare large variables as global, and then pass them to routines by reference. For example:

```
char buffer[10240];
void routine(char *buffer)
{
    //do stuff
}
void main()
{
    routine(buffer);
}
```

Instead of taking up 10 kilobytes of space on the stack every time that routine() is invoked, the buffer takes up 10 kilobytes of space (once and only once) in the data segment. Every time that routine() is invoked, the pointer to buffer takes only up 4 bytes of stack space.

5.6 Heap

The stack allocates and frees memory dynamically. But the manner in which memory is allocated and freed exhibits a high degree of regularity. Memory on the stack will always be allocated or freed relative to the stack pointer (i.e., ESP on Intel). Specifically, when a routine is invoked, a new activation record is created and space on the stack is allocated. When program control returns from the routine, the corresponding storage space on the stack is freed and the activation record vanishes.

The heap segment is just a collection of bytes (i.e., a *heap* of bytes). The heap is a dynamic memory segment like the stack, but it lacks the structural requirements that make the stack predictable. There are no rules that dictate when memory must be allocated or freed. It's a memory free-for-all, and anything goes. The heap typically relies on user libraries to initiate allocation and collection (i.e., the malloc() and free() calls declared in stdlib.h). Engineers can invoke these routines in their code whenever they feel like it. This causes the libraries that manage the heap to be rather complicated because they have to be able to service memory requests in potentially unpredictable ways.

There are two ways to implement dynamic memory management (or heap management):

- Manual memory management (explicit memory management)

- Automatic memory management (garbage collection)

In the case of manual memory management, facilities are provided by calls like malloc() and free(). The engineer implementing with manual memory management is *completely* responsible for keeping track of what has been allocated and explicitly freeing memory when it is no longer needed. This can lead to problems like memory leaks and dangling pointers, which I discussed in Chapter 2.

In the case of automatic memory management, facilities will be provided to allocate memory, but none will be provided to free memory. An automatic memory management service will quietly keep track of memory usage behind the scenes and decide when to free storage using its own internal algorithms. Using a high-quality garbage collector prevents memory leaks and dangling points from cropping up.

From the standpoint of complexity, garbage collection is the more complicated solution of the two because it entails more responsibility. A garbage collector has to sweep the heap and decide what is still being used and what isn't. A manual memory manager does only what the user tells it to. It doesn't have to do any guesswork.

From the standpoint of heap usage, it doesn't matter which type of memory management you use. Don't confuse policy with mechanism. The real issue, from the viewpoint of memory consumption, is how you use the heap space that you allocate (not how you allocate it). In this section, I am going to assume you are using manual memory management, but the tactics that I will discuss would work just as well in an environment that uses automatic memory management.

5.6.1 Memory Pools

The motivation behind pooling resources is to enable multiple service requests while at the same time being protected from the threat of starvation. Pooling objects in memory is one variation of this theme (as are thread pools and socket connection pools). A pool of objects allows client code to request multiple instantiations, while also placing a ceiling on the number of objects available. This offers protection from a greedy client that might otherwise bring the system down with an unreasonable request.

Memory pooling is also fast. To truly appreciate the magnitude of this statement, it may help to look at a concrete example. Consider the following class:

```
/* Object.h -------------------------------------------------*/
#define BOOLEAN int
class Object
{
    private:
    BOOLEAN isFree;
    DWORD value;

    public:
    BOOLEAN getStatus();
    void setStatus(BOOLEAN status);
    DWORD getValue();
    void setValue(DWORD value);
};
```

```
BOOLEAN Object::getStatus()
{
    return(isFree);
}
void Object::setStatus(BOOLEAN status)
{
    switch(status)
    {
        case TRUE:
        case FALSE:{ isFree= status; }break;
        default:{ isFree = FALSE; }
    }
}
DWORD Object::getValue()
{
    return(value);
}
void Object::setValue(DWORD value)
{
     (*this).value = value;
}
```

The isFree field indicates if the current object is being used, and the value field is a generic field implemented for demonstration purposes. One way to allocate and free instances of this class is to directly invoke malloc() and free().

```
#include<stdio.h>
#include<stdlib.h>
#include<windows.h>
#include<object.h>

#define LIMIT 1000*100
Object *object[LIMIT];

void main()
{
    long i;
    unsigned long start;
    unsigned long finish;

    start = GetTickCount();

    for(i=0;i<LIMIT;i++)
    {
        object[i]= (Object*)malloc(sizeof(Object));
    }
```

```
for(i=0;i<LIMIT;i++)
{
     (*object[i]).setValue(0xAABBCCDD);
     (*object[i]).setStatus(TRUE);
}

 for(i=(LIMIT-1);i>=0;i--)
{
    free(object[i]);
}

finish = GetTickCount();
printf("msecs elapsed=%lu\n",(finish-start));
return;
}
```

When this code is run, the following output is produced:

```
msecs elapsed=217
```

An alternative to the direct approach is to maintain a pool of instances. The following code is a variant of the previous example that uses a Pool object to provide faster service:

```
/* Pool.cpp-------------------------------------------------------*/
#include<stdio.h>
#include<stdlib.h>
#include<windows.h>
#include<object.h>


/*++++++++++++++++++++++++++++++++++++++++++++++++++++++++++++++++++
+ Declaration                                                      +
++++++++++++++++++++++++++++++++++++++++++++++++++++++++++++++++++*/

class Pool
{
    private:
    Object *object;
    Object *first;
    Object *last;
    unsigned long size;
    unsigned long currentIndex;

    public:
    Pool(unsigned long size);
    ~Pool();
    Object *allocate();
    void free(Object *address);
    void printArray();
```

```
};


/*++++++++++++++++++++++++++++++++++++++++++++++++++++++++++++++++++++++++
+ Definitions                                                           +
++++++++++++++++++++++++++++++++++++++++++++++++++++++++++++++++++++++++*/

Pool::Pool(unsigned long size)
{
    unsigned long i;

     (*this).size =size;
    object = (Object*)malloc(size*sizeof(Object));
    if(object==NULL){ printf("malloc() failed\n"); }
    for(i=0;i<size;i++)
    {
        object[i].setStatus(TRUE);
    }
    currentIndex=0;
    first = &((*this).object[0]);
    last  = &((*this).object[size-1]);
    return;
}/*end constructor------------------------------------------------*/
Pool::~Pool()
{
    free(object);
}/*end destructor-------------------------------------------------*/
Object* Pool::allocate()
{
    unsigned long i;

    if(currentIndex==size){ currentIndex=0; }

    for(i=currentIndex;i<size;i++)
    {
        if(object[currentIndex].getStatus())
        {
            object[currentIndex].setStatus(FALSE);
            currentIndex++;
            return(&object[currentIndex-1]);
        }
    }
    return(NULL);
}/*end allocate---------------------------------------------------*/
void Pool::free(Object *address)
{
    if((address>=first)&&(address<=last))
    {
        (*address).setStatus(TRUE);
    }
```

```
        else
        {
            printf("release out of range");
        }
        return;
}/*end free---------------------------------------------------------*/
void Pool::printArray()
{
    unsigned long i;
    printf("--------------------------\n");
    for(i=0;i<size;i++)
    {
        if(object[i].getStatus())
        {
            printf("[%6lu]=FREE\n",i);
        }
        else
        {
            printf("[%6lu]=OCCUPIED\n",i);
        }
    }
}/*end printArray--------------------------------------------------*/

#define LIMIT 1000*100
Object *object[LIMIT];

void main()
{
    long i;
    unsigned long start;
    unsigned long finish;

    start = GetTickCount();
    for(i=0;i<LIMIT;i++)
    {
        object[i]= (Object*)malloc(sizeof(Object));
    }

    for(i=0;i<LIMIT;i++)
    {
        (*object[i]).setValue(0xAABBCCDD);
        (*object[i]).setStatus(TRUE);
    }

    for(i=(LIMIT-1);i>=0;i--)
    {
        free(object[i]);
    }
```

```
finish = GetTickCount();
printf("msecs elapsed=%lu\n",(finish-start));
return;
}
```

When this code is run, the following output is produced:

```
msecs elapsed=35
```

The pooled implementation is six times faster than the first. As some readers may have guessed, there is a catch. Memory pooling only works when you have a certain degree of predictability, which is to say that you know what you are going to allocate (e.g., "I know that I will be allocating objects of type XYZ, and a whole lot of them."). In certain cases, you will not know the size and type of memory that you are going to allocate, and in those cases pooling will not help.

5.6.2 Recycling

If you are going to implement a pooling scheme, it's a good idea to design your objects with a clear() function or reset() function so that you can return them to a ground state once they have been freed.

```
void Pool::free(Object *address)
{
    if((address>=first)&&(address<=last))
    {
        (*address).setStatus(TRUE);    // instance is "free"
        (*address).reset();            //send back to initial state
    }
    else
    {
        printf("release out of range");
    }
    return;
}
```

The details of the implementation of reset() are context sensitive. Returning an object to its initial state could include setting variables to their default values, closing open files, terminating network connections, etc.

5.6.3 Lazy Instantiation

Lazy instantiation is a form of just-in-time memory allocation. When a block of memory (e.g., an object, an array, a structure) is allocated via lazy instantiation, the block of memory is not actually allocated until it is used. This saves both time and memory by only granting resources to those constructs that actually need it.

Here is a simple illustration of what I'm talking about. The following class has an internal buffer that it allocates only after a request has been made to access it:

```cpp
/* LazyClass.cpp -------------------------------------------------*/
#include<stdio.h>
#include<stdlib.h>
#include<string.h>

#define DEFAULT_SIZE    8

/*++++++++++++++++++++++++++++++++++++++++++++++++++++++++++++++++++
+ Declaration                                                      +
+++++++++++++++++++++++++++++++++++++++++++++++++++++++++++++++++*/

class LazyClass
{
    private:
    char *buffer;
    int size;

    public:
    LazyClass();
    ~LazyClass();
    char *getBuffer();
    void setBuffer(char *buffer, int nbytes);
};

/*++++++++++++++++++++++++++++++++++++++++++++++++++++++++++++++++++
+ Definitions                                                      +
+++++++++++++++++++++++++++++++++++++++++++++++++++++++++++++++++*/

LazyClass::LazyClass()
{
    buffer = NULL;
    size = DEFAULT_SIZE;
}/*end constructor-------------------------------------------------*/
LazyClass::~LazyClass()
```

```
{
    if(buffer!=NULL)
    {
        printf("destructor()\n");
        free(buffer);
    }
}/*end destructor-------------------------------------------------*/
char *LazyClass::getBuffer()
{
    if(buffer==NULL)
    {
        printf("NULL, allocating\n");
        buffer = (char*)malloc(size);
        buffer[size-1]=0x00;
    }
    return(buffer);
}/*end getBuffer-------------------------------------------------*/
void LazyClass::setBuffer(char *buffer, int nbytes)
{
    if((*this).buffer==NULL)
    {
        printf("NULL, allocating\n");
        (*this).buffer = (char*)malloc(nbytes);
        (*this).size = nbytes;
    }

    if((*this).size<nbytes)
    {
        printf("resizing\n");
        free((*this).buffer);
        (*this).buffer = (char*)malloc(nbytes);
        (*this).size = nbytes;
    }
    strcpy((*this).buffer,buffer);
}/*end setBuffer-------------------------------------------------*/
```

Microsoft Windows utilizes lazy instantiation in its memory management services. For example, my laptop has only 128MB of physical RAM, but the following program runs without even affecting my machine:

```
#include<stdio.h>
#include<stdlib.h>
#define KB      1024
#define MB      1024*KB
#define LIMIT   512
void main()
{
    int i;
    char *array[LIMIT];
```

```
    for(i=0;i<LIMIT;i++)
    {
        printf("allocated MB[%d]\n",i);
        array[i] = (char*)malloc(MB);
    }
    return;
}
```

The reason that this program runs without a hitch is that it doesn't use any of the memory that it allocates. Every time that a new megabyte is allocated, the Windows memory management service performs a few basic accounting operations and goes about its business with little or no interruption.

Contrast the previous program with this one:

```
#include<stdio.h>
#include<stdlib.h>
#define KB      1024
#define MB      1024*KB
#define LIMIT      256
void main()
{
    int i;
    int j;
    char *array[LIMIT];
    char *cptr;

    for(i=0;i<LIMIT;i++)
    {
        printf("allocated MB[%d]\n",i);
        array[i] = (char*)malloc(MB);
        cptr = array[i];
        for(j=0;j<MB;j++)
        {
            cptr[j] = 'a';
        }
    }
    return;
}
```

In this program, you actually manipulate the memory that is allocated. This program should cause your hard drive to buzz a little as Windows starts relying on disk storage to simulate memory. If you have less than 256MB of RAM, I would warn you against running this program (it basically creates a giant memory leak).

5.6.4 Tracking Memory Usage

Most operating systems have special commands or utility programs that will let you view the memory consumption of a program. From the standpoint of optimization, these tools are useful because they will give you an idea of how much memory your efforts have bought you. It's like getting a report card from school.

On Linux, you can use the ps command.

```
# ps -o sz,vsz,pmem,pid -C init
SZ          VSZ         %MEM            PID
350         1411        .2                      6
```

This command takes a running process, named init, and displays its byte size in physical memory, the size of the process in the virtual address space (which includes physical memory and secondary storage), the percentage of the total virtual address space being used, and the process ID.

On Windows, the Task Manager can offer a decent view of process memory usage (if you configure it correctly). You can begin by pressing Ctrl-Alt-Del to open up the task manager. Select the Processes tab pane (see Figure 5-7).

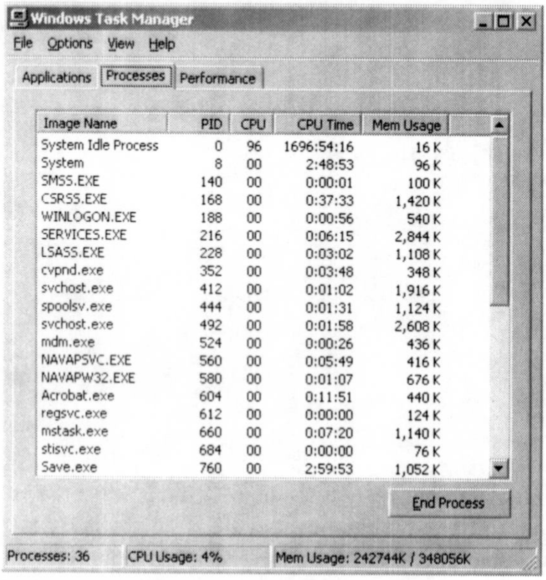

Figure 5-7. The Windows Task Manager

Once the Processes Tab pane has focus, click the View menu and then select the Select Columns menu item. This will bring up a dialog box that will

allow you to choose the type of process metadata that you want the Task
Manager to display (see Figure 5-8).

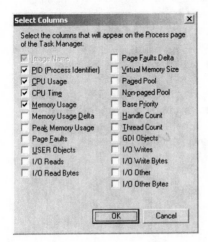

Figure 5-8. Select Columns dialog box

A number of columns offer memory statistics:

- *Memory Usage:* Number of kilobytes in physical RAM

- *Memory Usage Delta:* Change since the last update

- *Peak Memory Usage:* Maximum since the process started

- *Virtual Memory Size:* Total memory used (RAM and disk)

- *Paged Pool:* Allocations from the kernel's paged pool

- *Non-paged Pool:* Allocations from the nonpaged pool

All columns display values that are measured in kilobytes. Microsoft's
documentation on paged pool and nonpaged pool memory differs depending
on where you look (hint: the Windows Glossary led me around in circles).
Most of the useful information that I found was in the MSDN documentation
for the Windows Process Status API (PSAPI). There are also a couple of decent
books that you can reference, such as the one by David A. Solomon and Mark
Russinovich.[8]

---

8.   David A. Solomon and Mark Russinovich, *Inside Microsoft Windows 2000, Third
     Edition* (Microsoft Press, 2000. ISBN: 0-735-61021-5)

The paged and nonpaged columns correspond to regions of memory owned by the operating system in kernel space. Specifically, a pool of memory in the kernel gets used on the behalf of a process when the process executes. Paged pool memory can be paged to disk if necessary, and nonpaged pool memory cannot.

To view memory usage on a finer level of granularity, you will need to rely on API calls that are native to your host operating system. For example, almost every system API provides library calls to determine the size of a program's heap. If your application is running on an interpreter, like the JVM, there may be platform-neutral ways of determining the size of different memory segments. There are also add-ons, like the BDW conservative garbage collector, that I discussed earlier in the book, which can be used to track memory usage.

5.7 Summary

A program has two basic resources at its disposal:

- Processor time (i.e., CPU cycles)

- Memory

In this chapter, we looked at ways to make efficient use of memory.
Running programs are organized as blocks of memory called *segments*. Four types of program segments are available:

- *Code segments:* Store program instructions

- *Data segments:* Store global variables

- *Stack segments:* Store local variables, function arguments

- *Heap segments:* Provide storage for dynamic allocation

Various techniques can be used to minimize the size of the each segment type.

Code Segments

- State each logical operation in a single place.

- Replace macro-based operations with functions.

- Periodically trim dead code from the source tree.

Data Segments

- Utilize dual-use data structures.

- Use compression algorithms to condense storage.

Stack Segments

- Limit the number of arguments that you pass to a function.

- Consolidate lengthy argument lists into a dedicated structure.

- Pass arguments by reference, instead of by value.

- Avoid defining large local variables.

Heap Segments

- Utilize a suballocator (i.e., a memory pool), if possible.

- Permit lazy instantiation.

- Recycle your objects.

- Periodically check for sinks and leaks.

CHAPTER 6

Optimization: CPU Cycles

The devil hath power to assume a pleasing shape.

—William Shakespeare, *Hamlet*, act 2, scene 2

A program has two basic resources at its disposal:

- Processor time (i.e., CPU cycles)

- Memory

In this chapter, I will demonstrate ways to make efficient use of processor time—which is to say that I'll show you ways to make your program do the most, in the smallest amount of time, by pruning away unnecessary operations.

Don't forget Vilfredo Pareto's heuristic, which I introduced in the last chapter. Unless your code is a complete mess, most of your performance problems will arise in a small number of places. Always use a profiler to identify bottlenecks so that you don't make the mistake of blindly optimizing everything. Optimization makes code brittle. If you optimize your entire program, you are likely to drastically undermine its structural integrity. As I mentioned in the last chapter, it's like making a pact with Lucifer. Sure, your code will be faster, but only at a steep price.

WARNING   *In this section, more than a few of the techniques that I present will directly contradict some of the things I talked about in the previous chapter. This is because optimization involves trade-offs. No perfect solution exists for every problem, but rather solutions that are successful under certain conditions. You can make your program smaller, but it will probably cost you CPU cycles. Likewise, you can make your program faster if you don't mind putting up with memory bloat. Rarely can you have your cake and eat it too. Instead, you will need to strike a balance between speed and size. The approach that you adopt ultimately will depend upon your priorities.*

6.1 Program Control Jumps

The fastest way for a processor to execute operations is sequentially, one after another. Naturally, when you start forcing the processor to jump around from one place to the next in memory, everything goes to hell. Not only can a jump instruction require the processor to leave the confines of the cache, but it usually also entails the overhead of setting up an activation record.

6.1.1 Labels and GOTO

Consider the following function definition:

```
int orderEntry
(
    char *customerID,
    char *productID,
    int quantity,
    float total,
    char *salesRep
)
{
    //perform order entry
}
```

The sheer overhead involved in calling this function is nontrivial. You can see this by looking at the Intel assembly code used to call this function:

```
; returnVal = orderEntry(custormerID, productID, quantity, total, salesRep);
mov     eax, DWORD PTR _salesRep$[ebp]
push    eax
mov     ecx, DWORD PTR _total$[ebp]
push    ecx
mov     edx, DWORD PTR _quantity$[ebp]
push    edx
mov     eax, DWORD PTR _productID$[ebp]
push    eax
mov     ecx, DWORD PTR _customerID$[ebp]
push    ecx
call    orderEntry
add     esp, 20
mov     DWORD PTR _returnVal$[ebp], eax
```

The mere act of invoking this routine costs 13 machine instructions. One way to get around having to build a stack frame is to use the goto statement. With a goto statement, all the push instructions necessary to set up the stack frame disappear.

```
goto orderEntry;
```

In assembly language this translates into a single instruction.

```
JMP orderEntry
```

Two conditions make this technique viable:

- The routine that you jump to is not recursive.

- The label being jumped to is in the current routine.

A stack frame is what facilitates recursion. Once you take the stack frame away, the ability to implement recursion is also abolished. In other words, the code that you jump to cannot be recursive. If you decide to use a goto statement, you must pass arguments and process return values, via mutually accessible variables.

Labels in C are visible only within the function in which they are defined. This means that you may have to consolidate related operations inside of a common function so that they can access the same set of variables and jump around freely.

```
void primaryLoop()
{
    char *customerID;
    char *productID;
    int quantity;
    float total;
    char *salesRep;

    begin:
    goto    waitForOrder;
    endWaitForOrder:

    goto    orderEntry;
    endOrderEntry:

    goto    confirm;
    endConfirm:
    goto begin;

    waitForOrder:
        //wait for data entry
    goto endWaitForOrder;

    orderEntry:
        //perform DB transaction
    goto endOrderEntry;

    confirm:
        //display confirmation to user
    goto endConfirm;

    exitLoop:
    return;
}
```

You may find using the goto statement distasteful, and I would not blame you. Using goto liberally makes source code more difficult to read and harder to maintain. I like to think of goto as the nuclear warfare of software engineering. It is the final option, and one that tends to result in a Pyrrhic victory.

6.1.2 Function Parameters

One alternative to going nuclear is to try and minimize the amount of code that gets generated to manage the activation record. You can do this by wrapping function arguments in a structure and then passing the structure by reference. This condenses all the arguments into a single address, which can be passed to functions rather easily.

For example, you can replace the following:

```
int orderEntry
(
    char *customerID,
    char *productID,
    int quantity,
    float total,
    char *salesRep
)
{
    //perform order entry
}
```

with something like this:

```
struct OrderInfo
{
    char *customerID;
    char *productID;
    int quantity;
    float total;
    char *salesRep;
};

int orderEntry2(struct OrderInfo *orderInfo)
{
    //perform order entry
}
```

If you do so, invoking the following function:

```
returnVal = orderEntry(&orderInfo);
```

translates into the following Intel assembly code:

```
lea     edx, DWORD PTR _orderInfo$[ebp]
push    edx
call    orderEntry2
add     esp, 4
mov     DWORD PTR _returnVal$[ebp], eax
```

The original version of this invocation required 13 machine instructions, and this one requires only 5. This is just a little bit more work intensive than goto with all the additional benefits of abstraction and scope. Thus, not only does passing structures by reference lower memory footprint (as you saw in the previous chapter), but it also consumes fewer CPU cycles.

6.1.3 Functions with a Varying Number of Arguments

Several macro routines (i.e., va_start(), va_arg(), and va_end()) declared in the ANSI C header file stdarg.h allow you to define a function that has a variable number of arguments. The best way to understand how these routines operate is to look at an example. The following source code defines a function named average() that takes a variable number of floating-point values and computes their average:

```c
/* varyArgs.c ------------------------------------------------*/
#include<stdio.h>
#include <stdarg.h>
double average(double value,...)
{
    int size;
    double sum;
    va_list marker;

    size=0;

    //set marker to the first argument
    va_start(marker,value);

    while(value!=0.0)
    {
        sum += value;
        size++;
        printf("value=%f\n",value);

        //get the next argument
        value = va_arg(marker,double);
    }

    //clean up and go home
    va_end(marker);
    return(sum/size);
}
void main()
{
    printf("sampleMean=%f\n",average(1.01,34.02,7.45,0.0));
}
```

NOTE *The basic operation of this scheme requires you to place a sentinel value at the end of the list of arguments so that you know when to stop reading arguments. In the previous code, that sentinel value is zero.*

The problem with using variable argument functions is that a significant amount of overhead is incurred to locate and access function parameters. You can see this by looking at an implementation of the macros in stdarg.h:

```
typedef char * va_list;
#define INTSIZEOF(n)   ((sizeof(n)+sizeof(int)-1)&~(sizeof(int)-1))
#define va_start(ap,v)  (ap = (va_list)&v + INTSIZEOF(v))
#define va_arg(ap,t)   (*(t *)((ap += INTSIZEOF(t)) - INTSIZEOF(t)))
#define va_end(ap)   (ap = (va_list)0)
```

While things are not as bad as they could be, because macros are being used, you can see how many extra steps a routine has to take in order to process a variable number of arguments. In most cases, the flexibility of this approach is not worth the additional overhead.

6.1.4 System Calls

Back in the 1990s, I worked as an actuary for an insurance company in beautiful downtown Cleveland. One of the other actuaries that I worked with was making the switch from APL to C. He complained to me, at one point, that C was way too slow for performing statistical calculations. I asked him to prove it to me, and he showed me his code and handed me a printout that contained the following snippet of source code:

```
for(i=0;i<nRows;i++)
{
    for(j=0;j<nColumns;j++)
    {
        result[i] = result[i] + ((matrix[i][j])*vector[j]);
        printf("result[%d]=%d\n",i,result[i]);
    }
}
```

He told me, "It's just simple arithmetic, so why is it taking several seconds to execute?"

I tried not to laugh out loud. Such is the plight of the novice programmer. The problem was not with C, but rather the fact that he had made a system call in the middle of a performance-sensitive chunk of code. System calls, particularly ones that communicate with hardware, are expensive operations.

The System Call Architecture

Most programs are blissfully ignorant of what's going on behind the scenes to support their execution. It's like making a telephone call: you dial in a number and the telecom's massive network of computers does the rest. Likewise, programs request operating system services without really caring about how things actually get done. Programs that execute in user space see the operating system from an outsider's view. From this vantage point, the system call interface is all that they see.

The *system call interface* is the collection of routines that an operating system kernel exposes to the outside world (i.e., programs running in user space). Every service that an operating system offers can be spelled out in terms of the system call interface. The system call interface is like the kernel's formal job description. It dictates what the kernel is responsible for and can do. Some people would argue that an operating system is defined in terms of its system call interface, seeing as how an operating system is really nothing more than the implementation of its system call interface.

Taking the system call routines of the original OS and constructing a clean room implementation of them produces an operating system *clone*. The clone may differ in terms of the underlying data structures and algorithms that it uses, but to a program running in user space, it feels like the real McCoy. Cloning PC operating systems was manageable back when DOS was just a few thousands lines of assembly code; but I doubt very highly if anyone could clone Windows XP today. Not even a giant like IBM can stand toe-to-toe with Microsoft (in fact, they tried with OS/2 and got their clock cleaned). One can only imagine the kind of consistency and discipline it takes to manage Windows successfully.

The more features that an operating system implements, the larger the system call interface. For example, NACHOS (Not Just Another Completely Heuristic Operating System)[1] is a small demo OS designed by Tom Paterson. NACHOS has a system call interface that consists of only eleven routines.

Process Management

- `SpaceId Exec(char *name);`

- `int Join(SpaceId id);`

- `void Halt();`

- `void Exit(int status);`

---

[1] http://www.cs.washington.edu/homes/tom/nachos/

Threads

- void Fork(void (*function)());

- void Yield();

File Input/Output

- void Create(char *name);

- OpenFileId Open(char *name);

- void Write(char *buffer, int size, OpenFileId id);

- int Read(char *buffer, int size, OpenFileId id);

- void Close(OpenFileId id);

Linux, on the other hand, has a system call interface that consists of well over 200 routines.

System calls are not always spelled out using easy-to-read C prototypes. Some operating systems, like DOS, specify system calls using bare-bones interrupt primitives.[2] For instance, the following DOS system call prints a string of characters terminated by a dollar sign:

```
Interrupt: 0x21
Function: 0x09
Inputs: AH = 0x9, DS:DX = segment:offset address of string
```

Operating systems like Linux actually use interrupts too. It's just that they have the good sense to hide them in the basement and then wrap them completely in C code so that they can be dealt with in a civilized fashion. The MINIX operating system[3] does a particularly good job of wrapping the assembly code that configures the Intel 8259 programmable interrupt controller (PIC).[4]

System calls are the primitives upon which user libraries are built (see Figure 6-1). User libraries access system calls through a checkpoint known as the *system gate*. The kernel sits in a protected region of memory. The details of this protection mechanism are hardware dependent, but suffice it to say that the user libraries cannot simply jump to the kernel code. Like a teenager asking

---

2.   See Ralph Brown's Comprehensive DOS Interrupt List at
     http://www.ctyme.com/intr/cat-010.htm.

3.   http://www.minix.org/

4.   Joe McGivern, *Interrupt Driven PC System Design* (Annabooks, 1998. ISBN: 0-929-39250-7)

to use the car, user libraries must make a polite request via the system gate. The system gate is the only way in and out of the kernel. Every path of execution that uses kernel services must eventually pass through this channel.

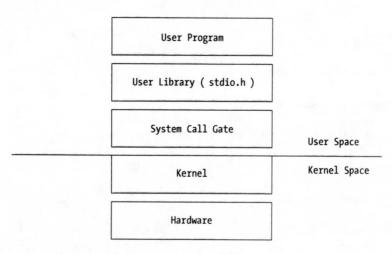

Figure 6-1. The system gate

Systems implemented on Intel processors, like Linux or Windows, use the system call gate as an interrupt handler. Specifically, the user library will generate a software interrupt, and the system call gate will respond by checking to see if the request for service is valid. If the service request looks kosher, the system call gate will then redirect the request to the appropriate system call in the kernel proper. When the system call in the kernel is done, it hands things back to the call gate, which in turn passes the results back to the user library. The system call gate is, in essence, a broker between the kernel and the user libraries (where the kernel pays the broker's paycheck).

The C standard library uses this tactic. Let's look at a hypothetical implementation of putchar() to see how user libraries communicate with the kernel. Most ANSI C implementations of putchar() rely on the putc() function.

```
#define putchar(c)  putc(c,stdout)
```

The putc() function is implemented in terms of a hypothetical write() function.

```
int putc(int ch, FILE *stream)
{
    int ret;
    ret = write(stream,&ch,1);
    return((ret!=TRUE)?EOF:ch);
}
```

The write() function executes the software interrupt that invokes the system call gate code. It is here that the user code hits the metal:

```
int write(FILE *stream, void *buffer, int nbytes)
{
    struct CallGate callGate;

    callGate.function = FILE_SYSTEM;
    callGate.type = BUFFERED_OUPUT;
    callGate.arg1 = (long)stream;
    callGate.arg2 = (long)buffer;
    callGate.arg3 = (long)nbytes;

    asm
    {
        MOV  EDX, USER_LIB
        LEA  EAX, OFFSET callGate
        INT  0x18
    }
}
```

The write() function is very general. It would, no doubt, be used to facilitate various other input/output calls in stdio.h. This is how the standard C library is built. It is very general at the bottom and very specialized at the top.

Recommendations

You may be wondering why I spent so much time explaining how system calls work. My goals were to

- Satisfy your curiosity.

- Show you how much work the processor has to perform.

A system call might not seem like much from the outside, but (trust me) it is like the tip of a very large iceberg.

My recommendations are very simple: avoid making a system call in the middle of code that needs to execute quickly. In particular, make a point to avoid system calls that perform input/output operations. I used to work for a VP who fined developers $50 if they inserted extraneous disk reads or writes in their code. Talk about high-pressure code reviews! There were engineers who used to sneak through the source tree and delete their names from files.

6.1.5 Recursion

Recursion looks elegant in computer science textbooks, where the author usually presents a short example that computes a factorial or a Fibonacci number. The author is probably trying to give you a simple example to help you climb a learning curve. One alternative to recursion is to use precomputed results.

```
#define MIN_FACTORIAL    0
#define MAX_FACTORIAL    9
unsigned long factorials[] = { 1, 1, 2, 6, 24, 120, 720, 5040, 40320, 362880};
#define MIN_FIBONACCI    0
#define MAX_FIBONACCI    12
unsigned long Fibonacci[] = { 0, 1, 1, 2, 3, 5, 8, 13, 21, 34, 55, 89, 144 };
```

> **NOTE**   *In general, relying on precomputed results is a habit that will serve you well. There are dozens of elaborate algorithms dedicated to computing π to an arbitrary number of decimal places.[5] Believe it or not, some people have devoted their lives to it.[6] But why waste hundreds of CPU cycles when you can just rely on a #define constant that is accurate enough for most purposes?*

If you are able, always try to replace recursion with strict iteration using for(), while(), and do-while(). In the real world, elegant recursive solutions are a rare breed. Those who use recursion are more likely to implement code that is difficult to decipher and inclined towards bugs.

For example, if a recursive function does not have a circuit breaker installed to prevent infinite recursion, it could overflow the stack and bring its host application to an abrupt halt. Or, even worse, a spiteful engineer might decide to nest multiple recursive functions within each other. Try tracing that execution path in your head!

6.2 Program Control Branching

As I stated earlier, the type of code that the processor executes the quickest is straight sequential execution: one instruction after the next. The minute that the processor has to jump to another location in memory, or evaluate a condition to see which way to go, everything slows down. In this section, I will

---

5.   David Blatner, *The Joy of Pi* (Walker & Company, 1999. ISBN: 0-8027-7562-4)

6.   Richard Preston, "The Mountains of Pi," *The New Yorker*, March 2, 1992

discuss ways to avoid program branching and ways to make branching statements more efficient (if you have no choice but to use them).

6.2.1 Lookup Tables

The best way to avoid the overhead associated with a branching statement is not to perform one in the first place. For example, take a look at the following code:

```
BOOLEAN editName(char *name)
{
    if(strlen(name)>0){ return(TRUE); }
    else{ return(FALSE); }
}
```

This could easily be rewritten to avoid using an if-else statement.

```
BOOLEAN editName(char *name)
{
    return(strlen(name));
}
```

Granted, this example was trivial. Now let's examine something that offers more bang per buck: lookup tables. A *lookup table* is a tool that allows you to assign values using a table structure instead of using selective statements. For example, the following code uses an if-else statement to assign token types in a compiler:

```
#define LETTER      0
#define DIGIT       1
#define DELIMITER   2
#define WHITESPACE  3
#define UNKNOWN     4
int getCharType(char ch)
{
    int type;
    if((ch>='a')&&(ch<='z'))
    {
        type = LETTER;
    }
    else if((ch>='A')&&(ch<='Z'))
    {
        type = LETTER;
    }
    else if((ch==' ')||(ch=='\t')||(ch=='\n'))
    {
        type = WHITESPACE;
    }
```

```
    else if((ch>='0')&&(ch<='9'))
    {
        type = DIGIT;
    }
    else if((ch==';')||(ch==':')||(ch=='\"'))
    {
        type = DELIMITER;
    }
    else
    {
        type = UNKNOWN;
    }
    return(type);
}
```

This routine of 20+ lines could be replaced with a single statement if you used a lookup table as follows:

```
#define CHARS_SIZE    127
int charType[CHARS_SIZE];
int getCharType(char ch)
{
    return(charType[(int)ch]);
}
```

In this case, the lookup table is an array, which you can assume has been initialized earlier.

```
void initCharType()
{
    int i;
    for(i=0;i<CHARS_SIZE;i++){ charType[i]=UNKNOWN; }

    for(i='a';i<='z';i++){ charType[i]=LETTER; }
    for(i='A';i<='Z';i++){ charType[i]=LETTER; }
    for(i='0';i<='9';i++){ charType[i]=DIGIT; }

    charType[(int)' ']=WHITESPACE;
    charType[(int)'\t']=WHITESPACE;
    charType[(int)'\n']=WHITESPACE;

    charType[(int)';']=DELIMITER;
    charType[(int)':']=DELIMITER;
    charType[(int)'\"']=DELIMITER;
    return;
}
```

Lookup tables are essentially a way to eliminate conditional expressions by relying on a set of precomputed values to perform assignment operations. Here is another example:

```
#define STATUS_1    0
#define STATUS_2    1
#define STATUS_3    2
int getStatus(BOOLEAN A, BOOLEAN B)
{
    int status;
    if(A&&B)
    {
        status = STATUS_1;
    }
    else if((!A)&&(!B))
    {
        status = STATUS_2;
    }
    else
    {
        status = STATUS_3;
    }
    return(status);
}
```

A simple two-dimensional lookup table can replace the previous code.

```
int statusType[2][2] = { {STATUS_2, STATUS_3},{STATUS_3, STATUS_1}};
int getStatus2(BOOLEAN A, BOOLEAN B)
{
    return(statusType[A][B]);
}
```

6.2.2 switch vs. if-else

You've probably heard that you should always use switch statements instead of if-else because switch statements are always faster. This is *not necessarily true*. To understand this, let's take the following statements in C:

```
// if-else version
int flag;
if(flag==0){flag++;}
else{flag = 1;}
```

```
//switch version
switch(flag)
{
    case 0:{flag++;}break;
    default:{flag = 1;}break;
}
```

Now examine the corresponding Intel assembly code:

```
; if-else statement------------------
cmp    DWORD PTR _flag$[ebp], 0
jne    SHORT $L142

mov    eax, DWORD PTR _flag$[ebp]
add    eax, 1
mov    DWORD PTR _flag$[ebp], eax
jmp    SHORT $L143

$L142:
mov    DWORD PTR _flag$[ebp], 1
$L143:

; switch-statement------------------
mov    ecx, DWORD PTR _flag$[ebp]
mov    DWORD PTR -8+[ebp], ecx
cmp    DWORD PTR -8+[ebp], 0
je     SHORT $L148
jmp    SHORT $L149
$L148:
mov    edx, DWORD PTR _flag$[ebp]
add    edx, 1
mov    DWORD PTR _flag$[ebp], edx
jmp    SHORT $L145

$L149:
mov    DWORD PTR _flag$[ebp], 1
$L145:
```

Surprise! The two snippets of code cost roughly the same amount of execution time. The catch is that if-else statements are rarely ever this simple. A typical if-else condition can involve multiple conditional evaluations, like the following:

```
if((flag<100)&&((flag%2==0)||(flag%5==1)))
{
    flag=-1;
}
```

which in Intel assembler looks like this:

```
cmp     DWORD PTR _flag$[ebp], 100
jge     SHORT $L142
mov     eax, DWORD PTR _flag$[ebp]
cdq
xor     eax, edx
sub     eax, edx
and     eax, 1
xor     eax, edx
sub     eax, edx
test    eax, eax
je      SHORT $L143
mov     eax, DWORD PTR _flag$[ebp]
cdq
mov     ecx, 5
idiv    ecx
cmp     edx, 1
jne     SHORT $L142
$L143:
mov     DWORD PTR _flag$[ebp], -1
$L142:
```

Yikes. Because the switch statement, unlike if-else, is syntactically constrained to simple integer comparisons, it will *usually* be faster than anything but the most basic if-else statement. Always read the fine print.

6.2.3 Common Case First, Infrequent Case Last

If you are in a situation where you have no choice but to implement a switch statement, or an if-else ladder, always evaluate in order of frequency. In other words, evaluate the most common case first and the least common case last. The problem with this advice is that it assumes that you know how to determine the relative frequency of the different branching conditions. I can't offer you a general solution to this dilemma, but there are a few special situations. For example, if one case is normal and the others are all exceptional cases, put the normal case first.

```
if(type==NORMAL){ /*handle normal case*/ }
else if(type==EXCEPTION_1){ /*handle exception #1*/ }
else if(type==EXCEPYION_2){ /*handle exception #2*/ }
```

If the cases are all equally likely, then I would urge you to order things in a way that makes your code readable (e.g., alphabetical order, numeric order, etc.).

```
switch(charType)
{
    case ALPHA:{ /*...*/ }break;
    case COLON:{ /*...*/ }break;
    case COMMA:{ /*...*/ }break;
    case DIGIT:{ /*...*/ }break;
    case LEFT_PAREN:{ /*...*/ }break;
    case PERIOD:{ /*...*/ }break;
    case RIGHT_PAREN:{ /*...*/ }break;
    case SEMI_COLON:{ /*...*/ }break;
    case WHITE_SPACE:{ /*...*/ }break;
}
```

6.3 Program Control Loops

Loops provide fertile ground for improvement. This is because the operations that are performed inside of a loop have the potential to be repeated thousands of times. One small change can yield significant performance gains. In this section, I will present a collection of techniques for speeding up the execution of loops.

6.3.1 Loop Invariants

Any expression that does not depend upon the loop variable, or side effects produced by the loop variable, are *loop invariant* and can be relocated outside the loop. For example, consider the following code; it uses a Fourier series approximation to model a square wave (see Figure 6-2):

```
#include<math.h>
#define     PI     3.1415926535897932384626433832795
double FourierSquareWave
(
    double value,     //value at which to evaluate the function
    long limit,       //number of terms to sum
    double halfLength //half the period of the wave
)
{
    long i;
    double sum=0.0;
    double n;

    for(i=1;i<limit;i=i+2)
    {
        n = (double)i;
        sum = sum + ((4/PI)*((1/n)*(sin((n*value*PI)/halfLength))));
    }
    return(sum);
}
```

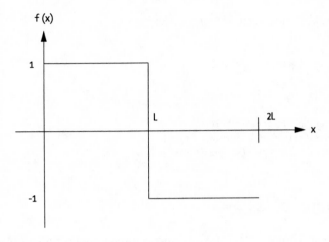

Figure 6-2. Square wave with period 2

You can speed this loop up by moving the two different invariants outside the summation loop:

```
#include<math.h>
#define     PI     3.14159265358979323846264338327950
double FourierSquareWave
(
    double value,
    long limit,
    double halfLength
)
{
    long i;
    double sum=0.0;
    double n;

    double const1 = 4/PI;
    double const2 = value*PI;

    for(i=1;i<limit;i=i+2)
    {
        n = (double)i;
        sum = sum + ((const1)*((1/n)*(sin((n*const2)/halfLength))));
    }
    return(sum);
}
```

To be honest, this example is somewhat artificial (for the sake of illustration). If you wanted a really fast way to get the same basic results, you could use the following:

```
double FourierSquareWave(double value, double halfLength)
{
    double remainder;
    double epsilon = 1.0e-20;

    remainder = fmod(value,2*halfLength);
    if(remainder<epsilon){ return(0.0); }
    else if(remainder<halfLength){ return(1.0); }
    else if(remainder>halfLength){ return(-1.0); }
    else if(remainder==halfLength){ return(0.0); }
}
```

6.3.2 Function Calls

Making a function call involves setting up a stack frame and jumping to another region of memory. If you have to make a function call inside of a loop, see if you can substitute it with a macro or an inline function. Recall what I said about function calls causing the processor to flush its cache. By using a macro, you are allowing the processor to stay inside of its cache and also sidestepping stack frame management.

Consider the following source code; it computes values for the exponential function near zero using a Maclaurin series:

```
#define MAX_FACTORIAL    9
unsigned long factorials[] = { 1, 1, 2, 6, 24, 120, 720, 5040, 40320, 362880};
double power(double value, int power)
{
    double product=1.0;
    int i;
    for(i=0;i<power;i++){ product*=value; }
    return(product);
}
double computeTerm(double value,int index)
{
    return((power(value,index)/factorials[index]));
}
double expSeries(double value,int limit)
{
    double sum=0.0;
    int i;

    if(limit>MAX_FACTORIAL){ limit =MAX_FACTORIAL; }

    for(i=0;i<=limit;i++)
    {
        sum = sum + computeTerm(value,i);
    }
    return(sum);
}
```

You can enhance the speed of this function using macros and inline functions.

```
#define MAX_FACTORIAL    9
unsigned long factorials[] = { 1, 1, 2, 6, 24, 120, 720, 5040, 40320, 362880};
inline double power(double value, int power)
{
    double product=1.0;
    int i;

    for(i=0;i<power;i++){ product*=value; }
    return(product);
}
#define TERM(value,index) power(value,index)/factorials[index]
double expSeries(double value,int limit)
{
    double sum=0.0;
    int i;

    if(limit>MAX_FACTORIAL){ limit =MAX_FACTORIAL; }

    for(i=0;i<=limit;i++)
    {
        sum = sum + TERM(value,i);
    }
    return(sum);
}
```

The `inline` keyword was introduced by C++ and was intended to allow class member functions to be expanded inline. Some C/C++ compilers, however, allow you to apply the `inline` keyword to stand-alone routines.

6.3.3 Array References

Consider the following code:

```
value = 0xFF;
array[5] = 0xFF;
threeDArray[4][5][6] = 0xFF;
```

Strictly speaking, the array assignment is a more expensive operation. This discrepancy can become nontrivial inside of a tightly nested loop. To understand the reason behind this, it helps to look at the assembly code that gets generated:

```
; value = 0xFF;
mov      DWORD PTR _value$[ebp], 255
; array[5] = 0xFF;
mov      DWORD PTR _array$[ebp+20], 255
; threeDArray[4][5][6] = 0xFF;
mov      DWORD PTR _threeDArray$[ebp+1824], 255
```

When an array element is accessed, the processor has to perform arithmetic at runtime (e.g., add an integer to the contents of the EBP register) to determine the exact address of the array element. For normal variables, the processor doesn't have to do this.

Obviously, most of the time it is impossible not to mention an array element as shown here:

```
double average(double *array, unsigned long size)
{
    unsigned long i;
    double sum=0.0;

    for(i=0;i<size;i++){ sum += array[i]; }
    return(sum/((double)size));
}
```

However, in some instances an array element can be moved outside of a loop and replaced by a variable. For example, take the following nested loop:

```
for(i=0;i<nRows;i++)
{
    for(j=0;j<nColumns;j++)
    {
        result[i] = result[i] + ((matrix[i][j])*vector[j]);
    }
}
```

This nested loop can be rewritten as shown here:

```
for(i=0;i<nRows;i++)
{
    double resultVal = 0.0;

    for(j=0;j<nColumns;j++)
    {
        resultVal = resultVal + ((matrix[i][j])*vector[j]);
    }

    result[i] = resultVal;
}
```

6.3.4 Breaking Up Compound Boolean Expressions

The ANSI C standard specifies a form of "short circuit" condition evaluation, where the compiler emits code such that the program will stop evaluating a condition as soon as it knows the condition will be false. Here is an example:

```
if((value<52)&&(value%2==0))
{
      /*do some work*/
}
```

In terms of Intel assembly language, this will look like the following:

```
cmp    DWORD PTR _value$[ebp], 52
jge    SHORT $L22001
mov    eax, DWORD PTR _value$[ebp]
cdq
xor    eax, edx
sub    eax, edx
and    eax, 1
xor    eax, edx
sub    eax, edx
test   eax, eax
jne    SHORT $L22001
;-------------------------
; do some work
;-------------------------
$L22001
```

As you can see, if the first expression in the condition is false, the program will stop evaluating the condition and skip the corresponding block of code.

If you are working with a language or some oddball compiler that does not support short circuit evaluation, then you can simulate it as follows:

```
if(value<52)
{
    if(value%2==0)
    {
        /*do some work*/
    }
}
```

The idea behind this technique is to prevent the processor from doing unnecessary work by allowing it to stop as soon as it realizes that a condition is false.

6.3.5 Loop Unrolling

In the average `for()` loop, there is overhead associated with managing the loop control variable. For example, in the following snippet of code, the processor has to take the time to initialize the loop index, increment it, and compare it against the terminal value:

```
for(i=0;i<9;i++)
{
    doWork(i);
}
```

One way to avoid spending processor time on this overhead, if the number of loop iterations is fixed, is to manually perform the loop operation.

```
doWork(0);
doWork(1);
doWork(2);
doWork(3);
doWork(4);
doWork(5);
doWork(6);
doWork(7);
doWork(8);
```

There is a caveat to this technique. If the unrolled instructions are too large to fit into the processor's cache, then it could cause the processor to flush and reload the cache. This could slow things down.

6.3.6 Loop Jamming

Loop jamming is exactly what it sounds like: taking as many operations as you can and jamming them into the same loop. Specifically, loop jamming involves taking neighboring loops that iterate over a common range and merging them into a single loop. This cuts down on loop bookkeeping and makes your code more efficient. For example, you could take the following two loops that initialize two arrays:

```
for(i=0; i<n; i++)
{
    productID[i]=NULL;
}
for(i=0; i<n; i++)
{
    perUnitCost[i]=0;
}
```

and merge them:

```
for(i=0; i<n; i++)
{
    productID[i]=NULL;
    perUnitCost[i]=0;
}
```

6.3.7 Extracting Program Branching Statements

As stated earlier, program branching statements are an inefficient use of processor time and should be avoided if possible. This is particularly true when it comes to the body of a program loop. If at all possible, try to move if-else and switch statements outside of program loops.

For example, given the following source code:

```
for(i=0; i<limit; i++)
{
    if(isUserNameValid(name))
    {
        commitTransaction(order[i]);
    }
    else
    {
        logFailure(order[i]);
    }
}
```

you can move the if-else statement outside of the while loop, as shown in the following code snippet, to save the processor from having to execute the if-else statement each time the loop iterates:

```
if(isUserNameValid(name))
{
    for(i=0;i<limit;i++)
    {
        commitTransaction(order[i]);
    }
}
else
{
    for(i=0;i<limit;i++)
    {
        logFailure(order[i]);
    }
}
```

6.4 Memory Management

Memory management routines rely very heavily on native system calls to do their dirty work. As such, they are very expensive to invoke. The resident memory manager has to take care of a lot of bookkeeping when memory is allocated or freed. It doesn't matter whether the memory manager uses manual or automatic collection; both approaches do a significant amount of work behind the scenes to track free and allocated blocks of memory.

> **NOTE** *The question of whether manual memory management is more efficient than automatic memory management (i.e., garbage collection) is a thorny issue. The difficulty lies in the fact that there are dozens of different algorithms[7] on both sides of the tracks and a variety of special implementations.[8] This makes it damn near impossible to come to any universal conclusions. The only concrete statement that you can make is that memory allocation is costly.*

6.4.1 Dealing with the Overhead

The first, and best, solution to dealing with the overhead associated with memory allocation is not to do it. Specifically, I would recommend pooling as an agreeable alternative to making repeated calls to `malloc()` and `free()` (I discussed pooling extensively in the previous chapter). The only problem with the pooling strategy is that it assumes you know ahead of time what, and how much, you are going to allocate. Sometimes you can't make these kinds of predictions.

There will be times when you have no alternative but to dynamically allocate memory. For these situations, I have one good piece of advice: be thrifty. Specifically, try to see if you can allocate a large chunk of memory, which you then break into an arbitrary number of smaller chunks, so that you can amortize the cost of allocation over as many bytes as possible. By allocating in large lots, you effectively lower the cost per byte.

Extendable arrays are a variation of this theme. An extendable array is an array that allocates memory in large blocks when it starts to run out of storage space. String tables in compilers often are built using extendable arrays.

---

7. Richard Jones and Rafael Lins, *Garbage Collection: Algorithms for Automatic Dynamic Memory Management* (John Wiley & Sons, 1996. ISBN: 0-471-94148-4)

8. Bill Blunden, *Memory Management: Algorithms and Implementation in C/C++* (Wordware, 2002. ISBN: 1-55622-347-1)

The following source code implements an extendable array:

```
/* ExtendableArray.cpp --------------------------------------------*/
#include<stdio.h>
#include<stdlib.h>
#include<string.h>
/*+++++++++++++++++++++++++++++++++++++++++++++++++++++++++++++++++++
+ Declaration                                                       +
+++++++++++++++++++++++++++++++++++++++++++++++++++++++++++++++++++*/
class ExtendableArray
{
    private:
    int increment;    /*controls re-allocation size*/
    int *start;       /*pointer to start of list*/
    int capacity;     /*current capacity*/
    int nextIndex;    /*next free space*/

    public:
    ExtendableArray(int initialSize,int increment);
    ~ExtendableArray();
    void addToList(int value);
    int getArrayElement(int index);
    void printList();
};
/*+++++++++++++++++++++++++++++++++++++++++++++++++++++++++++++++++++
+ Definitions                                                       +
+++++++++++++++++++++++++++++++++++++++++++++++++++++++++++++++++++*/
ExtendableArray::ExtendableArray
(
    int initialSize,
    int increment
)
{
    (*this).increment = increment;

    start = (int*)malloc(initialSize*sizeof(int));

    if(start==NULL)
    {
        printf("constructor(): cannot allocate memory\n");
        exit(1);
    }
    nextIndex = 0;
    capacity = initialSize;
    return;
}/*end constructor------------------------------------------------*/
ExtendableArray::~ExtendableArray()
```

```
{
    free(start);
    return;
}/*end destructor-------------------------------------------------*/
void ExtendableArray::addToList(int value)
{
    int *temp;
    int mallocSize;

    if(nextIndex >= capacity)
    {
        mallocSize = capacity + increment;
        temp = (int*)malloc(mallocSize*sizeof(int));
        if(temp==NULL)
        {
            printf("addToList(): cannot allocate more memory\n");
            exit(1);
        }
        else
        {
            printf("addToList(): not enough room for %d\n",value);
            printf("addToList(): allocating %d more cells\n",increment);
            memcpy(temp,start,capacity*sizeof(int));
            free(start);
            start = temp;
            capacity = capacity+increment;
        }
    }

    start[nextIndex]=value;
    nextIndex++;
    return;
}/*end addToList-------------------------------------------------*/
int ExtendableArray::getArrayElement(int index)
{
    if((index>=0)&&(index<capacity))
    {
        return(start[index]);
    }
    printf("getArrayElement(): index %d out of bounds\n",index);
    return(0);
}/*end getArrayElement-------------------------------------------*/
void ExtendableArray::printList()
{
    int i;

    printf("capacity =%d\n",capacity);
    printf("next index     =%d\n",nextIndex);
```

```
        for(i=0;i<nextIndex;i++)
        {
            printf("%d) %d\n",i,start[i]);
        }
        return;
}/*printList--------------------------------------------------------*/
void main()
{
    ExtendableArray array(4,4);
    array.addToList(4);
    array.addToList(-5);
    array.addToList(1);
    array.addToList(11);

    array.addToList(7);
    array.addToList(8);
    array.addToList(-12);
    array.addToList(122);

    array.addToList(4);
    array.addToList(5);
    array.addToList(5);
    array.addToList(-101);

    array.addToList(3);

    array.printList();

    printf("array[2]=%d\n",array.getArrayElement(2));

    return;
}/*end main---------------------------------------------------------*/
```

When the driver in `main()` is run, the following output will be produced:

```
C:\>extendableArray
addToList(): not enough room for 7
addToList(): allocating 4 more cells
addToList(): not enough room for 4
addToList(): allocating 4 more cells
addToList(): not enough room for 3
addToList(): allocating 4 more cells
capacity =16
next index =13
0) 4
1) -5
2) 1
3) 11
4) 7
```

```
5) 8
6) -12
7) 122
8) 4
9) 5
10) 5
11) -101
12) 3
array[2]=1
```

I have sprinkled `printf()` statements in this code to makes its operation more obvious. You would need to remove these invocations, or deactivate them with a `#define`, in a production scenario.

6.4.2 Locality of Reference

This is a subtle point that you can leverage for speed. All of the current enterprise operating systems (HP-UX, Linux, Windows, z/OS, OpenBSD, etc.) maintain a virtual address space that is a combination of physical memory and disk storage. Under this scheme, the address space of an application is broken up into units called *pages*. A page of virtual memory can be either in physical memory or may reside on disk. The motivation behind this is that disk storage can be used to simulate physical memory if the machine runs low on physical memory (see Figure 6-3).

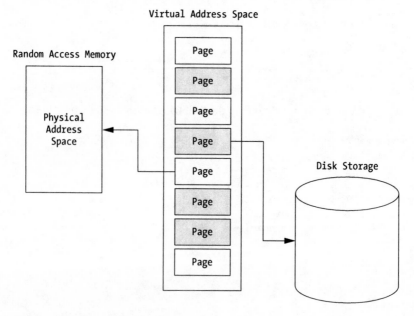

Figure 6-3. Virtual address space

NOTE   *In my opinion, using disk storage to simulate memory is an anachronism from the old days, back when 16KB of memory cost a few hundred dollars. Today you can buy 2GB of RAM for less than a thousand dollars and there's no need to use disk storage. Not only that, but the performance hit associated with performing disk I/O is exorbitant (10,000 to 100,000 times slower than accessing physical memory).*

If your program references a variable that has been persisted to the disk drive, a *page fault* will occur. This page fault will force the processor to load the page of storage (i.e., 4096 bytes on Intel) from the disk drive and into physical memory. It just so happens that disk I/O is one of the most expensive operations that a computer can perform. By forcing your program to access simulated storage on disk, you are killing your program's performance.

One way around this is to design your program so that it avoids accessing remote global data. The problem with this prescription is that it's much harder than it sounds. Placing everything that you need in the current activation record not only wastes memory, but also can make the activation record so large that part of it gets paged to disk.

In fact, it is almost impossible to design a program such that you can *guarantee* that the data you access will not be paged to disk. Program design often has nothing to do with it (surprise!). The percentage of a program's address space that an operating system persists to disk storage can vary based on the workload that the operating system is currently carrying. For instance, if your server is loaded down with 800 running programs, the operating system may decide to lower the size of each program's working set such that each program has less than a megabyte of actual space in physical memory. This makes disk I/O inevitable, regardless of a program's implementation.

Having said that, there is one approach that will protect you against page fault disk I/O: install enough physical memory to support your application load and then disable paging to disk. Most operating systems have a configuration switch hidden away somewhere that will allow you to disable the use of disk storage by the memory manager. For example, Windows uses a special system file, known as a *page file*, to use disk storage to simulate physical memory. On Windows, you can completely disable the page file by toggling the No paging file radio button in the Virtual Memory dialog box (see Figure 6-4).

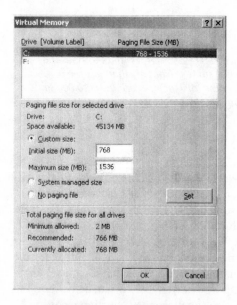

Figure 6-4. Disabling the page file on windows

6.5 Input/Output

In every computer there exists what is known as a *memory hierarchy*. Types of memory storage are placed in the hierarchy relative to how quickly the processor can access them. In other words, each level in the hierarchy has a certain lag time (or *latency*). Data stored in the processor's registers can be accessed the fastest, and data stored by external hardware has the slowest access time (see Figure 6-5).

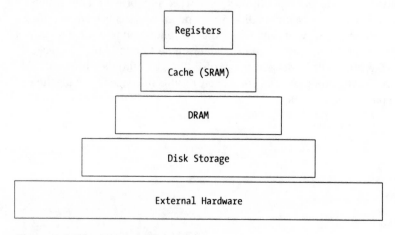

Figure 6-5. The memory hierarchy

In the old days, primary memory (referred to, back then, as *the core*) consisted of little ferrite loops that could be magnetized in one of two directions. In 1955, IBM's 705 was the first computer to utilize ferrite core memory. Primary memory today, which is referred to as *random access memory* (RAM), uses submicron electronic circuits to store data. Two basic types of RAM exist: dynamic RAM (DRAM) and static RAM (SRAM). DRAM needs to be recharged periodically to safeguard the integrity of its data; SRAM does not. Because SRAM is more expensive than DRAM, it tends to be used for caches located on the processor itself. The memory chips that get inserted into the motherboard's onboard slots use DRAM.

Most processors have an internal oscillator that oscillates at a certain number of cycles per second (e.g., a 1 GHz processor has an oscillator that performs 1,000,000,000 cycles per second). This oscillator sets the tempo of the song that the processor dances to. The number of cycles per second performed by the oscillator is known as the processor's *clock speed.*

Accessing data in the registers typically requires an amount of time on the order of a single cycle (e.g., a nanosecond on a 1 GHz processor). Accessing data on disk can easily consume an amount of time on the order of 10,000 or even 100,000 processor cycles. Disk access and network traffic are usually measured in terms of milliseconds.

The moral of the story is that disk input/output is one of the most expensive operations that a computer can perform. It should be avoided at all costs. In this section, I will discuss a few techniques you can use to make disk I/O less expensive. While reading through this section, keep the following mantra in the back of your mind:

Minimize the number of disk accesses.

Minimize the number of disk accesses.

Minimize the number of disk accesses.

6.5.1 Caching

The best way to avoid disk I/O is not to do it to begin with. One strategy to prevent unnecessary disk access is simply to cache data, which is normally stored on disk, in memory. Every time that a data element is requested, its copy in RAM can be referenced instead of having to perform a disk read. Caching works best if the data being cached is read frequently but relatively static. When it does work, caching can offer dramatic performance improvements.

Web servers make extensive use of caching. A solitary Web server besieged by thousands of requests doesn't have time to constantly access disk storage for the same page. Caching Web pages can easily double or triple throughput. For example, the Apache Web server uses the mod_cache module to implement

RFC 2616 HTTP content caching.[9] The `mod_cache` module uses the services of the `mod_mem_cache` module to cache objects in the heap or cache open file descriptors.

Database systems maintain a *data dictionary*, which describes the organization of the database. The data dictionary tracks all of the tables in the database, the columns that those tables use, and the data type of those columns, in addition to any conditions or relationships associated with the tables. In other words, the data dictionary is a repository of table metadata. The data dictionary is typically implemented as a set of system-defined database tables. To boost performance, most database systems cache the data dictionary in memory to service database requests more efficiently.

6.5.2 Buffering

When CIOs open up the corporate war chest and invest in a multimillion-dollar mainframe, their goal is to use the machine long enough so that they can distribute the purchase price over as many years as possible. The ultimate goal is to decrease the total cost per year to a reasonable level. This explains why some companies are still using machines that they bought back in the 1980s.

Data buffering is based on similar reasoning. The initial cost of reading or writing to disk storage is very high. To offset this charge, you need to read and write a large number of bytes such that the price of performing I/O can be amortized over as many bytes as possible, yielding a reasonable cost per byte.

Caveat emptor! There are a few tricky points that you should be aware of when buffering. Specifically, you should observe the following two conventions:

- Be careful when buffering user libraries.

- Do not use buffers that are too small or too large.

Both the operating system and the user library calls buffer the data that they read and write. If you add buffering on top of this, you are just slapping on another layer of additional overhead. If you are going to take the trouble to buffer data, then make sure that you are dealing with primitive system calls that do not buffer themselves. For example, Windows provides a low-level API (declared in io.h) for disk access that does not buffer or format data, and this is shown in Table 6-1.

---

9.   http://httpd.apache.org/docs-2.0/mod/mod_cache.html

Table 6-1. Low-Level Windows I/O

Format	Use
_close	Closes a file
_commit	Forces a file's contents to be flushed to disk
_create	Creates a new file
_eof	Tests for the end of a file
_lseek	Sets the position of the file pointer
_open	Opens a file (creation is optional)
_read	Reads from a file
_tell	Returns the current location of the file pointer
_write	Writes to a file

Hard drives consist of a vertical stack of metal platters that spin rapidly about a central spindle. Each side, on a given platter, is divided into concentric circular *tracks* (see Figure 6-6). Each track is subdivided into units of storage called *sectors*. The sector is the smallest unit of storage on a disk drive. The size of a sector can vary, depending on the type of disk storage being utilized, but for personal computers a sector will usually be 512 bytes in size.

Operating systems will read and write disk data in terms of sectors. Hence, a buffer should be no less than a sector in size. If you try to write less than a sector's worth of data to disk, the operating system will pad the data until it is as big as a sector and write the sector to disk. It is a good idea to define buffers that are a multiple number of sectors in size. At the same time, you should be careful not to make your buffers too large. If a buffer gets too big, it can end up being (partially or entirely) paged to disk. This would ruin performance, because in order to flush the buffer to disk you would first need to read the parts of the buffer that had been paged to disk. Picking the optimal buffer size is a context-sensitive problem; there is no closed form answer. I can only tell you that your best bet is to leave buffer size configurable so that your program is flexible enough to adapt to its surroundings and the workload that it has to process.

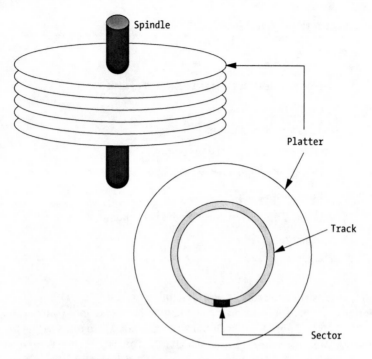

Figure 6-6. Hard disk layout

6.5.3 Advanced Techniques

Caching and buffering are two fairly universal solutions that work in a wide variety of situations. However, advanced techniques are available that can be used in a couple of special scenarios.

Data Compression

One way to minimize disk accesses is to compress the information that you are storing on disk. To this end, the zlib library that I mentioned in the previous chapter can be utilized. The processor *does* have to take extra time to compress and decompress the data, *but* the time needed to process the data in memory is nowhere near as great as the time needed for larger disk accesses. So, in a sense, compression is an approach that pays for itself, kind of like solar energy panels. In the future, disk drive controllers may automatically compress and decompress data stored on disk to take advantage of this space/time exchange.

Manual Disk Layout

A device known as a *read/write head* accesses each usable side of a disk platter. These heads are like phonograph needles, only they do not touch the platter. They hover slightly above the surface (see Figure 6-7). The only read/write heads that actually do make contact are those for 3.5-inch floppy disks (which accounts for their slow access speed).

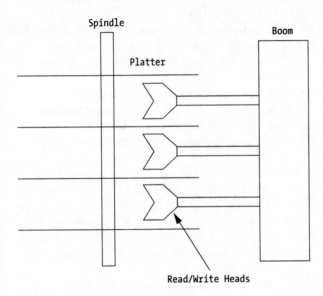

Figure 6-7. A disk drive head setup

The read/write heads of a hard drive are all attached to a boom, which moves the read/write heads in unison over the same track on each platter. The collection of tracks, which all have the same radius from the central spindle, is known as a *cylinder*. At any point in time, the read/write heads are limited to manipulating the sectors of a specific cylinder.

In order to read or write a certain disk sector, the head must perform three operations:

- The head must perform a seek.

- The head must experience a rotational delay.

- The head must read/write the disk sector.

During a *seek* operation the boom must move the heads so that they are in line with the track that contains the sector. Given that the platters are spinning rapidly about the spindle, the head adjacent to the track containing the sector must then wait until the sector rotates to the head. The lag time is known as *rotational delay*. Of the three operations, the seek operation is the most time intensive.

Normally, the native operating system controls which sectors a file's data is written to. The problem with this is that the operating system often allows a file's sectors to become spread out over different tracks in different cylinders. This fragmentation can slow down disk I/O significantly. Most operating systems ship with tools to defragment disk drives, but it would be nice if the file system component of the operating system could take care of this problem as a part of its normal operations.

With database systems, storage access time is a big issue (because this is what database systems basically do: manipulate data on disk storage). In fact, disk access time is a big enough issue that many vendors ship their databases with a customized file manager that sidesteps the operating system's native facilities.[10]

These special-purpose file managers cater to the needs of the database by ensuring that the sectors that make up a file are as close to each other physically as possible. In an ideal case, the sectors of a file would all lie on the same track, or at least in the same cylinder so that the heads do not have to seek at all. For larger files that require multiple cylinders, the database's file manager would try to minimize seek time by locating the cylinders as closely together as possible.

Reverting to manual disk layout is an extreme solution. Not only does it require an incredible investment of time (you are basically building your own file system driver), but also it can tie you irrevocably to the hardware that you're working with. Your code will be complicated and very difficult to port. The only engineers that fall back on this technique are the ones who stand to reap enough benefits to justify the initial expenditure. Typically database vendors, like Oracle, who need to push the performance envelope to its limits, will take this type of measure.

Speaking of Oracle, Larry Ellison tried to take this concept of sidestepping the native operating system to a higher level. At Comdex in November of 1998, during a keynote address, Ellison announced that he was going to bypass the native operating system entirely by shipping Oracle's database software with its own microkernel operating system. This initiative was labeled the Raw Iron project because Oracle would essentially be interfacing directly with the hardware, with only a thin layer of system code in between.

---

10. Thomas Connolly and Carolyn Begg, *Database Systems: A Practical Approach* (Addison-Wesley, 2001. ISBN: 0-201-70857-4)

The Raw Iron project, later rechristened as the Oracle8i Appliance, fizzled out quietly.[11] As META Group analyst Anthony Bradley put it:

> *One of the big initiatives going forward in the industry is database and server consolidation, the ability to manage multiple databases on the same box. (Raw Iron) increases server proliferation and decreases flexibility and manageability. So it seems to fly in the face of the market trends.*

6.6 Exceptions

Back when C was king, programmers had to rely on return values and global variables to propagate news about a program error. The problem with this approach is threefold:

- Source code is less readable.

- State information is lost.

- Crashes result from ignored return values.

If you handle every single possible return value that the C standard library returns, then you risk having your code's train of logic being mired in a swamp of details. This kind of code is not readable. If you don't believe me, take the following routine as an example:

```
int readString()
{
    int returnValue;
    char string[64];

    returnValue = scanf("%s",string);
    if((returnValue==0)||(returnValue==EOF))
    {
        returnValue = printf("error reading string\n");
        if(returnValue<0)
        {
            returnValue = fprintf(stderr,"unable to printf()\n");
            if(returnValue<0)
            {
                exit(1);
            }
        }
    }
}
```

---

11. Mike Ricciuti, "Lack of Interest Sinking Oracle's Raw Iron?" *CNET News.com*, January 24, 2000

```
returnValue = printf("%s\n",string);
if(returnValue<0)
{
    returnValue = fprintf(stderr,"could not printf()\n");
    if(returnValue<0)
    {
        exit(1);
    }
}
return(returnValue);
}
```

To make matters worse, a single error value rarely offers enough information. Most programmers would be hard pressed to figure out why and how a function fails when all they get is a return value of –1. Information about the state of the program is lost.

Finally, like everyone else, programmers suffer from deadlines. Unreasonable time constraints can lead programmers to forget to handle the function return values. This type of oversight can bring everything crashing down.

```
void readFile(char *fileName)
{
    FILE *filePointer;
    int byte;

    filePointer = fopen(fileName,"rb");

    //forget to check for filePointer==NULL

    byte = fgetc(filePointer);
    while(byte!=EOF)
    {
        printf("%c",(char)byte);
        byte = fgetc(filePointer);
    }

    fclose(filePointer);
}
```

Exception handling offers a solution to these three problems.

Exceptions, Throws, and Catches

An *exception* is a programmatic entity that is constructed when a program tries to perform an abnormal operation. This does not mean that every exception represents an error; rather, an exception is intended to represent a condition that the programmer views as unusual.

When an exception is created, a potentially nonlocal jump will be performed from the code producing the exception to the code that has been registered to handle the exception. An exception is *thrown* by the code that generates it and *caught* by the code that processes it. In C++, exception-handling services are implemented using the try, catch, and throw keywords.

```c
#define DIVIDE_BY_ZERO    1
#define MSG_SIZE    64
struct Exception
{
    char location[MSG_SIZE];
    char message[MSG_SIZE];
    int type;
};
void performDivision(int *i, int * j)
{
    if((*j)==0)
    {
        struct Exception exception;
        strcpy(exception.location,"createException");
        strcpy(exception.message,"divide by zero");
        exception.type = DIVIDE_BY_ZERO;
        throw(&exception);
    }
     (*i) = (*i)/(*j);
    return;
}
void createException()
{
    int i;
    int j;
    i = 5;
    j=0;
    try
    {
        performDivision(&i,&j);
    }
    catch(struct Exception *exception)
    {
        printf("%s(): ",(*exception).location);
        printf("%s\n",(*exception).message);
        i = 0;
    }
}
```

There are two ways that I have seen exception handling implemented:

- Dynamic registration approach

- Static table approach

I am using the terminology adopted by Christensen.[12] Different researchers have used other terms for these two approaches, like *portable* and *nonportable*. In the following sections I will look at both of these approaches.

6.6.1 Dynamic Registration Model

The dynamic registration model uses a stack-based data structure to track the location and type of active exception handlers. I will refer to this data structure as the *exception-handling stack*. When a try-catch statement is first entered, the program will push this statement's metadata on to the exception-handling stack. When program control leaves the try-catch statement, the program will pop this statement's information off the exception-handling stack. This guarantees that the exception-handling stack will only include information on handlers that currently enclose the instruction pointer.

When an exception is thrown, the runtime environment will query the exception-handling stack for an exception handler that processes the type of exception being thrown. If such a handler is found, a potentially nonlocal jump will be made to the handler. This is illustrated in Figure 6-8.

One of the performance issues with this approach is that the compiler has to generate special code to manage the exception-handling stack. This translates into extra instructions, which translates into more CPU time. If an exception happens only rarely, then a lot of this stack management work is a waste of effort.

Oddly enough, some implementations of this approach use the operating system to keep track of exception-handling metadata. This is not exactly a good idea, because it adds the overhead of making a system call to the already expensive task of managing the exception data structure. Most of the time, however, the dynamic registration approach does not rely at all on the native operating system, and this allows the dynamic registration approach to be fairly portable.

---

12. Morten Mikael Christensen, "Methods for Handling Exceptions," M.Sc. thesis, Odense University, 1995

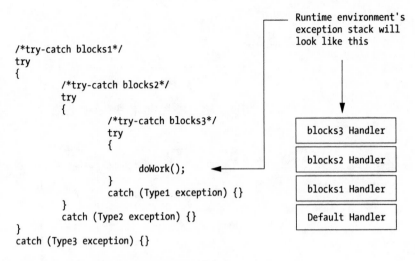

```
                                              ── Runtime environment's
                                                 exception stack will
/*try-catch blocks1*/                            look like this
try
{
        /*try-catch blocks2*/
        try
        {
                /*try-catch blocks3*/
                try                           ┌──────────────────┐
                {                             │  blocks3 Handler  │
                                              ├──────────────────┤
                        doWork();   ◄────     │  blocks2 Handler  │
                }                             ├──────────────────┤
                catch (Type1 exception) {}    │  blocks1 Handler  │
        }                                     ├──────────────────┤
        catch (Type2 exception) {}            │  Default Handler  │
}                                             └──────────────────┘
catch (Type3 exception) {}
```

Figure 6-8. Dynamic registration model

6.6.2 Static Table Model

The static table model relies on the compiler to create a special table to index exception handlers. Each exception handler gets an entry in the table. Among other things, the table entry records the address range over which the exception handler is valid. The table stores other types of information, but the address range is the crucial piece of metadata.

When an exception is thrown, the value of the instruction pointer (e.g., the EIP register on the Intel) is examined. The instruction pointer stores the address of the current instruction being executed. If there is a handler that is capable of processing the exception being thrown, and whose address range encloses the current value of the instruction pointer, then a (potentially) non-local goto will be performed that transfers program control to the exception handler. This operation is displayed in Figure 6-9.

If an exception handler cannot be found for the current instruction pointer value, then the return address of the current procedure will be extracted from its activation record. This return address will then be processed in a manner similar to the instruction pointer. In other words, the return address is treated like a new instruction pointer value. This process will continue until the call stack unwinds to the program's point of entry. If this is the case, then a default exception will usually be invoked.

Because the exception-handling table is created at compile time, there is little or no overhead associated with its maintenance (unlike the exception-handling stack, it has already been built). The overhead that occurs can be attributed to the handling of the execution.

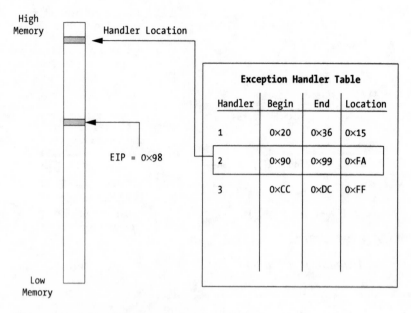

Figure 6-9. Table-driven exceptions

6.6.3 Dealing with Overhead

As I've mentioned many times already, there are no perfect answers, only trade-offs and personal values. Which is to say that choosing a particular technique has a lot to do with your worldview. Table 6-2 provides a comparison of the dynamic registration and static table approach.

Table 6-2. Exception Scheme Trade-Offs

Attribute	Stack-Driven	Table-Driven
Construction	Runtime	Compile time
Handler index	Cheap	Expensive
Portability	Good	Poor
Platform support	No	Sometimes

From our perspective, both approaches are suspicious because they both can slow down the processor. Given that applications are only supposed to rarely fail, some people would argue that the overhead associated with handling an exception is a nonissue. To an extent, I would have to agree with these people. However, if a program frequently uses exceptions as an opportunity to correct itself, instead of heading to the nearest exit, then the performance of exception handling is pertinent.

Both approaches to handling exceptions cost more than using a simple return value. Accessing a function's return value is as simple as popping a value off of the stack. Handling exceptions is a lot more involved, regardless of how they are implemented. To prove this, let's look at the following two function definitions:

```
void function0()
{
    throw(1);
}
int function1()
{
    return(1);
}
```

In Intel assembler, function0() looks like this:

```
push    ebp
mov     ebp, esp
push    ecx
; throw(1);
mov     DWORD PTR $T1123[ebp], 1
push    OFFSET FLAT:__TI1H
lea     eax, DWORD PTR $T1123[ebp]
push    eax
call    _CxxThrowException@8
mov     esp, ebp
pop     ebp
ret     0
```

There's a lot of extraneous stuff going on here. In particular, there's a call to some function named __CxxThrowException@8, which could involve any number of extra instructions. Now compare this to function1(), which looks like the following:

```
push    ebp
mov     ebp, esp
; return(1);
mov     eax, 1
pop     ebp
ret     0
```

Because this function is not recursive and returns a single integer value, the function places its return value in the EAX register. This is much quicker and more direct than exception handling.

The bottom line is this: if you are hell-bent on execution speed, you should use return values instead of exceptions. However, you should be prepared to sacrifice readability and be willing to deal with global variables to recover machine state information.

6.6.4 Abusing Exceptions

Like any other language feature, exceptions can be abused. Some less scrupulous programmers have been known to use exception handling as a way to implement a nonlocal goto statement. In other words, instead of submitting to the normal chain of invocations, a function can jump several functions back with return value information stored in the exception.

The difference between this and the intended use of exception handling is that exception handling is intended to imply that an unusual event has occurred. If you use exception handling casually, you might cause someone reading your code to wonder, "Hey, where's the emergency?"

6.7 Expensive Operations

As I stated earlier, the processor executes straight-line, sequential code the fastest. Even if you have been able to minimize the number of program jumps, branches, loops, and input/output requests, there are still things that you can do to tighten up whatever remains. In this section, I will present techniques that can be used to optimize sequential instructions.

6.7.1 Eliminate Common Subexpressions

If you can identify an expression that gets performed repeatedly in a block of code, it's a good idea to assign the expression to a variable and then use the variable in the block of code, as opposed to repeatedly performing the operation.

For example, the following snippet of code:

```
triangleArea = 0.5*length*width;
volume =  length*width*height;
```

can be rewritten as

```
squareArea = length*width;
triangleArea = 0.5*squareArea;
volume =  squareArea*height;
```

This is a variation of the precompute theme. Realizations of this theme that you have seen so far include

- Replacing well-known values with hard-coded results

- Replacing Boolean expressions with lookup tables

- Calculating values once at runtime and then referencing them

6.7.2 Floating Point Calculation Myths

Originally, the PC did not support floating-point calculations. The owner of an Intel 8086, 80286, or 80386 would have to choose between

- Installing a coprocessor (e.g., the 8087, 80287, 80387)

- Using an emulation library

The emulation routines implemented floating-point calculations using software, and this could significantly slow things down. Typically a compiler, like Borland's Turbo C, would have command-line options to give you the alternative of generating coprocessor instructions or using emulation routines. It should come as no surprise that the mathematics coprocessor was much faster. The emulation routines executed in memory, and the coprocessor executed floating-point calculations at the machine level. Starting with the Intel 80486, the floating-point coprocessor was built into the main processor. Thus, emulation libraries are not as widespread as they used to be.

The floating-point coprocessor embedded in the Intel Pentium (also known as the x87 floating-point unit, or x87 FPU) has its own set of dedicated registers.[13] However, it is also a distinct execution environment relative to the processor, such that normal system instructions and floating-point instructions can be executed concurrently. The FPU cannot read or write to external devices, so it must access memory to obtain data. Thus, the processor and the FPU communicate by exchanging values in memory.

The presence of a dedicated coprocessor to perform floating-point calculations, which can run in parallel with the main processor, discredits the idea that performing floating-point calculations is expensive. This is the case only when emulation libraries are being used (otherwise it is just a myth). If anything, the presence of an independent FPU speeds up the main processor by

---

13. *IA-32 Intel Architecture Software Developer's Manual, Volume 1: Basic Architecture,* Order No: 245470-011 (downloadable from http://www.intel.com)

allowing it to offload work that it would otherwise have to do. If any operation is expensive, it is conversion, because the two processors don't normally speak the same language.

Here's an example that can demonstrate this:

```c
/* floatingPoint.c ------------------------------------------------*/
#include<stdio.h>
#include<windows.h>
#define BEGIN    begin = GetTickCount()
#define END    end = GetTickCount()
#define TIME    printf("msecs=%lu\n",end-begin)
#define MILLION    1000000
void main()
{
    unsigned long begin;
    unsigned long end;
    unsigned long i;
    long value1;
    long value2 = 42;
    long value3 = 7;
    double fvalue1;
    double fvalue2 = 54645.23423;
    double fvalue3 = 343245.324234;

    BEGIN;
    for(i=0;i<MILLION;i++)
    {
        value1 = value2+value3;
        value1 = value2-value3;
        value1 = value2*value3;
        value1 = value2/value3;
    }
    END;
    TIME;

    BEGIN;
    for(i=0;i<MILLION;i++)
    {
        fvalue1 = fvalue2+fvalue3;
        fvalue1 = fvalue2-fvalue3;
        fvalue1 = fvalue2*fvalue3;
        fvalue1 = fvalue2/fvalue3;
    }
    END;
    TIME;

    BEGIN;
    for(i=0;i<MILLION;i++)
```

```
    {
        fvalue1 = (double)value1;
        fvalue2 = (double)value2;
        fvalue3 = (double)value3;
        value1 = (long)fvalue1;
    }
    END;
    TIME;
}
```

When I ran this code, I received the following output:

```
msecs=52
msecs=45
msecs=195
```

As you can see, the conversion routines took up the most time. Keep this is mind when someone tells you that you can save time by converting a floating-point value into an integer. Don't be afraid to write a little disposable program to test what people tell you.

6.7.3 Strength Reduction

The *strength* of an arithmetic operation specifies how much processor time is needed to complete the operation. Strength reduction involves taking a relatively expensive operation and substituting it with a cheaper operation.

Table 6-3 provides a list of potential strength reduction techniques.

Table 6-3. Strength Reduction Tactics

Operation	Replace With	Example
Exponentiation	Multiplication	`y = pow(x,3.0);` becomes `y = x*x*x;`
Multiplication	Addition	`y = x*5;` becomes `y = x+x+x+x+x;`
Multiplication/ Division by 2	Bit-wise shifting	`y = x*34;` becomes `y = (x<<5) + x + x;`
Division	Multiplication	`y = x/4;` becomes `y = x*(0.25);`

6.7.4 Synchronization

The ANSI C standard is conspicuously silent when it comes to multithreading and synchronization. Traditionally, these topics have been left for the native operating system to specify. One of the reasons behind this is that different operating systems have different ways of defining and managing threads. Some operating systems don't support threads, such that a threading model has to be implemented entirely in user space. More sophisticated operating systems, like Windows, not only support threads but also support a lightweight thread construct known as a *fiber*.

Multithreading by itself is not a very taxing activity; it's when the threads share data (e.g., variables) that things start to get expensive. When threads share data, mechanisms have to be used to preserve the integrity of that data by limiting access to it. In other words, primitives must exist so that access to the shared data can be synchronized. Typically the goal of these primitives is to provide mutually exclusive access, so that only one thread at a time can manipulate the data. For example, the Windows Win32 API supports three mutual exclusion primitives: critical sections, mutexes, and semaphores.

From a performance standpoint, these tools are expensive because they are managed at the kernel level, and accessing them means making a system call and sending the program's path of execution on a lengthy journey through the system call gate. On Windows, both semaphores and mutexes are managed at the kernel level. Critical sections on Windows, however, are intraprocess constructs that can be accessed without going through the kernel. Still, even critical sections require a certain degree of behind-the-scenes bookkeeping that incurs a charge with respect to processor time.

As it turns out, while uncontended synchronization translates into a fixed cost, a *serious* penalty occurs when threads contend for a synchronized resource. The more threads that contend, the more behind-the-scenes code that gets executed, and the greater the performance hit.

Let's look at an example to help demonstrate this:

```c
/*synchronize.c -------------------------------------------------*/
#include<stdio.h>
#include<windows.h>

//NOTA BENE - make sure to link with multithreaded libraries!

#define BEGIN     begin = GetTickCount()
#define END       end = GetTickCount()
#define TIME      printf("msecs=%lu\n",end-begin)
#define nLOOPS    500000

void routine(char *string)
{
    /*empty*/
}


CRITICAL_SECTION criticalSection;
```

```
void synchRoutine(char *string)
{
    EnterCriticalSection(&criticalSection);
    LeaveCriticalSection(&criticalSection);
}


#define     NAME_LENGTH     8      /* [t][h][r][e][a][d][#][0x00] */
#define     OK      0

DWORD threadFunc(int *index)
{
    char name[NAME_LENGTH];
    long begin;
    long end;
    unsigned long i;

    strcpy(name,"thread");
    name[NAME_LENGTH-2]='0'+((char)(*index));
    name[NAME_LENGTH-1]=0x00;
    printf("created %s\n",name);

    BEGIN;
    for(i=0;i<nLOOPS;i++)
    {
        synchRoutine(name);
    }
    END;
    printf("END thread %d msecs=%lu\n",*index,(end-begin));
    return(OK);
}


#define     nTHREADS     5

void main()
{
    long begin;
    long end;
    unsigned long i;

    HANDLE hThread[nTHREADS];
    DWORD  threadID[nTHREADS];
    int    argument[nTHREADS];
    DWORD (*functionPointer)(int *index);

    //no synchronization
```

```
BEGIN;
for(i=0;i<nLOOPS;i++){ routine("main()"); }
END;
TIME;

InitializeCriticalSection(&criticalSection);

//uncontended synchronization

BEGIN;
for(i=0;i<nLOOPS;i++){ synchRoutine("main()"); }
END;
TIME;

//now add some contention

functionPointer = threadFunc;

for(i=0;i<nTHREADS;i++)
{
    argument[i]=i;
    hThread[i] = CreateThread
     (
        NULL,
        0,
        (LPTHREAD_START_ROUTINE)functionPointer,
        (LPVOID)&argument[i],
        0,
        &threadID[i]
     );
}

WaitForMultipleObjects(nTHREADS,hThread,TRUE,INFINITE);
for(i=0;i<nTHREADS;i++)
{
    CloseHandle(hThread[i]);
}

DeleteCriticalSection(&criticalSection);
}
```

When this code is run, the following output is produced:

```
msecs=9
msecs=46
created thread0
created thread1
created thread2
```

```
created thread3
created thread4
END thread 1 msecs=635
END thread 0 msecs=1301
END thread 3 msecs=1544
END thread 4 msecs=1509
END thread 2 msecs=1585
```

In the previous code, I invoke a routine with no synchronization
(a bunch of times), then I invoke a routine with uncontended synchronization (a bunch of times), and finally I create five threads and let them contend
for the same routine (a bunch of times).

The uncontested synchronized routine costs about five times as much as
the routine that was not synchronized. The contested synchronized routine
calls were at least 13 times as expensive as the uncontended routine calls.
This should demonstrate how costly it is to implement synchronized code
that is heavily contended.

Given the preceding results, it is obvious that you should try to

- Minimize the total amount of synchronized code.

- Make synchronized blocks of code as small as possible.

- Limit amount of data shared across threads.

- Use separate locks to synchronize different variables, if possible.

6.7.5 Shorthand Operator Myths

I have often seen the op= shorthand operators abused by engineers who
thought it would make their code faster. This is *not necessarily* true. If anything, all it does is hurt readability. For example, consider the following two
statements:

```
value1 = value1 + 0xFF;
value1 += 0xFF;
```

It just so happens that there is no tangible performance differential
between these two statements. Both of these statements get translated into
the same assembly code:

```
; value1 = value1 + 0xFF;----------------------------
mov     eax, DWORD PTR _value1$[ebp]
add     eax, 255
mov     DWORD PTR _value1$[ebp], eax
```

```
; value1 += 0xFF;----------------------------------------
mov     ecx, DWORD PTR _value1$[ebp]
add     ecx, 255
mov     DWORD PTR _value1$[ebp], ecx
```

6.8 Quick Fixes

If you don't have the time to revisit your implementation, there are a couple of quick fixes that you can use that yield immediate improvements.

6.8.1 Better Hardware

If you can afford to buy your way out of a problem, you don't have problem.

—Harvey Mackay, *Swim with the Sharks Without Being Eaten Alive*

If worst comes to worst, you can always open up your wallet and try to buy your way out of a problem. It works for the Mafia, it works for Harvey, and it can work for you, too. Those hardware vendors are just begging for you to visit the showroom. If you don't believe me, see what happens when you call up Big Blue and ask to speak to a sales rep about their mainframe servers. Tell them that you are a CIO from a Fortune 500 company looking to replace your aging legacy systems. Get out a stopwatch and see how many minutes you have to wait before they call you back. Then change your phone number because those sales reps will not stop calling you.

The problem with relying on faster hardware is that it is only a short-term fix. If your application is using weak algorithms, it won't be long until you consume all of the available resources. I don't care if you are running your program on a z900 with 32 processors blazing away; if your program is using bubble sort to repeatedly tackle a list of a million items, you are sunk.

If the hardware manufacturers are able to keep up with Moore's Law (and this is a big "if"), in 20 years it won't be so simple to just go out and buy a faster processor. There might not be any. Parallel processing might come to the rescue, for a short while, but even then Amdahl's Law places a limit to the improvements that parallel processing can provide.[14] Inevitably, the only way to speed things up will be to develop and use better algorithms.

6.8.2 Constrain the Problem

Sometimes you can improve performance by imposing constraints on a program. The basic idea behind this technique is to make your code do one thing, and do it well, by taking advantage of underlying assumptions. The

---

14. Ted G. Lewis et al., *Introduction to Parallel Computing* (Prentice Hall, 1992. ISBN: 0-13-498924-4)

downside to this approach is that your code becomes very brittle and cannot adapt well to more general scenarios.

For example, let's say you want to sort a list of n 32-bit integers (where n is some integer). You could use a general, in-place sorting algorithm like quick-sort or heap-sort. These algorithms, in the average case, require processor time that is $O(n\log_2(n))$. However, *if* you could make the assumption that the list lies within a given range (e.g., 0 to 1000), and each value occurs only once, you could use the Binsort algorithm and achieve performance that is $O(n)$.

Here's another example: in the general case of indexing an arbitrarily large number of records, and supporting advanced search features like range queries, the B*-tree is the data structure of choice. The asymptotic cost of searching, inserting, and deleting records in a B*-tree is $O(\log_B n))$, where n is the total number of records being indexed and B is an integer much larger than 2.

However, *if* you could constrain your indexing problem to a list of key values that was small enough to fit into memory, and you could also constrain record searches to the form "find me the record that has key K," then you could replace the B*-tree with a hash table. The average search time for a record in a hash table is $O(1)$, which is pretty damn good if you can get away with it.

6.8.3 Compiler Settings

A compiler capable of generating optimized object code can automatically implement many of the techniques that I described in this chapter. Some optimizing compilers are quite impressive, and perform as many as 29 separate passes of a given source file. Thus, before you initiate manual optimization, you should see if your compiler has any options that support generating object code that is geared towards execution speed.

The GNU gcc compiler provides a multitude of command-line optimization switches. Table 6-4 lists a few of the more notable ones.

Table 6-4. gcc *Optimization Switches*

Option	Use
-O0	Do not perform optimization.
-O1	The compiler tries to reduce code size and execution time.
-O2	Nearly all supported optimizations are performed except loop unrolling and function inlining.
-O3	Include optimizations specified by -O2 and also turn on function inlining.
-Os	Optimize to reduce code size.
-funroll-loops	Unroll loops if the iterations can be determined at compile time.
-finline-functions	Integrate all simple functions into their callers.

6.9 Summary

A program has two basic resources at its disposal:

- Processor time (i.e., CPU cycles)

- Memory

You can use certain techniques to minimize the amount of time that the processor spends executing an operation. These techniques can result in code that is more difficult to maintain and that may have a larger footprint. Use these techniques as a last resort, only after you have debugged the code thoroughly, profiled it to find bottlenecks, and looked for better algorithms.

Function Calls

- Replace routine calls with goto statements *sparingly.*

- Condense parameters into a structure and pass it by reference.

- Avoid functions that use a varying number of parameters.

- Use system calls sparingly; they are expensive.

- Replace recursion with iteration.

- Use return values instead of exceptions.

Program Branching

- Use lookup tables to replace if-else and switch statements.

- Switch statements are usually cheaper than if-else statements.

- Handle the common case first.

Loops

- Pull out loop invariant instructions.

- Use inline functions when possible.

- Replace array references with atomic variables.

- Use short-circuit condition evaluation.

- Utilize loop unrolling and loop jamming.

- Pull if-else statements outside loops.

Memory Management

- Pool memory for quicker allocation and collection.

- Install enough memory so that you can disable paging to disk.

Input/Output

- Cache static data in memory.

- Buffer data in multiples of the disk sector size.

- Compress data to minimize disk access.

- Use manual disk layout to improve sector proximity.

Straight-Line Code

- Precompute.

- Avoid conversion between floating-point values and integers.

- Use strength reduction techniques.

- Steer clear of synchronized code that is heavily contended.

Quick Fixes

- Buy a faster computer.

- Take advantage of context-sensitive assumptions.

- Use the compiler's built-in optimization facilities.

- Do a rain dance.

6.10 Putting It All Together

In this chapter and the previous one, I looked at ways to improve performance. I have tried to summarize the major points of both chapters in Figure 6-10.

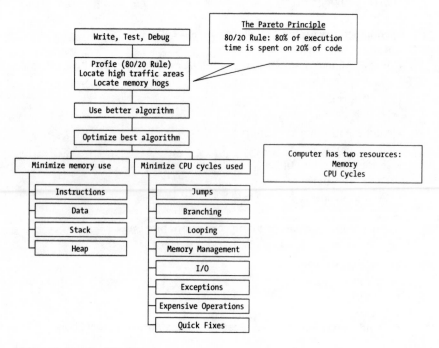

Figure 6-10. The Big Picture

CHAPTER 7

Final Words of Advice

For the listener who's enjoying my stuff, I would hope that they just take everything they're told by authority figures less seriously—not believe what their parents say, what their teachers say, not believe clergymen, law enforcement people, legislators, business leaders. Because they're being bullsh**ted at every corner.

—George Carlin, *Inside Borders* interview

Back in 1990, I took an introductory political science course taught by Theodore Lowi and Ben Ginsberg. It was one of those classes where they crammed 500 students into an auditorium. Class felt more like a circus than a lecture. I distinctly remember the last day of class. Ginsberg walked up to the lectern and announced, *"Up until now, there probably hasn't been anyone who has been out to get you. This will change the minute you graduate and go out into the real world."*

As far as I can tell, this was the only useful thing that I learned at Cornell (contrary to popular belief, knowing all about quantum mechanics is not horribly practical). People who are paranoid have enemies that are imaginary. Victims have enemies that they think are imaginary. Both groups of people suffer from their delusions. The only meaningful distinction is that victims tend to suffer more from their mistakes than paranoids.

For those of you about to enter the corporate landscape for the first time, college graduates in particular, I would urge you to consider what Ginsberg had to say. It may sound paranoid, but it's not. Do not be fooled by the cotton-candy fluff that the human resources people feed you, or the glossy brochures that they pass out. There will be people who see you as a threat to their jobs, managers who want to treat you like a disposable diaper, and disgruntled workers who want to vent their frustration on you. In other words, there will be people out to get you.

One of the themes that this book examines is the impact of human behavior. While I have spent much of the book discussing technical issues, I have also tried to address some of the social and environmental forces that can influence the outcome of a software project. Most of the projects that I have seen fail did not fail due to technical challenges. They failed because of behavioral challenges: politics, infighting, witch-hunts, nepotism, backstabbing, and sabotage, just to name a few.

One of my primary motivations for writing this book has been to alert newcomers so that they can learn to spot trouble before it ambushes them. If I can prevent just one person from being victimized, then I will have accomplished my mission. Having said that, I would like to end this book with a few words of advice—advice that I wish someone had given to me back in 1988.

7.1 Other Threats to Source Code Integrity

One of the greatest and least talked about threats to the stability of your source code is fashionable technology. Revamping a code base to cater to the latest flavor of the month will waste more man-hours than any memory leak or race condition. Once more, the return on investment is awful, because six months later something new will come out. Engineers who chase after the next big thing are constantly playing a game of catch-up, and it is a game they can never win.

The most dangerous thing about adopting a fashionable technology is that it tends to constrain your options. When some commercial software vendor is marketing a new development technology, it's in their best interest to sell you something that anchors you to their platform. Anyone who's worked at a movie theater knows that it's easier to gouge a customer for candy when you have a captive audience. By putting the family heirloom (i.e., your code base) in the hands of a third party, you are surrendering control of important, long-term features like portability and flexibility.

Fashionable Technology: A Case Study

Let's take a look at the evolution of Microsoft's development technology. Back in 1987, Windows 2.0 supported Dynamic Data Exchange (DDE), which was basically an interprocess communication (IPC) mechanism that allowed applications to share data. The object linking and embedding (OLE) framework replaced DDE. OLE was geared towards supporting document components that could be cut and pasted between applications. OLE-related tools were first made available to developers in 1991. Two years later, in 1993, OLE 2.0 was released. OLE 2.0 objects were based on a core infrastructure known as the Component Object Model (COM). As time passed, COM became a buzzword in its own right, serving as a foundation for implementing software components in general (not just those related to application documents).

In 1996, Microsoft introduced two new terms: DCOM and ActiveX. ActiveX was a branding name used to describe COM components that provided interactive Web content. ActiveX was Microsoft's response to Java applets. DCOM was Distributed COM, a framework that allowed COM objects on different machines to interact. DCOM was Microsoft's response to CORBA, through which Windows NT 4.0 supplied ORB-like services. DCOM had a couple of serious shortcomings that prevented it from being a serious threat to CORBA, like the inability to support distributed transactions. Microsoft went back to the drawing board and, in late 1997, announced the creation of COM+, which was a merger of COM technology and the Microsoft Transaction Server (MTS). With COM+, Microsoft seemed to be moving away from the client-server topology of DCOM towards a Web-based, server-centric model.

In every case, going with Microsoft meant handcuffing your code to Windows. Sure, there were attempts to provide support on Unix platforms, but they were nothing more than token gestures. Microsoft proponents may claim that the recent .NET initiative, with its virtual machine approach, offers more alternatives. After all, the nature of a virtual machine is that it can be implemented anywhere, using any set of tools, just as long as the implementation obeys the virtual machine's specification. I suspect, however, that Microsoft's *common language runtime* (CLR) is just a thinly veiled attempt to counter the rising popularity of Java, which has done an admirable job of offering *true* cross-platform support. In my opinion, Microsoft's marketing hype is paying lip service to portability, while at the same time quietly conveying the notion that .NET applications "run best on Windows."

You'd pay to know what you really think.

—J.R. "Bob" Dobbs

Brainwashing 101

In the end, fashionable technology is a ruse, an excuse for you to spend money. The big corporations want your cash, and they will tell you damn near anything to get you to part with it. Everything that they say is tainted with this ulterior motive.

Marketing hype can be very seductive. Even worse, it's everywhere. Half of the technical magazines that you see at the newsstand are nothing more than oversized brochures. On a superficial level, the technical articles that you read may seem like they are trying to "educate" you. The actual agenda is not so philanthropic. This propaganda is intended to subliminally give you the impression of what is "current."

By bombarding you with the same acronym enough times, the media is hoping to encourage the notion that "everyone" is moving to technology XYZ. Their ability to convince people of this is what ⌐'' s them to charge millions of dollars for advertising space. In so m⌐ ⌐echnology is "current" only because the corporate sr⌐ to make it look that way.

As a junior engineer in ⌐id in a candy store. The release of Windows 3.1 w⌐ f slick, sexy-sounding engineering technologies. Th⌐ it that I didn't love. At 20 years of age, I was very ir⌐ ⌐oking down on all of the veteran engineers and th⌐ seemed like crotchety old men who had falle⌐ d. In reality, I was the one who was out of touch.

The Real Issue

The salient issue is not "which solution is current;" this is just a trick that the marketing people use to distract you. The real issue is about *return on investment* (ROI). It's not about being trendy; it's about getting the most bangs per buck. Other than the research firms, like Gartner, Inc. or Forrester Research,

Inc., none of the periodicals seems to pay homage to this topic. Why? The reason that the software industry periodicals shy away from ROI is that their corporate sponsors have expensive products that they want to sell you.

When a CIO decides to roll out a new platform, a venture that can make or break some businesses, the last thing they are worried about is being in fashion. Instead, they have their eyes on long-term financial repercussions. They're focused on satisfying business requirements, minimizing total cost of ownership, availability, compatibility, and safeguarding against vendor lock-in. As John Schindler, CIO of Kichler Lighting, put it, *"If I caught a CIO reading* Byte *magazine, I'd fire him."*

Your goal, as an engineer, should be to adopt this mindset and apply it to software development. Don't be a victim of marketing hype. Renovating significant portions of your code base just to be fashionable is an expensive waste of resources. Ask yourself: "What is this technology really going to buy me? Am I going to get tangible benefits from this new technology, or am I just following the rest of the herd?"

7.2 Maintaining a Paper Trail

When the proverbial crap hits the fan, the best way to defend yourself against fallout, as I have stressed before, is to maintain a well-documented paper trail. Concrete documentation can be used to assign responsibility, and responsibility transforms into blame if a project heads south.

Some managers have been known to save their own skin by blaming things on the other guy. A manager who was rooting and hollering for your project last week, in a staff meeting, can suddenly turn around and stick a shank in your back: "I knew those guys would screw it up, they wouldn't listen to me. I told them it wouldn't work."

Quietly Keep Records

If you are going to maintain a paper trail, do so as inconspicuously as possible. This kind of record keeping can be serious business. People can get fired. You don't want to make your allies nervous, and at the same time you don't want to alert your enemies. Do all of your strategic thinking and analysis at home. Granted, you will still have to collect and record information at work, but there are steps you can take to minimize your footprints when you do.

If you need to huddle with team members to discuss a sensitive issue, go to a bar or a restaurant or any other place in a remote area of town, and do it there. Eavesdropping has been honed to a fine art among cube denizens (which is one reason why managers have offices). Not to mention that a number of financial institutions are required to record telephone conversations to guard against insider trading and disclosure violations.

The Myth of Privacy

When I walked into my first software gig, there was a grizzled old-timer sitting in the cube next to me. He had been with the company for almost 15 years. He had some impressive hardware humming away in his cube, including a fiber optic network connection. Yet, there he was, reading a cheap paperback novel when he could have been surfing the Internet. I was just a little confused at how this technologically savvy early adopter could resist playing with his toys. As I was to find out, he had his reasons . . .

This may sound a little too cloak-and-dagger, but the growing threat of industrial espionage has led many software companies to closely monitor their employees. The idea of privacy in the workplace is a myth. Everything that your employer supplies you with (e.g., a computer, a network connection, a chair, a desk, office supplies) is their property and they can do whatever they want to with it. If they want to, your employer can install a keyboard logger on your workstation to see what you're typing in. They can also legally intercept traffic that you send over the network. This includes e-mails, Web browser downloads, and chat messages. In extreme cases, they can use remote desktop software or TEMPEST equipment to observe everything that you do in real time.

WARNING *The prevalence of IP snooping is one reason why e-mail can be particularly dangerous. Don't EVER e-mail anything at work unless you feel comfortable with the whole world reading it.*

If you want privacy at work, you'll need to buy a laptop and bring it with you. This laptop is your property, not theirs. They have no legal right to install logging software on it. If you suspect that network traffic is being monitored, for $150 you can buy a firewall appliance and set up a VPN tunnel between your laptop and your home computer (assuming you have a home computer). Depending on how your home LAN is set up, you can then reroute incoming traffic from your laptop back out onto the Internet through your home connection, and achieve a modicum of privacy.

NOTE *I'm not sure what to tell you when it comes to TEMPEST equipment. Most companies that manufacture EMF shielding products sell only to the government.*

The bottom line is this: if you are going to keep records so that you can defend yourself later on, collect information unobtrusively and then process it away from prying eyes.

7.3 History Repeats Itself

Silicon Valley is like Hollywood; everyone wants to be a movie star. Yet for every company that makes it to an IPO, a thousand go down in flames.

—Howie Ernesti

In the aftermath of the dot-com bust, the outlook for the software industry doesn't seem very good. Some people are even claiming that the recent collapse of the software industry is an omen of more far-reaching changes. For example, in April 2003, Larry Ellison announced, *"What's going on ... is the end of Silicon Valley as we know it."*[1]

Ellison predicts that the software industry will mature, in the same way that our steel industry did decades ago. The growing standardization of products will result in thinner profit margins, as larger companies rely on economies of scale to squeeze out the smaller companies and gain dominant market positions. To boost efficiency, the survivors will move operations overseas to take advantage of cheaper labor.

There are those who agree, in part, with Ellison. In November 2002, researchers at Gartner[2] predicted that by the end of 2004, half of the world's software vendors will be acquired or be put out of business. IBM has already embraced the idea of "grid computing," where products are standardized to the extent that they are more like utilities. In October 2002, Sam Palmisano stated that IBM would be committing $10 billion towards "on-demand computing," which aims to turn software services into a commodity.[3]

Then again, Larry has been wrong in the past. In the previous chapter I mentioned his failed Raw Iron initiative, which attempted to replace monolithic database servers with appliances that used a microkernel OS. In the mid-1990s, Ellison also backed two companies to build a "network computer," which would execute all of its programs on a remote service (i.e., essentially the 1990s' equivalent of the serial terminal). Neither of the two companies succeeded.

---

1. Mylene Mangalindan, "Larry Ellison's Sober Vision," *The Wall Street Journal*, April 8, 2003

2. Thomas Topolinski and Joanne Correia, "Prediction 2003: Continued Challenges for Software Industry," Gartner Research, AV-18-8042, November 20, 2002

3. Ludwig Siegele, "At Your Service: Despite Early Failures, Computing Will Eventually Become a Utility," *The Economist*, May 16, 2003

The "New Economy" Hits Home

Ed Yourdon once predicted the demise of the American programmer.[4] While the fate of the entire industry has yet to be seen, I think that Ed has hit the bull's-eye (even if he was a little premature). The sad fact is that software engineering in the U.S., as a career path, has become a quaint anachronism.

Look around you—how many 55-year-old software architects do you see? If anything, software is a young man's game. This is due to two reasons:

• The constantly shifting skill set

• The availability of cheaper substitutes

The skill set that you learn today can be completely supplanted within a year. I remember taking the better part of six months to become comfortable with DCOM, and then "poof," it vanished off the radar as soon as the next fashionable technology (i.e., COM+) appeared. This makes taking the time to understand the latest tools a poor investment in the long run.

I know some older engineers who try to counter this by claiming, "Well, I like to think that my years of experience give me a leg up when it comes to the bigger picture of implementing a solid design and getting a stable product out the door." This may be true, but only as long as you understand the technology being used. All it takes is a year or two to get out of touch with the industry, and that "big picture" explanation sounds more like an excuse for not having to stay up to date. Before you know it, the junior engineers are sneering at you as if you were a COBOL programmer. Hence, even the "big picture" guys will have to relearn everything periodically to keep from looking outmoded.

The short-lived utility of software engineering job skills is compounded by the availability of cheaper substitutes. Every year a whole new batch of kiddies enter the workforce knowing the latest thing. My guess is that they would be willing to do your job for a fraction of what you make. They don't have a mortgage, they don't have children, and they're too naive to be bothered by working 15 hours a day. Most college graduates see pulling a 15-hour workday as heroic, just like charging a machine gun nest (now you know why they draft 18-year-olds).

Thus, software engineering is a great field to go into if you're young. Harried managers are always looking for new blood they can put to work (ahem, exploit). However, after you have spent a few years building up your market value, you will discover that you have morphed into a target for the efficiency experts. If you decide to enter the workforce as a programmer, you should do so with your eyes open. Like professional football, programming is

---

4. Ed Yourdon, *Decline and Fall of the American Programmer* (Prentice Hall, 1992. ISBN: 0-132-03670-3)

strictly a short-term occupation. Have an exit strategy in place so that your transition out of programming is as smooth as your entrance.

The really big threat to the future of software engineering in the U.S., however, is not here at home. It's overseas. The GNP per capita in India and China is a fraction of what it is in the U.S. Not only that, but the emphasis placed on education in these countries has produced an army of highly trained engineers. This glut of relatively cheap labor is an awful temptation for software vendors. With the availability of gigabit networking equipment, teleconferencing, instant messaging, and e-mail, a branch office in another country can seem like it's right next door.

In 2002, Bank of America laid off 3,700 of its 25,000 IT and back-office employees. That's about 15 percent. In 2003, Bank of America will outsource 1,100 jobs to India.[5] This is by no means an isolated incident. Hardware manufacturers like Intel have been frantically hiring Chinese and Indian engineers, with advanced degrees, to design new processors. Hewlett-Packard, for instance, has 3,300 software engineers in India. Then there's Microsoft. Over the next three years, Microsoft will invest $400 million in India and $750 million in China. Over a billion dollars of capital; think about that.

NOTE *To give you an idea of how bleak things look: John C. McCarthy, an analyst for Forrester Research, predicts that more than 3.3 million white-collar jobs will leave the U.S. for other countries by 2015.[6]*

We've seen this before. Decades ago, this happened to the U.S. steel industry when the means of production moved overseas. History is repeating itself. Only this time it's the white-collar workers who are getting sold out. Back then, political and business leaders proclaimed that the blue-collar workers who lost their jobs would be retrained and redeployed in the IT industry. As we all know, this never happened. What are they going to tell us this time? If I may, I would suggest that you revisit the George Carlin quote that I began the chapter with.

---

5.   Peter Engardio et al., "The New Global Job Shift," *Business Week*, February 3, 2003

6.   Ibid.

Index

Numbers and Symbols

32-bit Windows console program
  illustrating how a debugger operates,
  193–195
80:20 rule
  use of in computer science, 216–217

A

abstraction
  design problems created by excessive,
  125
activation records
  example of a generic, 240
  function of, 239–245
  limiting size of local variables in,
  247–248
  minimizing amount of code generated
  to manage, 266–268
  modified, 21
Adams, Scott
  quotation from Dilbert and the Way of
  the Weasel, 8
address space pages, 292
admin() member function
  invoking to generate log messages,
  28–30
ADMIN severity field
  for LogMessage object normal system
  events, 28
Adobe PDF viewer
  Web site address for, 154
allSegments.c program
  segment occupants in, 224
American National Standards Institute
  (ANSI) C Standard
  reader need for when obscure
  language features are used in code,
  133
ANSI clock() routine
  using to measure small amounts of
  time, 54
ANSI C Standard. *See* American National
  Standards Institute (ANSI) C
  Standard
*AntiPatterns: Refactoring Software,
  Architectures, and Projects in Crisis*
  (John Wiley & Sons, 1998)
  by William J. Brown, et al., 3

"AOL buys Netscape, joins Sun in Java
  Deal"
  by Rebecca Sykes, IDG News Service,
  November 24, 1998, 5
Apache Web server
  use of mod_cache module by, 295–296
  using for a Web-enabled knowledge
  base, 154–155
  Web site address for, 154
APL (A Programming Language)
  vs. C language merging statements,
  131
  invented by Ken Iverson, 131
arguments
  types of bad, 17–18
  use of a function with a variable
  number of in C, 131
arithmatic operation
  strength reduction techniques, 311
array elements
  moving outside of a loop and
  replacing with a variable, 284
array references
  using, 283–284
ASCII text
  using Huffman coding to compress,
  235
assembly language
  translation of goto statement, 265
"At Long Last Windows 2000 Operating
  System to Ship in February,"
  Associated Press, December 15, 1999
  by Michael Martinez, 11
"At Your Service: Despite Early Failures,
  Computing Will Eventually Become a
  Utility," *The Economist*, May 16, 2003
  by Ludwig Siegele, 327
AT&T's long distance system
  crash of due to switch statement error,
  130
atomic data types
  searching out, 140–142
attrition
  countertactics to, 118–119
auto keyword
  use of in C, 131
automated testing
  motivation behind, 44–46'
"Automatic Detection and Prevention of
  Buffer-Overflow Attacks" paper
  by Crispen Cowen, et al., 91